DICKENS'S VILLAINS

Dickens's Villains
Melodrama, Character, Popular Culture

JULIET JOHN

OXFORD
UNIVERSITY PRESS

OXFORD

UNIVERSITY PRESS

Great Clarendon Street, Oxford, OX2 6DP

Oxford University Press is a department of the University of Oxford.
It furthers the University's objective of excellence in research, scholarship,
and education by publishing worldwide in

Oxford New York

Athens Auckland Bangkok Bogotá Buenos Aires Cape Town
Chennai Dar es Salaam Delhi Florence Hong Kong Istanbul Karachi
Kolkata Kuala Lumpur Madrid Melbourne Mexico City Mumbai
Nairobi Paris São Paulo Shanghai Singapore Taipei Tokyo Toronto Warsaw

and associated companies in Berlin Ibadan

Oxford is a registered trade mark of Oxford University Press
in the UK and certain other countries

Published in the United States
by Oxford University Press Inc., New York

© Juliet John 2001

British Library Cataloguing in Publication Data

Data available

Library of Congress Cataloging in Publication Data

John, Juliet 1967–
    Dickens's villains : melodrama, character, popular culture / Juliet John.
    p. cm.
    Includes bibliographical references (p.) and index.
    1. Dickens, Charles, 1812–1870—Characters—Villains. 2. Popular culture
—England—History—19th century. 3. Villains in literature. 4. Melodrama.
I. Title.
    PR4592.V54J65 2002   823'.8—dc21   00-053038

ISBN 0-19-818461-1

1 3 5 7 9 10 8 6 4 2

Typeset by Regent Typesetting, London
Printed in Great Britain
on acid-free paper by
Biddles Ltd,
Guildford and King's Lynn

To Calum and Iona,
with Love

Acknowledgements

This book started life as an undergraduate dissertation, became a doctoral thesis, and has followed me round various teaching posts as an embryonic book. Because of the time it has taken to materialize in book form, I will inevitably forget to acknowledge everybody who has helped it on its way, and for that I apologize in advance. My thanks are largely given chronologically: to Tim Cribb, who supervised my undergraduate dissertation on Dickens, to Jean Chothia, who fuelled my interest in theatre, my enthusiasm for literature, and my academic confidence throughout my time at Cambridge, and to Andy Brooks, who had to compete with Dickens for quite some time. Max Saunders and Wilbur Sanders set me early examples of dedication in both scholarship and teaching. As a postgraduate and since, I have profited continuously from my supervisor Dan Jacobson's intellectual rigour, incisive editorial skills, moral support, and honesty. During my time at UCL and beyond, I benefited from the friendship and/or academic support of the following individuals: Rosemary Ashton, David Brauner, Helen Hackett, Nicki Hitchcott, Stephen James, Richard Lansdown, Richard North, Dominic Rainsford, Phil Robins, Lee Sands, Ashley Tauchert, and Hugh White. From Manchester University, I owe thanks to the students on my Dickens course and to the following friends and colleagues: John Anderson, Carson Bergstrom, Brian Cox, Matt Jordan, Matthew Nilan, Anita Pacheco, John Stachniewski, Kathryn Sutherland, and Kathy Taylor. From Liverpool University, I am grateful to the students on my Dickens course, and to Bernard Beatty, Phil Davis, and Jill Rudd; from Edge Hill, my thanks are to Gill Davies, Margaret Forsyth, and Jo Sadler. Among my current colleagues at Salford University, Avril Horner, Scott McCracken, and Antony Rowland have been thorough and obliging readers of sections of this book, and I have benefited from Daniel Duffy's expertise on melodrama. I am also indebted to my Ph.D. examiners, Andrew Sanders and Angus Easson, to Clive Bloom, Margaret Darby, John Sutherland, and the Oxford University Press readers for taking the time to read sections or all of this book. Research was conducted at the British Library (old and new), the University of London library, the John Rylands Library, University of Manchester, and the libraries of the University of Liverpool, Edge Hill University College, Lancashire, and the University of Salford: I owe thanks to the librarians in all these libraries who helped me to improve my research skills. Jason Freeman and Sophie Goldsworthy have been extremely patient and understanding editors. I am also grateful to the following for their friendship: Iain Bennett, Andrew Cooper, Sarah Francis, Paola Grenier, Steve Mawer, and Francis O'Gorman.

In terms of direct academic involvement with this book, I owe most thanks to four readers and friends who did their best to help me revise large sections of it in the final stages and to buoy my flagging spirits: to Gregory Dart, Dan Jacobson (again), Alice Jenkins (for academic and telephonic support), and Susan Rowland. My biggest debt of gratitude goes to my families: to David, Jackie, and Rebecca for help and support always; and to my new family; to Calum, for his unwavering support and his belief in (as well as influence on) the argument of this book; and to Iona, for making its last days special as well as very unpredictable, and for smiling throughout her difficulties.

A version of Chapter 5 has appeared as '*Twist*ing the Newgate tale: Dickens, Popular Culture and the Politics of Genre', in Juliet John and Alice Jenkins (eds.), *Rethinking Victorian Culture* (Houndmills: Macmillan, 2000), 126–45. A section of Chapter 7 has appeared as 'Byronic Steerforth: Sincerity and Self-Fashioning in *David Copperfield*', in Sara Thornton (ed.), *Lectures d'une œuvre: 'David Copperfield'* (Paris: Éditions du Temps, 1996), 70–82. A version of Chapter 8 has appeared as 'Dickens's Deviant Women: A Reassessment', *Critical Review*, 34 (1994), 68–84.

Contents

x   *Contents*

A Note on the Text

References to Dickens's novels are to the Clarendon Edition (Oxford, 1966–) for *David Copperfield, Dombey and Son, Great Expectations, Little Dorrit, Martin Chuzzlewit, The Mystery of Edwin Drood, Oliver Twist, The Old Curiosity Shop,* and *The Pickwick Papers,* and to the (New) Oxford Illustrated Dickens (London, 1947–) for all other volumes. References to Dickens's letters are to the Pilgrim edition, ed. Madeline House and Graham Storey, 11 vols. (Oxford: Clarendon Press, 1965–) where available, and otherwise to the Nonesuch edition, ed. Walter Dexter, 3 vols. (Bloomsbury: Nonesuch Press, 1938), iii. References are cited in the text, as are other references throughout this book, where this is helpful and possible. Unless otherwise stated, dates given in the text are dates of first publication in the case of fiction and poetry, and dates of first performance in the case of drama.

Abbreviations

Drama

The abbreviations employed for both editions of plays and the names of theatres are taken from Allardyce Nicoll's *A History of Early Nineteenth-Century Drama, 1800–1850*, 2 vols. (Cambridge: Cambridge University Press, 1930).

and *French's Minor NY* refer to the New York edition of
French's series of plays)

Lacy	*Lacy's Acting Edition* (*c.*1850–60)
LC	Lord Chamberlain's Collection (British Library)
LC Add. MS	Lord Chamberlain's Collection Additional Manuscript (British Library)
Richardson Minor	*Richardson's New Minor Drama* (1828–31)

Theatres

Adel.	The Adelphi
CG	Covent Garden, Theatre Royal
CL	The Royal City of London Theatre
Cob.	The Royal Coburg Theatre
DL	Drury Lane, Theatre Royal
EOH	English Opera House
H.2	Theatre Royal, Haymarket
Lyc.	The Lyceum
Olym.	The Olympic Theatre
P'cess	The Princess's Theatre
Queen's	The Queen's Theatre
Stand.	The Standard Theatre
St. J.	The St James's Theatre
Surrey	The Surrey Theatre
SW	Sadler's Wells Theatre
Vic.	The Royal Victoria Theatre

Introduction

> [Bradley Headstone is] a type which begins to appear in these
> later novels of Dickens and which originally derives from those
> early theatrical villains, of the type of the elder Rudge or Monks
> in *Oliver Twist*, skulking figures with black looks and ravaged
> faces, a literary convention of which one would suppose it
> would be impossible to make anything plausible.
>
> (Edmund Wilson, 'Dickens: The Two Scrooges', 1941)

> When one thinks of Mr Micawber, one is reminded of the frogs
> whose brains have been taken out for physiological purposes.
>
> (G. H. Lewes, 'Dickens in Relation to Criticism', 1872)

The brain is a marginal part of the Dickens character's anatomy.
This case has been argued many times in Dickens criticism, not least
of his melodramatic villains.[1] Since Wilson stimulated interest in the
macabre side of Dickens's work, for example, many notable critics
have dismissed Dickens's villains as 'melodramatic' and 'stagy', while
at the same time praising Dickens's complex understanding of
deviant psychology.[2] This book was born in response to the false logic
of such arguments; if Dickens's villains are nothing more than
theatrical stereotypes, I asked myself, how do his novels convey what

---

[1] For criticism of the unreality of the melodramatic villain in Dickens, see G. K.
Chesterton, *Appreciations and Criticisms of the Works of Charles Dickens* (London: Dent, 1911),
179, Earle Davis, *The Flint and the Flame: The Artistry of Charles Dickens* (London: Gollancz,
1964), 234, George Gissing, *Charles Dickens: A Critical Study* (London: Gresham, 1903), 112, R.
H. Horne (ed.), *A New Spirit of the Age*, The World's Classics, CXXVII (London: Oxford
University Press, 1907), 14, T. H. Lister, 'Dickens's Tales', *Edinburgh Review*, 68 (1838), 75–97
(p. 96), '*Oliver Twist*', *Quarterly Review*, 64 (1839), 83–102 (p. 94), J. C. Reid, *Charles Dickens:
'Little Dorrit'*, Studies in English Literature, XXVIIII (London: Arnold, 1967), 17, 37,
Michael Slater, *Dickens and Women* (London: Dent, 1983), 291, Edmund Wilson, 'Dickens:
The Two Scrooges', in *The Wound and the Bow: Seven Studies in Literature* (Cambridge, Mass.:
Riverside Press, 1941), 1–104 (pp. 56, 82).

[2] Wilson's pioneering essay is a classic example of this critical response to Dickens, as is
Humphry House's essay 'The Macabre Dickens', in *All in Due Time: The Collected Essays and
Broadcast Talks of Humphry House* (London: Rupert Hart-Davis, 1955), 183–9. This tendency
to sideline the theatre has persisted in criticism of the 'macabre' Dickens, even in the most
recent Foucauldian approaches to the issue—see for example D. A. Miller's *The Novel and
the Police* (Berkeley and Los Angeles: University of California Press, 1988), Natalie
McKnight's *Idiots, Madmen and Other Prisoners in Dickens* (New York: St Martin's Press, 1993),
and Jeremy Tambling's *Dickens, Violence and the Modern State* (Houndmills: Macmillan, 1995).

Humphry House calls an 'intimate understanding of morbid and near morbid psychology'?[3] It is no accident, for example, that the passages in Dickens most commonly praised for their psychological power are invariably projected through the consciousness of exactly those 'skulking figures' of theatrical convention dismissed by Wilson: we think of Sikes after the murder of Nancy, Fagin at his trial, Jonas after the murder of Tigg, and even Rudge remembering the murder of Reuben.[4] It is similarly significant that Dickens's first novelistic villain, Jingle in *The Pickwick Papers*, is an actor. There has been a great deal of fruitful criticism of both the macabre and the theatrical elements of Dickens's writing.[5] What is striking, however, is the extent to which these two key strands in Dickens studies have regarded themselves as mutually exclusive. While critics of the 'macabre' Dickens routinely disparage the theatre, among the vast body of work which has grown up around Dickens's fascination with the theatre, virtually no notice has been taken of the deviant Dickens.[6] I aim to illuminate the crucial symbiosis which exists between the 'deviant' and the 'theatrical' aspects of Dickens's writing and, in so doing, to pinpoint some of the contradictions that are endemic in the current state of understanding of his art.

[3] 'The Macabre Dickens', 187.

[4] See Chapter 4 for a fuller discussion of the 'psychological' exploration of the stagy villain. Even the psyche, I argue, is melodramatically rendered.

[5] For analyses of the 'deviant' Dickens, see John Carey, *The Violent Effigy: A Study of Dickens' Imagination* (London: Faber & Faber, 1973); see also Edgar Johnson's *Charles Dickens: His Tragedy and his Triumph*, 2 vols. (London: Gollancz, 1953), John Lucas's *The Melancholy Man: A Study of Dickens's Novels* (London: Methuen, 1970), McKnight, *Idiots, Madmen and Other Prisoners in Dickens*, Steven Marcus, *Dickens: From Pickwick to Dombey* (London: Chatto & Windus, 1965), John Schad (ed.), *Dickens Refigured: Bodies, Desires and Other Histories* (Manchester: Manchester University Press, 1996), and Tambling's *Dickens, Violence and the Modern State*.

On the theatrical Dickens, see William Axton, *Circle of Fire: Dickens' Vision and Style and the Popular Victorian Theatre* (Lexington: University of Kentucky Press, 1966), Edwin M. Eigner, *The Dickens Pantomime* (Berkeley and Los Angeles: University of California Press, 1989), Robert Garis, *The Dickens Theatre: A Reassessment of the Novels* (Oxford: Clarendon Press, 1965), John Glavin, *After Dickens: Reading, Adaptation and Performance*, Cambridge Studies in Nineteenth-Century Literature and Culture, XX (Cambridge: Cambridge University Press, 1999), Paul Schlicke, *Dickens and Popular Entertainment* (London: Allen & Unwin, 1985), Deborah Vlock, *Dickens, Novel Reading and the Victorian Popular Theatre*, Cambridge Studies in Nineteenth-Century Literature and Culture, XIX (Cambridge: Cambridge University Press, 1998), George Worth, *Dickensian Melodrama: A Reading of the Novels*, University of Kansas Humanistic Studies, L (Lawrence: University of Kansas, 1978).

[6] A notable exception to the latter statement is Claire Tomalin's excellent *The Invisible Woman: The Story of Nelly Ternan and Charles Dickens* (Harmondsworth: Penguin, 1991). John Glavin's *After Dickens* also looks at Dickens's ambivalent or negative feelings about the theatre, using psychoanalysis among other theoretical tools.

It is customary to account for the extreme imbalance between Dickens's ability to render the 'bad' psyche and his inability to animate the 'good' psyche with recourse either to the attractiveness of deviance to artists generally, or—in the tradition of Wilson and House—to Dickens's difficult childhood. While structuralism and post-structuralism have both, in their different ways, shifted critical debates away from the notion that characters are unmediated representations of people, this book argues for a further paradigm shift. In Dickens's works, 'psychology' is synonymous with deviance, I would argue, because Dickens was instinctively opposed to the privileging of the individualized psyche which was becoming so crucial an element of the nineteenth-century understanding of selfhood and society.[7] In other words, the notion of 'psychology', as we have since come to understand it, is itself deviant in the Dickens world. Dickens's belief in the principles of communality and cultural inclusivity made the notion of a psyche-centred approach to people and society seem individualistic, divisive, and potentially elitist.

It is hardly novel to argue that Dickens dramatizes rather than analyses the psyche. What is new is the attempt to explain why. Steven Connor, for example, incisively identifies what he regards as Dickens's unique feature as a writer, while remaining clearly baffled by it:

it is hard to think of an art that is less secretive than Dickens's; perhaps the uncomfortable thing about his writing is not its sense of hidden depths, but its inexplicable and monstrous [. . .] *ostension*. Unlike other writers, Dickens keeps his underside clearly and flagrantly on display.[8]

This book locates the rationale for Dickens's 'ostension' in his populism and his belief that 'dramatic' forms of entertainment best serve the purposes of cultural inclusivity. Dickens's belief in cultural inclusivity was held with uncharacteristic consistency. In fact, one might go so far as to say that a belief in 'popular' culture was Dickens's most firmly held political view.[9] Dickens's two-part essay 'The

[7] Edwin M. Eigner makes a similar point about writers (including Dickens) of the 'metaphysical novel', who regarded Lockean thought as 'the principal curse of their century, a psychology which their own fiction was specifically written to defeat'—*The Metaphysical Novel in England and America: Dickens, Bulwer, Melville, and Hawthorne* (Berkeley and Los Angeles: University of California Press, 1978), 88. The implications of Eigner's observation have not, however, been explored in Dickens studies.

[8] Review essay on Harry Stone's *The Night Side of Dickens: Cannibalism, Passion, Necessity* (Columbus: Ohio State University Press, 1994), *Dickensian*, 91 (1995), 127–30 (p. 127).

[9] See Schlicke, *Dickens and Popular Entertainment*.

Amusements of the People' is one of his clearest statements of his belief in, and vision of, popular culture; more importantly, for our purposes, it is a lucid articulation of his vision of 'dramatic entertainment' as the most effective instrument of cultural cohesion and somehow the natural imaginative outlet for the 'common people'.[10] 'It is probable', he begins, 'that nothing will ever root out from among the common people an innate love they have for dramatic entertainment in some form or other. It would be a very doubtful benefit to society, we think, if it could be rooted out.' The theatre, for Dickens, is ideally a crucial site of communal imaginative experience; 'dramatic entertainments' have the socially cohesive potential to counter the forces of fragmentation at work in industrialized Britain.

'The Amusements of the People' argues that drama as an educational medium could be used to improve the taste and understanding of the 'common' person, helping to diminish the effects of mechanization and the class divisions which attended it. 'The lower we go', Dickens writes, 'the more natural it is that the best-relished provision for this [imagination] should be found in dramatic entertainments; as at once the most obvious, the least troublesome, and the most real, of all the escapes out of the literal world' (p. 13). 'Dramatic entertainments' are 'escapes' that are also 'real'; imagination is both a social salve and an escape from the 'literal world'. Though the terms of Dickens's invocation of imaginative escapism appear almost Keatsian in their emphasis, their context is anything but Romantic. Dickens's positioning of the popular theatre as the site for the most rewarding and constructive imaginative experiences for the lower classes is consistent with his view of the imagination as, ideally, an externalizing force. The need for escape is not exclusive to the sensitive, artistic individual, as Dickens makes clear in his elucidation of the communal function of 'Fancy' in the 'Preliminary Word' to *Household Words*:

In the bosoms of the young and old, of the well-to-do and of the poor, we would tenderly cherish that light of Fancy which is inherent in the human breast [. . .] to teach the hardest workers at this whirling wheel of toil, that their lot is not necessarily a moody, brutal fact, excluded from the sympathies of imagination.[11]

Escape from the self is thus often, to Dickens, a social rather than an antisocial urge.

---

[10] *HW* i (30 Mar. 1850), 13–15; *HW* i (13 Apr. 1850), 57–60.
[11] *HW* i (30 Mar. 1850), 1. 'The 'Prelimary Word' is also a remarkably lucid account of the populism which informs Dickens's art.

Dickens's understanding of the need that the lower classes especially possess to escape '*out of* the literal world' (italics mine) means just that. The imagination as it exercises itself in dramatic experience—whether this involves the actor or spectator—takes one outside, rather than inside, the self. What Dickens seems to value is the pleasure the actor or spectator derives from escaping from him- or herself in the company of others. It is as if Dickens associates pain with privacy, with the isolated individual; the theatre provides representation of such individuals, but simultaneously helps the audience and actors to escape from themselves. Imagination, in Dickens's view, should theoretically make for a better society. In 'Two Views of a Cheap Theatre', for example, Dickens refers to 'the natural inborn desire of the mass of mankind to recreate themselves and to be amused'.[12] The language in which he expresses himself is significant: the phrase 'to recreate' means 'entertain' but also carries the root sense of to 're-create', or to create the self anew. Imaginative role-playing, Dickens suggests, underpins the emotional pleasure we derive from 'dramatic entertainment'. Dickens approves of such imaginative performativity in the context of the theatre because the acts of sympathy or empathy we so often perform in the theatre take us out of ourselves. A positive imaginative experience of the theatre encourages externally focused emotions and personalities (hence the theatre's function in lessening class conflict). What Dickens is projecting, then, is an anti-individualistic, communal model of the ideal theatrical (and, by implication, social) experience.

'Ostension' in character is a fundamental means by which Dickens imitates the popular theatre's externality. His belief in the appropriateness of 'ostension' to a poorly educated, lower-class audience is made explicit, in 'The Amusements of the People', when we are first introduced to the working-class archetype Joe Whelks:

Joe Whelks, of the New Cut, Lambeth, is not much of a reader, has no great store of books, no very commodious room to read in, no very decided inclination to read, and no power at all of presenting vividly before his mind's eye what he reads about. But, put Joe in the gallery of the Victoria Theatre; [. . .] tell him a story [. . .] by the help of live men and women dressed up, confiding to him their innermost secrets, in voices audible half a mile off; and Joe will unravel a story through all its entanglements, and sit there as long after midnight as you have anything left to show him. ('The Amusements of the People', 13)

[12] In *The Uncommercial Traveller and Reprinted Pieces* (Oxford: Oxford University Press, 1958; repr. 1987), 29–39 (p. 38).

To Dickens, it is in the ability of the theatre to embody, externalize, and objectify its representations that its social and cultural import-ance resides. My argument is that his novels appropriate, imitate, and interrogate the objectification which he regards as crucial to the theatre's ability to entertain and instruct the lower classes. His belief that mimetic fiction cannot be culturally inclusive is voiced explicitly in a fascinating letter to Forster:

> It does not seem to me to be enough to say of any description that it is the exact truth. The exact truth must be there; but the merit or art in the narra-tor, is the manner of stating the truth. As to which thing in literature, it always seems to me that there is a world to be done. [. . .] I have an idea [. . .] that the very holding of popular literature through a kind of popular dark age, may depend on such fanciful treatment.[13]

'Fanciful' or imaginative treatment in Dickens is, as we have seen, largely synonymous with a 'dramatic' or externalized 'manner of stating the exact truth'.

While Dickens sees imaginative role-playing and escape from the self as crucial to the education and cultural inclusion of the masses, those officially responsible for the improvement of the workers assume, in Dickens's accounts of them, that instruction starts inside the individual mind. Dickens's defence of the theatre as an educa-tional instrument is frequently linked to his attacks on the centrality of the intellect in the establishment's view of social and cultural integration. To Dickens, valorization of the mind, the intellect, or the private self is ineffective as an educational strategy and therefore leads inevitably to the perpetuation of established cultural hierarchies and divisions. Dickens's populism is therefore inextricable from his anti-intellectualism. In 'Dullborough Town', for example, Dickens reveals his dislike of the intellectual snobbery which, he believes, informs 'anti-theatrical' prejudice.[14] Finding that no mechanics belong to the Dullborough Mechanics Institution, the narrator takes a closer look at its activities, concluding: 'I fancied I detected a shy-ness in admitting that human nature when at leisure has any desire whatever to be relieved and diverted; and a furtive sliding in of any poor make-weight piece of amusement, shamefacedly and edge-

---

[13] John Forster, *The Life of Charles Dickens*, ed. J. W. T. Ley (London: Palmer, 1928), 727–8.

[14] In the debate about the desirable nature of Sunday recreations in the Victorian period, a vociferous lobby were anti-theatrical, upholding the church, religious meetings, or polytechnic lectures as morally superior recreations to the theatre—see Schlicke, *Dickens and Popular Entertainment*, 191–225.

wise.'[15] Dickens despises what he calls, in the same article, 'the mask-
ing of entertainment, and pretending it was something else—as
people mask bedsteads [. . .] and make believe that they are book-
cases' (p. 122). The Polytechnic Institution is an object of particular
opprobrium for Dickens, symbolizing a Utilitarian view of education
and a mechanized vision of humanity.

Dickens's writings attempt to collapse the artificial opposition
between 'high' and 'popular' culture by exposing the mindset which
upholds it. In post-Enlightenment, post-Romantic Britain, the
dichotomy between the mind and the emotions is particularly prominent in debates about the education of the masses. The privileging of
the mind above emotion underpins, for Dickens, the misguided
intellectual elitism which, far from improving the lot of the workers,
compounds their cultural alienation. Dickens does not deconstruct
this opposition, however; rather, he reverses the hierarchy which
underpins it. He values emotion above reason, conscious that the
former was less valued in the cultural market place—at least in the
melodramatic garb in which he himself commonly dressed it. The
upward mobility of Mr Whelks demands the cultivation of his intellectual faculties; but, as Dickens makes particularly clear in *Hard
Times*, the kind of intellectual development which is socially constructive necessarily begins with the imagination and the feelings.
Dickens's sense of emotion as the key to social and cultural cohesion
is made clear in 'The Amusements of the People' when he concludes
with reference to the 'conventional passion' common to both melodrama and 'the Italian Opera' by saying: 'So do extremes meet; and
so there is some hopeful congeniality between what will excite MR.
WHELKS, and what will rouse a Duchess' (p. 60).

Dickens mediates the mind through 'conventional', externalized,
or theatrical expressions of emotion—even, this book argues, when
the impression created is one of interiority or subjectivity.[16] It is the
'turn inwards' effected by high Romanticism, however, which has
become naturalized in western high culture. Of particular importance has been the Romantic contribution to the development and
cultural prominence of 'psychology', and to the foregrounding of

[15] In *The Uncommercial Traveller and Reprinted Pieces*, 116–26 (p. 122).

[16] John Kucich maintains correctly that 'Dickens always conceives inwardness as
inextricable from the ways it is consciously or unconsciously presented to others'—
'Dickens', in John Richetti (ed.), *The Columbia History of the British Novel* (New York:
Columbia University Press, 1994), 381–406 (p. 399). See Chapter 4 below for a full discussion of the melodramatic poetics which inform Dickens's rendering of the 'inner' life.

personal emotional experience in explorations of selfhood.[17] High
Romanticism—with the important exception of the *Lyrical Ballads*—
tends to valorize internalized, intellectualized feeling; it values
emotion, in other words, principally when it is mediated by the
mind. The realist novel, psychoanalysis, and modernism have all perpetuated and intensified the high Romantic elevation of the psyche
as the site, and analysis as the instrument, of the most culturally
valuable expressions of 'reality'. Jonathan Arac, for example, convincingly foregrounds the formative role of Romantic readings of
Shakespeare in the development of 'modern' concepts of individualism and character. Discussing Mill's definition of character in *On
Liberty*, he argues: 'In the literary development of character in the
nineteenth century the depths, recesses, and alienation made possible
by such self-alienation [. . .] became the model for what it was to *be* a
character.'[18] This book argues that literary criticism of character, in
the tradition of high Romanticism, has internalized the very high
cultural values that Dickens was writing against. Even critical theory,
whilst largely rejecting the subject-centred, mimetic perspective on
literary texts which it associates with liberal humanism, is frequently
guilty of intellectual elitism in its dealings with popular culture—
another form, in other words, of privileging of the mind.[19]

Dickens's 'dramatic' techniques of characterization have correctly
been linked to the eighteenth-century comic novel and to contemporary forms of popular theatre like pantomime. It is no accident,
however, that the form of 'dramatic entertainment' most extensively
discussed in 'The Amusements of the People' is melodrama—in
particular 'an attractive Melo-Drama called MAY MORNING; OR THE
MYSTERY OF 1715, AND THE MURDER!' (p. 13). Melodrama was arguably
the most popular form of theatre in the nineteenth century—particularly with the lower classes. Melodramatic aesthetics offered Dickens
a specific set of characteristics fundamental to his anti-intellectual

---

[17] See Chapter 2 below.
[18] 'Hamlet, *Little Dorrit*, and the History of Character', in Michael Hays (ed.), *Critical
Conditions: Regarding the Historical Moment* (Minneapolis: University of Minnesota Press, 1992),
82–96 (p. 89). Mill defines character thus: 'A person whose desires and impulses are his
own—are the expressions of his own nature, as it has been developed and modified by his
own culture—is said to have character. One whose desires and impulses are not his own,
has no character, no more than a steam engine has a character'—John Stuart Mill, 'Of
Individuality, as One of the Elements of Well-Being', in *On Liberty and Other Essays* (1859),
ed. John Gray (Oxford: Oxford University Press, 1991), 62–82 (p. 67). There is some
slippage here between Arac's discussion of literary character and Mill's comment, which is
about moral character.   [19] See Chapter 1 below.

marginalization of 'psychology' and interiority: melodrama publicizes the private, privileges spontaneous emotions, and marginalizes the mind. Most importantly, melodrama depends on excessively passional models of character and an unrivalled 'ostension' or objectification in its modes of representation. In terms of its overt ideologies, its dramatization of working-class concerns as well as its emphasis on family and community are in keeping with Dickens's own politics. Most attractive of all to Dickens perhaps is melodrama's assumption that passionate ostension or transparency of character is crucial to the survival of community. Dickens appropriates melodramatic aesthetics, in my account, as a point of ideological principle—the principle of cultural inclusivity.

The melodramatic villain both confirms and threatens melodrama's aesthetics and ideologies. In 1856, Hippolyte Taine argued that 'all Dickens's characters belong to two classes—the people who have feelings and emotions, and the people who have none'.[20] Taine's claim is a little excessive when applied to the entire Dickens canon, but has some validity in relation to Dickens's melodramatic villains. The idea of *the* melodramatic villain is in fact a convenient misnomer. There is more than one model of melodramatic villainy, as this book makes clear, the most 'out-and-out' of which tend to emotional extremes. In this respect, melodramatic villainy is not new: from the Vice of the morality plays and Herod of the miracle plays, to Richardson's (appropriately named) Lovelace and the hotheads of the Gothic novel, absolute villainy tends to be either passionate or passionless. In Dickens, villains and deviants are often twinned with doubles or alter egos at the opposite end of the emotional scale to themselves; Fagin and Sikes spring to mind in an early novel like *Oliver Twist*; Headstone and Wrayburn are a more refined, obscured version of this opposition in *Our Mutual Friend*; and John Jasper in *Edwin Drood* embodies what psychoanalysis might regard as a 'psychopathic' fusion, or indeed split, between excessive passion and repression. There are countless examples of this passionate/passionless dialectic throughout the Dickens canon.

The use of doubles and character clusters is just one means by which Dickens subverts the subject-centred view of 'reality' common in the dominant cultural modes of high Romanticism and classic

[20] 'Charles Dickens, son talent et ses oeuvres', *Revue des deux mondes*, 1 (1 Feb. 1856), 618–47; repr. in Stephen Wall (ed.), *Charles Dickens Critical Anthology* (Harmondsworth: Penguin, 1970), 99–103 (p. 102).

realism. By definition, moreover, the villain is unrealistic. To speak accurately, she or he is pre-realistic. For the figure of *the* villain—defined by the *OED* as 'That character in a play, novel, etc., whose evil motives or actions form an important element in the plot'—derives from an allegorical tradition rooted, in British culture, in Christianity. The figure of the villain met its nemesis with the advent of realism—and the decline of the Christian faith. An increased interest in the effect of 'nurture' on deviant behaviour, and an increasing degree of religious scepticism, has made the idea of 'the villain' seem old-fashioned and incredible as a real-life concept and consequently simplistic or primitive in fiction. The rise of 'psychology' and 'psychoanalysis' as instruments by which to understand human conduct, moreover, shifted the emphasis away from action to motivation, and, in so doing, muddied moral absolutes. The fact that in a post-Romantic age we have no small difficulty distinguishing between a villain and a hero is testimony to the role of high Romanticism in the development of psychology (and vice versa).[21] The pre-realist roots of the villain perhaps explain the extreme neglect of the type as a subject for literary criticism.[22] The villain is a type before she or he is an individual, and as such appears to offer little to literary criticism which prioritizes the hidden over the ostensible, the ambiguous over the absolute, the complex over the simple.

Thus described, the villain appears perfectly consistent with Dickens's subversion of high cultural, psychological ways of seeing. In melodrama, as in any genre, however, villains are villains because

[21] See Chapter 2 below for more on psychology and Romanticism.

[22] One exception to this rule in Dickens studies is John Kucich's chapter 'Villains', in *Excess and Restraint in the Novels of Charles Dickens* (Athens: University of Georgia Press, 1981), 59–104. 'Villainy', he argues, 'is the focal point for the violent energies unleashed by Dickens's novels' (ibid. 61). Villainy in Dickens is a product, Kucich maintains, of this emotional economy. He identifies two main types of villain: the 'real melodramatic', excessive, or transcendent villain—a type whose violence is unmotivated by anything other than a desire to violate boundaries—and the restrained, 'bourgeois' villain who paradoxically affects transcendence for materialistic reasons which are socially circumscribed (ibid. 62–5). Kucich's typology to an extent confirms Taine's view of Dickens's emotional economy. Lionel Trilling's *Sincerity and Authenticity: The Charles Eliot Norton Lectures, 1969–70* (Oxford: Oxford University Press, 1972; rev. edn. 1974), 14–16, and Bernard Spivack's *Shakespeare and the Allegory of Evil: The History of Metaphor in Relation to his Major Villains* (New York: Columbia University Press, 1958), are further valuable contributions to our understanding of literary villainy. See also John Mortimer (ed.), *The Oxford Book of Villains* (Oxford: Oxford University Press, 1992).

For early studies of Dickens's deviants, see Walter Dexter, *Some Rogues and Vagabonds of Dickens* (London: Palmer, 1927), Irving W. Kreutz, 'Sly of Manner, Sharp of Tooth: A Study of Dickens's Villains', *Nineteenth Century Fiction*, 22 (1968), 331–48.

of the threat they pose to the value system upheld by the parent genre. This means that melodramatic villains subvert the dominant ethos of melodrama in ways crucial to this study: they can act duplicitously rather than 'ostensibly'; they are invariably individualistic rather than socially constructive; they expose the existence of the private self which melodrama works so hard to downplay; and, perhaps most importantly, they are often the most intelligent characters in the genre, threatening its general elevation of emotion over intellect. They can be (but need not be) role-players, dandies, intellectuals, or indeed Romantics. Melodramatic villains thus confirm and undermine the melodramatic world view simultaneously. In Dickens's novels, they are frequently the site of tensions and paradoxes which surround the attempt dramatically to marginalize the psyche underpinning Dickens's populist, anti-intellectual project.

This book is structured around melodramatic models of villainy that are passionally defined; needless to say, this typology is a heuristic device rather than a rigid system of categorization. The villain of Gothic melodrama, for instance, is excessively passionate, and comparatively 'honest' about his evil nature; it is this breed that colours popular conceptions of melodramatic villainy. The aristocratic villain of domestic melodrama, to use the pithy terms of many melodramatists, replaced 'heart' with 'art'. He is often a passionless manipulator, conscious of his abilities as an actor. The 'villains' of romantic melodrama tend to combine both principles (of 'heart' and 'art'), thus complicating the usually straightforward ethical scheme of the genre. Likewise the female villain, who is often passionate, repressed, and—like the Victorian actress—obliged to play certain roles. All these villains are products of the dialectical emotional economy governing melodrama, which revolves around the principles of excess and restraint. They are likewise creatures of a rigidly demarcated ethical landscape.

The absence of such inimitable villains as Quilp and Pecksniff from this study arises from the fact that they are comic and pantomimic, rather than melodramatic.[23] The importance of this generic

[23] There is in fact a general critical consensus that Quilp and Pecksniff are pantomimic. In *The Dickens Pantomime*, Eigner calls Pecksniff 'one of the greatest of Dickens' Pantaloons' (p. 72) and Quilp 'one of the most hateful of his Dandy Lovers' (p. 101). See also Coral Lansbury, 'Pecksniffs and Pratfalls', in Carol Hanbery MacKay (ed.), *Dramatic Dickens* (Houndmills: Macmillan, 1989), 45–51. James R. Kincaid has noted—with particular relevance to this discussion—the way that Pecksniff is villain on one page and pantomime buffoon on the next—*Dickens and the Rhetoric of Laughter* (Oxford: Clarendon Press, 1971),

distinction is that, as a consequence of their pantomimic roots, Quilp and Pecksniff are less relevant to the tensions between the 'psychological' and 'theatrical' tendencies under scrutiny here, or to the relationship between the emotions and the mind as figured in Dickens's work. Though inevitably pantomimic characters are open to psychological interpretation, they do not, like melodramatic villains, threaten to valorize interiority or the psyche. In pantomime, selfhood is metamorphic from the outset; the surreal nature of the spectacle demands that selfhood is not circumscribed but protean. As a result, we do not respond to pantomimic characters as emotional— or psychological—beings but as fantastical, kaleidoscopic figures. In other words, whereas melodramatic villains function both figurally and 'realistically'—hence the threat they pose to the parent genre— in pantomime, aesthetic pleasure derives from our sense that we are cocooned in the world of the imaginary. If comedy is to remain unambiguously comic, villainy must be registered intellectually or at a distance; to adapt Bergson, pantomimic villainy produces a 'momentary anaesthesia of the heart'.[24] Readers thus perceive Quilp and Pecksniff as characters in a novel; they are cosseted by their heightened consciousness of the characters' fictionality. They are not 'inferior' characters of lesser moral seriousness; but we respond to them as entertaining 'likenesses' or *symbols* of immorality—or, to quote Dickens on Pecksniff, as 'Great Abstractions' (*MC*, chapter 31, p. 498). John Carey would argue that they have 'no insides';[25] in G. K. Chesterton's terms, they possess an 'original innocence';[26] in the coinage of Bakhtinian theory, they are carnivalesque.[27]

Melodramatic villains threaten, in a variety of different ways, the idea of unitary selfhood. It is thus perhaps unsurprising that key

150–6. Paul Schlicke—in *Dickens and Popular Entertainment*, 125—lists various recent theories about sources for Quilp in popular culture: an actual dwarf named Prior who lived in Bath, the evil dwarf and devil of folklore, the comic devil of the English stage, a fairy tale called 'The Yellow Dwarf', the father of Joseph Grimaldi, and Punch.

[24] Henri Bergson, 'Laughter', in Wylie Sypher, (ed.), *Comedy*, trans. Fred Rothwell (Garden City, NY: Doubleday, 1956), 59–190 (pp. 63–4).

[25] *The Violent Effigy*, 64–5. Carey in fact maintains that it is not only Dickens's hypocrites who have 'no insides', arguing: 'Life customarily consists of physical proximity and mental distance, and this is the essence of Dickens' character creations.'

[26] *Appreciations and Criticisms of the Works of Charles Dickens*, 101. Wilson, in 'Dickens: The Two Scrooges', contrasts the 'innocence' of Dickens's earlier villains with the later, darker villains like Headstone (pp. 82–3).

[27] See Mikhail Bakhtin, *Rabelais and his World*, trans. Hélène Iswolsky (London: MIT Press, 1968).

models of melodramatic villainy closely resemble Romantic models of heroism; whereas melodrama attempts to uphold the fiction of the transparent, public self, high Romanticism explores the multiplicity and complexity of the private self. Melodramatic villains are thus not infrequently internally focused, guilty of self-violation as well as violation of the selfhood of others. Indeed, the dialectical emotional economy of the genre means externally focused violence is often synonymous with violence that is self-directed. In Dickens's novels, the Romantic individual is not infrequently deviant or villainous, and always ideologically and ethically problematic.

For much of his career, Dickens was no admirer of the inwardly focused personality, as is witnessed by his comments on that hero of the Romantics and symbol of 'modern' individualism, Hamlet. In his preface to the Folio Society publication of *A Christmas Carol* manuscript in facsimile, Frederick B. Adams, Jr., notes that after Dickens's early reference to 'Hamlet's Father' in *Carol*, he originally digressed as follows:

Perhaps you think that Hamlet's intellects were strong. I doubt it. If you could have such a son tomorrow, depend upon it, you would find him a poser. He would be a most impracticable fellow to deal with, and however creditable he might be to his family, after his decease, he would prove a special incumbrance in his lifetime, trust me.[28]

Dickens damns Hamlet as an empty emotional vessel when he brands him 'a poser'. To Dickens, Hamlet's understanding of the emotional life of others is impaired by his love affair with his own intellect, and thus, in consequence, his intellectual life is paradoxically incomplete. He is 'a poser' because he is trapped in obsessively self-conscious observance of his own role-playing and intellectual gymnastics. To poach and reapply the words of T. S. Eliot, Hamlet's self-consciousness makes him unable to 'experience' thought in a manner that modifies his sensibility; he is unable to 'feel [. . .] thought as immediately as the odour of a rose'.[29] Ultimately, Hamlet's performative angst makes him, to Dickens, inauthentic rather than sincere, superficial rather than complex.

[28] Quoted by Michael Slater in his notes to *A Christmas Carol* in *The Christmas Books*, 2 vols. (Harmondsworth: Penguin, 1971), i. 257.
[29] 'The Metaphysical Poets' (1921), in *Selected Prose*, ed. John Hayward (London: Penguin, 1953), 111–20 (p. 117). Professor Michael O'Neill has suggested to me that Dickens might be using 'poser' here to mean 'puzzle'. In support of this, *OED* supplies the definition 'A question that poses or puzzles; a puzzle', with citations from 1793 to 1894 (one of them

Dickens's dislike of Hamlet is of a piece with his rejection of the Romantic idea that 'depths, recesses and alienation' of personality make one person more important than another. His refusal of the notion that interiority consitutes authenticity goes some way towards explaining our reaction to Dickens's first person narratives. While these narrratives are nominally 'subjective', we do not feel that we know Dickens's first person narrators 'inside out'. This is particularly true of David and Esther, whose claims to goodness are related to their repression of subject-centred interiority. Pip's deviant characteristics, by contrast, can be read as directly linked to secrecy and self-obsession; his apparent growth to 'maturity', therefore, for the most part involves an attempt to escape from or even forget the self, rather than the kind of inwardly focused self-*analysis* so valued in our own therapy culture. Events or actions, rather than Hamlet-like introspection, are always the starting point for self-knowledge in *Great Expectations*.

To argue that Dickensian aesthetics are melodramatic rather than Romantic is not to argue, however, that Dickens is consciously and straightforwardly anti-romantic. In the preface to *Bleak House*, for example, Dickens emphasizes his intention to reveal 'the romantic side of familiar things'. In the 'Preliminary Word' to *Household Words*, Dickens announces a similar intention, 'To show to all, that in familiar things, and even in those which are repellant on the surface, there is Romance enough.'[30] While Dickens could embrace the terms 'romance' and the 'romantic' when these terms carried the sense of fantasy and adventure, he typically loathed a particular model of 'Romantic' masculinity which defined itself through internalized, intellectualized, and individualistic emotional response.[31] Though several studies of Dickens have emphasized the continuities between

from *Pickwick Papers*). Its first cited use of 'poser' to mean 'One who poses or attitudinizes' is in 1888 (and 'poseur' in 1872). The complicating factor is that the verb 'to pose', meaning 'To present oneself in a certain character (often implying that is assumed)', was used as early as 1840 by Dickens's great rival Thackeray. Moreover, as the *Christmas Carol*'s use of 'poser' exists in manuscript only, this usage would not have been available to the *OED*'s editors. The context of the world in the *Carol* manuscript seems to me to support the reading 'one who poses or attitudinizes'. However, even if one accepts that 'poser' means 'puzzle', Dickens is still rebutting the idea that unfathomable interiority of character is synonymous with intellectual ability. His general point remains that for the intellect to be valuable, it must be socially useful.

[30] *HW* I (30 Mar. 1850), I.

[31] See Chapter 5 below for a fuller discussion of Dickens in relation to both romance and realism.

Romantic and Dickensian models of selfhood, this approach often results in a reinforcement of the very values Dickens was writing against—the privileging, for example, of interiority and 'psychology'—and in a neglect of the melodramatic means by which Dickens renders his insights into character.[32] The introspective individual prominent in high Romanticism was to Dickens constitutive of, and constituted by, a culture of exclusivity.[33]

The potential radicalism of Dickens's melodramatic aesthetics (and villains) has largely eluded academics whose critical practices have remained steeped in the very intellectual elitism (itself rooted in the values of high Romanticism) which Dickens was trying to subvert. I am not arguing, then, that Dickens was pursuing a consciously anti-Romantic agenda in his work, but that the critical reception of Dickens—particularly of Dickensian character—has been distorted by the attempt to judge his work against inappropriately Romantic criteria. The influential biographical work of Wilson, for example, is clearly Romantic in its location of Dickens's personality as the key to Dickens's art: Scrooge, for example, represents 'a principle fundamental to the dynamics of Dickens's world and derived from his own emotional constitution'. Though Wilson concedes that Dickens's fondness for melodrama fuels this constitution, he is keen to position personality as the *origin* of the problem— for emotional extremes are definitely, to Wilson, a problem—and Dickens's poor aesthetic taste (for melodrama) as its superficial manifestation:

It was not *merely* that his passion for the theatre had given him a taste for melodramatic contrasts; it was *rather* that the lack of balance between the opposite impulses of his nature had stimulated an appetite for melodrama. [Previous italics mine.] For emotionally Dickens *was* unstable. Allowing for the English restraint, [. . .] he seems almost as unstable as Dostoevsky.[34]

---

[32] See Dirk Den Hartog's *Dickens and Romantic Psychology: The Self in Time in Nineteenth Century Literature* (Houndmills: Macmillan, 1987) for a comparatively recent example of this kind of character criticism: 'the mature Dickens had moved away from the eighteenth century tradition of static and self-contained characters [. . .]. Where earlier Dickensian comic characters had performed themselves as a spontaneous emanation of their being, the maturer intelligence moves away from this fictional convention to a sophisticated psychological realism' (p. 81). See also Donald D. Stone, *The Romantic Impulse in Victorian Fiction* (Cambridge, Mass.: Harvard University Press, 1980), Lawrence Frank, *Charles Dickens and the Romantic Self* (Lincoln: University of Nebraska Press, 1984).

[33] See Chapter 2 for more on the connection between high Romanticism and cultural exclusivity.

[34] 'Dickens: The Two Scrooges', 62.

Wilson's subordination of popular culture to 'interiority' as a means of making sense of Dickens is reinforced in most Dickens criticism. If we take a sample of the most infamous critical judgements on Dickens, for example, all utilize and reinforce the cultural hierarchies Romanticism did so much to establish. Henry James famously labelled Dickens 'the greatest of superficial novelists';[35] F. R. Leavis reified the contradictions inherent in his own value system by dubbing Dickens a 'great entertainer'.[36] G. H. Lewes maintained that there was not 'a single thoughtful remark' in the whole Dickens canon, adding: 'He never was and never would have been a student'.[37] Associating emotion with interiority, George Eliot argued that Dickens 'scarcely ever passed from the humorous and external to the emotional and tragic, without becoming [. . .] transcendent in his unreality'.[38] All uphold and perpetuate the Romantic elevation of 'depths' over surfaces, and of conscious intelligence over spontaneous emotion. All underestimate the epistemological sophistication informing Dickens's scepticism about 'depths' and the ideological significance of Dickens's refusal to valorize interiority. All read Dickens, in other words, in terms of cultural assumptions to which he was opposed.

Dickens's most consistent political aim was to counter cultural elitism. To counter cultural exclusivity is not as straightforward a task as it immediately appears, however, as contemporary cultural theory has made all too clear.[39] This introduction, for example, has outlined Dickens's *ideals* for both popular culture and 'dramatic entertainment', whereas the main body of the book also considers the contradictions and anxieties which attend these ideals. A significant body of melodrama criticism typifies a marked tendency within cultural theory to assume that popular cultural modes invariably peddle a

---

[35] '*Our Mutual Friend*', *Nation*, 1 (21 Dec. 1865), 786–8 (p. 787).

[36] F. R. Leavis, *The Great Tradition*, Peregrine (London: Chatto & Windus, 1948; Harmondsworth: Penguin, 1962), 29. Leavis, of course, later implies a change of heart about Dickens's 'greatness' as a 'serious' novelist without explicitly admitting the change— see F. R. and Q. D. Leavis, *Dickens the Novelist* (London: Chatto & Windus, 1970), p. ix.

[37] 'Dickens in Relation to Criticism', *Fortnightly Review*, 11 (Feb. 1872), 141–54 (pp. 151–4). Donald Stone points out interestingly that Lewes changes his position on Dickens's emphasis on emotion; in 1837, Lewes was a 'young Hegelian' who believed that 'the primary aim of art was not mimetic but emotive'. He hence praised *Oliver Twist* as 'pregnant with philosophy and feeling'—see Stone, *The Romantic Impulse in Victorian Fiction*, 253.

[38] 'The Natural History of German Life', *Westminster Review*, 10 (1 July 1856), 51–79; repr. in *Selected Essays, Poems and Other Writings*, ed. A. S. Byatt and Nicholas Warren (Harmondsworth: Penguin, 1990), 107–39 (p. 111).

[39] See Chapter 1 below.

popular conservatism which undermines the radical political potential of popular culture.[40] This book argues, first, that it is impossible to 'fix' the ideology of any genre—let alone popular culture in its entirety—as much depends on cultural context, which is itself metamorphic. It maintains further that the political significance of any work goes far beyond that work's overt ideologies; in the case of stage melodrama and Dickens's novels, for example, it is surely absurd to argue that the conservative ideologies inherent in both— the emphasis on family and community, for example—negate the potential radicalism of the fact that both were addressing an entirely new audience of workers and artisans in a language to which they could relate. Cultural politics, in other words, are not necessarily synonymous with politics *per se*. My view of the contradictions in Dickens's populist project, therefore, avoids the easy option of off-setting Dickens's populist aspirations against the conservative ideologies which arguably oppress that very populace he was trying to serve. Not even the most fervent Dickensian would argue that Dickens's strengths lie in his explicit political or sociological pronouncements or analysis. This book assumes that Dickens's most radical contribution to cultural politics is his aesthetic practice.

To be popular as well as radical is a contradictory, near impossible task. Dickens's stubborn reliance on populist melodramatic aesthetics constitutes, in my account, his attempt to revise established generic, literary, and cultural hierarchies. By catering for a commonly disenfranchized section of the cultural market place and forcing its existence on the attention of the intelligentsia, Dickens subverts the cultural status quo. To 'cater for' an audience is not, however, the same as to empower them. Through Dickens's villains, this book examines Dickens's shifting attitudes to interiority and theatricality, and the implications of these shifts for his attempt to empower, entertain, and instruct the populace through literature. The most obvious problem attending Dickens's populism consists in the fact that where the stage could cater for the illiterate, Dickens's main audience (readings aside) had to be literate. It is possible to argue that Dickens saw the potential of the novel to reach a far bigger audience than any theatre could contain, and indeed, Dickens's own career accelerated the process by which the novel became more widely read and widely available. This does not of course address the problem of literacy. A determined defence of Dickens's populist credentials could empha-

[40] See Chapter 1 below.

size the role of stage adaptations in delivering Dickens's stories to the masses, or that of Dickens's own reading tours. However, I do not wish to foreground any of these arguments: rather, I accept that Dickens's populism is predicated on a paradox, but reject the assumption that this paradox invalidates either Dickens's populism or academic attempts to understand it.

Another, less intransigent, problem with the association Dickens makes between externalized aesthetics and cultural inclusivity is that where the theatrical experience is public, novel reading is more often than not a private experience. Indeed, Foucauldian criticism—most notably D. A. Miller's *The Novel and the Police*—has argued forcefully that the novel reinforces the valorization of privacy to which Dickens (and melodramatic aesthetics) is opposed. My response to this should by now be clear: Dickens was conscious of the subject-centred bias of dominant cultural modes like the classic realist novel, and his own theatrical novels work to counter this tendency. Though Dickens is as hostile to the subject-centred view as Foucault, his novels subvert the idea (ironically reinforced by Foucauldian criticism) that privacy is solely synonymous with a carceral form of innerness.[41] His conception of the imagination is, as we have seen, that it should ideally help the individual to escape out of the prison of the self. The 'private' reading experience should be similarly outwardly focused; we think of David Copperfield, for example, reading eighteenth-century theatrical novels 'as if for life' (chapter 4, p. 48).

Neither imagination nor reading always function to aid selflessness and communality, of course, as Dickens's novels make clear. There are problems too with the idea of emotion as an egalitarian medium of communication.[42] As early as *Oliver Twist*, for example, Dickens was self-reflexively analysing the potential of emotion, the mainstay of melodramatic aesthetics, as an instrument of power as well as empowerment. Throughout his writings, Dickens's fascination with social role-playing typifies his un-Romantic 'outside in' approach to

[41] Deborah Vlock has persuasively pinpointed the way in which Foucauldian narratives have paradoxically reinforced 'an unexamined belief in the interiority of modern culture', erasing the spectacular and the theatrical. *Dickens, Novel Reading, and the Victorian Popular Theatre*, 2. I would add a couple of points by way of embellishment rather than argument: first, the belief that is unexamined in modern critical thought is in the interiority of *high* culture; the theatrical is thus often defined oppositionally as vulgar or low, hence its erasure from traditional and theoretical critical histories. Second, the tendency of Foucault and his followers is to use the idea of privacy monologically, associating it unquestionably with a repressive, fake subjectivity.

[42] See Chapter 5 below.

identity. Ultimately interiority is only as knowable, in Dickens, as its (frequently duplicitous) external or social manifestations. However, the fact that Dickens's 'ostensible', naive models of character are largely modelled on stage prototypes brought to life by actors gives some indication of Dickens's intense ambivalence about the ethical and social function both of acting itself and of melodramatic models of identity. Dickens's ideal externalized individual, in other words, is largely an act or an illusion. Again, in the later novels, the increasing sympathy with which Romantic individuals like Eugene Wrayburn are treated suggests a reassessment of the introspective individual and his contribution to a culture of exclusivity, as well as a related reassessment of the 'transparent', melodramatic personality to which, in Dickens's novels, he is so often contrasted.

Dickens's central anxiety about his populist project seems to concern the flagrant unreality of the melodramatic models underpinning it. The fact that Dickens continues to depend on such melodramatic models even in his late novels is testimony to his vision of the social and ethical function of art. The main function of art, to Dickens, is not necessarily to reflect reality but to improve that reality. But idealized versions of reality may constitute the same kind of staged illusion about which, in his responses to acting, Dickens was ambivalent. Dickens's anxieties about the imposition that utopian artistic models may represent is commonly attended, therefore, by a self-conscious exposure of the fictional nature of his ideals. Melodramatic models are filtered through a double perspective which draws attention to their desirability and unreality. The melodramatic villain, as both resident and alien in the melodramatic world, is frequently the key site of this double perspective.

Post-structuralist criticism has done much to draw attention to the sophistication of Dickens's self-reflexivity, and to counter the crude notion that Dickens was a failed realist or psychologist.[43] His texts expose the very structures—emotional, linguistic, and ideological— on which they rest. However, to expose is not the same as to reject, and Dickens's texts retain a distinctive tendency to uphold and undermine beliefs and structures simultaneously. Though post-structuralist readings provide ways of appreciating aspects of Dickens's writing commonly neglected by critics immersed in Romantic value systems, their characteristic emphasis on the

[43] Schad (ed.), *Dickens Re-Figured*, contains some good examples of post-structuralist criticism of Dickens.

fictionality of both texts and social experience can lead to a neglect of the ideological and ethical principles which underpin Dickens's literary gamesmanship. J. Hillis Miller's influential essay 'The Fiction of Realism', for example, sets the tone for subsequent accounts: Dickens's self-reflexivity, he maintains, draws attention to the never-ending hermeneutic process which comprises the relationship between text (including the critical text) and the social world. The interpretative chain on which Dickens's texts reflect 'creates illusion out of illusion and the appearance of reality out of illusion, in a play of language without beginning, end or extra linguistic foundation'.[44] Exclusive concentration on the self-conscious fictionality of Dickens's texts can turn both Dickens's works and literary criticism into a self-contained intellectual performance of little relevance to the social world—can lead, that is, to exactly the sort of cultural segregation to which Dickens was so opposed.

To talk generally, much Dickens criticism still seems to belong to either the post-structuralist or the mimetic school—one tending to stress the self-reflexive fictionality of Dickens's texts, and the other tending to treat the novels as representations of social and/or psychological realities. Dickens's novels in fact present a self-consciously idealized and problematized version of reality in which, most importantly, the mind is marginalized. Since G. H. Lewes complained of the apparent brainlessness of Dickens's characters, critics have been slow to investigate the political purposes informing Dickens's externalized aesthetics. In Dickens's ideal world, the brain should not be the most important part of either the individual or the cultural anatomy.

---

[44] In Lilian R. Furst (ed.), *Realism*, Modern Literatures in Perspective (London: Longman, 1992), 287–318 (p. 315); repr. from 'The Fiction of Realism: *Sketches by Boz, Oliver Twist*, and Cruikshank's Illustrations', in Ada Nisbet and Blake Nevius (eds.), *Dickens Centennial Essays* (Berkeley and Los Angeles: University of California Press, 1971), 85–126. See also Chapter 5 below.

PART I

Melodrama, Villainy, Acting

I

Intellectual Incorrectness: Melodrama, Populism, Cultural Hierarchies

MELODRAMA AND THE ACADEMY

For a century, melodrama was virtually ignored by literary criticism.[1] What makes this silence particularly strange is that melodrama was the most popular kind of theatrical entertainment for much of the nineteenth century, and 'more people went to the theatre during the nineteenth century than at any time in history'.[2] Its very popularity is indeed the 'problem'—the problem at least for the institutionalized disciplines of the academy. The history of the academic study of English literature, for example, provides ample explanation for the suppression of melodrama in literary histories before the 1960s. From

---

[1] In *The World of Melodrama*, published in 1967, Frank Rahill stated confidently: 'No serious and comprehensive study of melodrama has appeared in any language' (University Park: Pennsylvania State University Press, 1967), p. xiii. Though Disher's learned but poorly referenced *Blood and Thunder: Mid-Victorian Melodrama and its Origins* (London: Muller, 1949) poses a potential challenge to this claim, Rahill is largely correct in his assertion. There had been glimmers of interest before Rahill's work, of course. Bernard Shaw, for example, argued that if melodrama is of a high enough standard, 'why, then one has *Lear* or *Macbeth*'—Bernard Shaw to Ellen Terry (26 Mar. 1896), in *Ellen Terry and Bernard Shaw: A Correspondence*, ed. Christopher St John (New York, 1931), 21; quoted by Louis James, in 'Was Jerrold's *Black Ey'd Susan* More Popular than Wordsworth's *Lucy*?', in David Bradby, Louis James, and Bernard Sharratt (eds.), *Performance and Politics in Popular Drama: Aspects of Popular Entertainment in Theatre, Film and Television, 1800–1976* (Cambridge: Cambridge University Press, 1980), 3–16 (p. 3). T. S. Eliot's 'Wilkie Collins and Dickens' (1929) acknowledges the continuity—indeed potential synonymity—which exists between 'drama' and 'melodrama'—*Selected Essays*, 3rd edn. (London: Faber & Faber, 1951; repr. 1965), 460–70. In 1948, Wylie Sypher identified melodrama as the defining modality of the 19th century—'Aesthetic of Revolution: The Marxist Melodrama', *Kenyon Review*, 10 (1948), 431–44. And some of the most thoughtful insights into melodrama I have enountered are contained in Eric Bentley's *The Life of the Drama* (New York: Atheneum, 1964). None of these accounts are extended considerations of melodrama, however, and all except Sypher define melodrama loosely and trans-historically.

[2] Gabrielle Hyslop, 'Researching the Acting of French Melodrama, 1800–1830', *Nineteenth Century Theatre*, 15 (1987), 85–114 (p. 85).

Matthew Arnold, the 'founding father' of the discipline, to his disciple F. R. Leavis, the rationale informing English literary studies was that 'great' literature could and should refine and civilize the individual, regardless of his or her class background. Q. D. Leavis's contempt for twentieth-century popular culture typifies a larger contempt for popular culture *per se*: for her, it encourages 'a set of habits inimical to mental effort' and offers 'the temptation to accept [. . .] cheap and easy pleasures'.[3] This opposition between 'mental effort' and 'easy pleasures' is exactly that which Dickens attacked in his writings on the popular theatre. To his and our detriment, it has permeated university English for over a century. Melodrama has been an inevitable casualty of this kind of intellectual elitism, which places more importance on the educated individual than it does on either the uneducated person or the socially defined group.

In the last thirty years, however, academic enquiries into melodrama have proliferated, and continue to do so. Critical orthodoxy positions the publication of Peter Brooks's *The Melodramatic Imagination* as the initiating moment in the 'serious' study of melodrama.[4] Brooks's central thesis is by now familiar: 'the melodramatic mode', he argues, is a means of 'uncovering, demonstrating, and making operative the essential moral universe in a post-sacred era'.[5] Brooks's use of tools like psychoanalysis and expressionism to analyse the melodramatic 'mode' (rather than genre), as it manifested itself in the novels of canonical writers like Balzac and Henry James, was groundbreaking at the time in many different ways. However, as I shall argue in Chapter 2, *The Melodramatic Imagination* is a landmark volume because it makes melodrama acceptable to literary studies rather than accommodating literary studies to melodrama. The real breakthrough in the critical acceptability of melodrama should have come with the shifts in methodology effected by Cultural Studies and the critical theories informing it. The leftist politics underpinning much of critical theory and Cultural Studies make the study of popular culture imperative, and the individual less important than the politically or economically defined group. This is not to say, however, that Marxist—or indeed feminist—attitudes to popular culture

---

[3] *Fiction and the Reading Public* (London: Chatto & Windus, 1932), 224–5.

[4] For example, Jacky Bratton, Jim Cook, and Christine Gledhill (eds.), *Melodrama: Stage, Picture, Screen* (London: British Film Institute, 1994), structures itself around responses to Brooks's work.

[5] Peter Brooks, *The Melodramatic Imagination: Balzac, Henry James, Melodrama and the Mode of Excess* (New Haven: Yale University Press, 1976), p. 15.

are generally sympathetic. In shifting the critical emphasis away from questions of aesthetic value to ideological analyses of cultural formations, popular cultural studies, as Stuart Hall put it, 'has tended to oscillate wildly between two alternate poles of that dialectic— containment/resistance'.[6] In other words, does popular culture represent an authentic expression of the tastes and values of the populace, or is it an ideological instrument by which 'the people' are suppressed?

Though the theories of Gramsci and Bakhtin are potentially useful for left-wing optimists who want to argue that political resistance can be effected through popular culture, so far the dominant voice of the left has been pessimistic in its view of the liberating potential of popular culture. From the Frankfurt School to the currently influential work of Foucault, the politically credible view is that popular culture inculcates a 'false consciousness' in its consumers and functions as a formidable instrument of political control. Interestingly for our purposes, Foucault positions the transition between the eighteenth and nineteenth centuries—the same period that witnessed the emergence of melodrama as a 'new' genre—as the historical moment when 'the people' were stripped of their culture.[7] Characteristically, he does not give his theoretical meta-narrative textual flesh, but there is an abundance of critiques of melodrama—not necessarily Foucauldian—which reinforce the message that stage melodrama at this time peddled a popular conservatism which kept the people in their place.[8] Such blanket assumptions typify the intellectual elitism which has permeated a particular kind of politicized response to popular culture; such responses ironically uphold the

---

[6] 'Notes on Deconstructing the Popular', in Raphael Samuel (ed.), *People's History and Socialist Theory* (London: Routledge & Kegan Paul, 1981), 227–40 (p. 228).

[7] Foucault argues that crime fiction underwent 'a whole aesthetic rewriting' at the turn of the century, at first functioning as 'two-sided discourses' which spoke to both 'the people' and those in political control, and eventually emerging as the 'literature' of crime: 'The split was complete; the people was robbed of its old pride in its crimes; the great murders had become the quiet game of the well behaved'—*Discipline and Punish: The Birth of the Prison* (1975), trans. Alan Sheridan (London: Penguin, 1991), 68–9.

[8] A clear expression of this position is voiced by Gabrielle Hyslop, who generalizes on the basis of her research on Pixérécourt: 'melodrama is popular in the sense of being *for* the common people. [. . .] It is not proletarian art. Like other forms of mass media, Pixérécourt melodramas were presented in order to impose the views of the dominant social class on the common people. Melodrama expresses the conservative patriarchal ideas of the middle class who aim to control the opinions and life-styles of the men and women they regard as their inferiors'—'Deviant and Dangerous Behaviour: Women in Melodrama', *Journal of Popular Culture*, 19 (1985), 65–77 (p. 66). See also E. Ann Kaplan, 'Theories of Melodrama: A Feminist Perspective', *Women and Performance*, 1 (1983), 40–8.

Leavisite elevation of 'mental effort' over 'immediate pleasure'. Antony Easthope puts it bluntly: 'To liberal, Frankfurt and dominant ideology theories of the high/popular cultural divide the same single objection can be made—they assume that ordinary people are fools'[9].

Melodrama is an anti-intellectual genre which sets out to subvert, rather than replicate, the value systems most commonly used to condemn it. It is only by placing melodrama in the context of the cultural history which produced it that we can begin to gain an idea of the politics informing this anti-intellectualism—as it manifests itself both on the popular stage and in Dickens's melodramatic art.[10] In the aftermath of the French Revolution, melodrama values the simple passions of the many above the complex angst of the few. In this sense, melodrama is the alter ego of high Romanticism. While this book freely draws on recent theoretical instruments, it also contends that there remains a vast gap in our *knowledge* of the nineteenth-century stage and our understanding of the cultural and ideological significance of its modes of representation.

Melodrama and Populism: Aesthetics

The question of what made melodrama so popular is often explained in *either* historical or aesthetic terms. The reality is that both melo-drama's formal characteristics and the social and cultural conditions of its birth contributed to its popularity. As melodrama was originally

---

[9] Antony Easthope, *Literary into Cultural Studies* (London: Routledge, 1991), 79; on Marxist elitism see also the introduction to Jean Radford (ed.), *The Progress of Romance: The Politics of Popular Fiction* (London: Routledge & Kegan Paul, 1986), 1–20 (p. 13).

[10] I am of course not alone in calling for the historicization of melodramatic politics. Several recent studies have argued against monolithic interpretations of melodramatic ideologies as simply 'conservative' by contextualizing melodrama. See, for example, Michael Hays and Anastasia Nikolopoulou (eds.), *Melodrama: The Cultural Emergence of a Genre* (Basingstoke: Macmillan, 1996), and Elaine Hadley's *Melodramatic Tactics: Theatricalized Dissent in the English Marketplace, 1800–1885* (Stanford, Calif.: Stanford University Press, 1995), which is a brilliant mapping of the processes—textual, cultural, economic, and political—by which the ideology of a particular genre or 'mode' is mediated, appropriated, and metamorphosed. Again, there has also been a steady stream of readings of the infusion of radical politics in melodrama—for example, Anna Clark, 'The Politics of Seduction in English Popular Culture, 1748–1848', in Radford (ed.), *The Progress of Romance*, 47–70. Hays and Nikolopoulou discuss 'melodrama's early radical traces' in their introduction to *Melodrama: The Cultural Emergence of a Genre*, p. viii. What is disappointing, however, is the demonization of aesthetics which informs so many of these historical studies. My work is premised on the assumption that aesthetics remain integral to a detailed and nuanced understanding of the politics of cultural formations, as film and media studies have been particularly advanced in understanding.

designed for those who could not read, nineteenth-century stage melodrama offered Dickens an inclusive, populist, indeed anti-intellectual aesthetics. Melodrama fulfils the infamous definition of fiction supplied by Oscar Wilde's Miss Prism: 'The good ended happily, and the bad unhappily. That is what Fiction means.'[11] The structural backbone of melodrama is the battle between good and evil, a battle in which good invariably—though often unconvincingly —triumphs. The world of melodrama is 'a world of absolutes where virtue and vice coexist in pure whiteness and pure blackness'; it is 'a world of certainties',[12] in which evil is vanquished far more consistently than it is in reality. Melodrama's underlying pattern of ethical fantasy thus grows from the morality of fairyland. As Michael R. Booth puts it,

Essentially, melodrama is a dream world inhabited by dream people and dream justice, offering audiences the fulfilment and satisfaction found only in dreams. An idealization and simplification of reality, it is in fact what its audiences want but cannot get. Melodrama is [. . .] an allegory of human experience dramatically ordered, [a world] as it should be rather than as it is.[13]

Melodramatic 'simplification' functions primarily through the objectification or 'ostension' of that which is normally invisible or hidden. Character, for example, is normally 'transparent'. The audience cannot fail to understand immediately—through appearance, music, and sometimes language—a character's destined role in the play and his or her ethical substance. The presentation of character rests firmly on what can be neatly described as a 'pigeon-hole' system which allows little room for character development. To quote Booth, 'melodrama demands superficial "instant" characters who behave in the same way, think in the same way, and act in the same way'[14] throughout the play. Part of the appeal of melodramatic 'types' is that they are usually characterized by what Robert Heilman calls 'monopathy', or 'the singleness of feeling that gives one the sense of wholeness'—an emotional structure that pervades melodrama as a genre.[15]

[11] *The Importance of Being Earnest*, in *Complete Works of Oscar Wilde* (Glasgow: HarperCollins, 1994), 357–419 (p. 376); ii.
[12] Michael R. Booth, *English Melodrama* (London: Jenkins, 1965), 14.
[13] Ibid.
[14] Ibid. 15.
[15] *Tragedy and Melodrama: Versions of Experience* (Seattle: University of Washington Press, 1968), 243.

In keeping with its anti-intellectualism and its origins as 'illegitimate' (or non-verbal) drama, melodrama does not place any particular value on language other than as one tool of communication
among several. Melodramatic dialogue, therefore, for the most part
shuns complexity and lyricism. Most commentators emphasize that
'the dialogue of melodrama is, if nothing else, totally functional with
respect to action';[16] as a consequence of its functional purpose, 'melodramatic dialogue ranges in quality from the wooden to the smoothly
competent'.[17] The functional nature of melodramatic language does
not mean, however, that it imitates the language of social interaction.
Melodramatic language is functional with respect to the theatre;
paradoxically, it is thus often rhetoric with a 'literary ancestry'.[18]
Although critics are right to emphasize the direct link between
dialogue and action in melodrama, dialogue fulfils a second, equally
important purpose: the externalization of emotion. In most melodrama, no passion remains unexpressed, and each passion is
expressed unequivocally through music, the body, spectacle, and, not
invariably, words. The language of emotion is always extreme, and
seemingly exaggerated. In Watts Phillips's *Lost in London*, for example,
Job Armroyd, the injured husband, is so hurt that he cannot bear to
hear the voice of his fallen wife, pleading: 'Dunna speak! I canna
bear it! The soun' o' thy voice kills me'; despite the risk of her
husband's death, the fallen wife must express her feelings too, crying
'Job! Job! I love you, I love you.'[19] In W. H. Murrey's *Obi; or,
Three-Fingered Jack* (2 July 1800, H.2), the villain leaves the audience in
no doubt about his feelings. Jack tells his captive Rosa: 'you have
doubtless heard of Karfa's cruelties; but know, it is *not merely thirst of
blood that fires me*—a *nobler* passion nerves my arm—*vengeance*! [. . .]
Karfa's *word* is as his *hate*—unalterable!'[20] The rejection of secrecy is
one way in which melodrama collapses the dichotomy between
surfaces and depths prevalent in Romantic and post-Romantic intellectual activity.

Externalization is the melodramatic meta-technique by which

[16] Joseph Donohue, *Theatre in the Age of Kean* (Oxford: Blackwell, 1975), 114.

[17] Ibid.

[18] W. D. Howarth, 'Word and Image in Pixérécourt's Melodramas: The Dramaturgy of
the Strip-Cartoon', in Bradby et al. (eds.), *Performance and Politics in Popular Drama*, 17–32 (p.
22).

[19] In Michael R. Booth (ed.), *Hiss the Villain: Six English and American Melodramas* (London:
Eyre & Spottiswoode, 1964), 203–69 (p. 263; III. i).

[20] *Dicks*, [no.] 478 (London: Dicks, [1883]), 7 (II. iii).

depths and surfaces become synonymous; it therefore undermines the idea of the 'private' individual so crucial in nineteenth-century culture in general and the realist novel in particular. Externalization is perhaps most evident in melodrama in the use of physiognomy and gesture. Both physiognomy and gesture dramatize character, emotion, and moral fibre in visual, physical terms. They combine to form an accessible, bodily semiotics, more valuable in melodramatic aesthetics than the spoken word. It would be incorrect to claim that character is always evident from facial appearance, but it is true to say that physiognomy often corresponds with character—often enough, for instance, for exceptions to the physiognomy-equals-inner nature equation to be pointed out to the audience. In Douglas Jerrold's *Black-Eyed Susan; or, All in the Downs* (8 June 1829, Surrey), for example, Raker soliloquizes: 'I must look a villain, and that's the truth. Well, there is no help for an ugly countenance; but if my face be ill-favoured, I'll take care to keep my heart of the right colour.'[21] Again, in the same play, Jacob is accused of having 'a most Tyburn-like physiognomy' and reminds Gnatbrain 'of the Newgate Calendar' (p. 165; I. iii), but nonetheless, he finally turns his back on wickedness.

Gesture is arguably a more reliable index of inner nature in melo-drama. Although a century-long argument had been in progress about whether the actor should learn his trade by adopting the conventions of the stage or by confronting his own emotions, the tendency of early nineteenth-century acting, especially in melo-drama, was 'towards consistent objectification'.[22] Acting manuals were available which provided diagrammatic illustrations of the gestural 'translation' of numerous human emotions. One such manual, Henry Siddons's translation *Practical Illustrations of Rhetorical Gesture and Action*, divided 'all modifications of the body [. . .] into two ranks or classes—the gestures *picturesque* and the gestures *expressive*', enquiring:

Why would not a collection of expressive gestures and attitudes be as easy as a collection of drawings, plants, or shells? And if this affair should one day become an object of serious study, why should not technical words be in

---

[21] In Michael R. Booth (ed.), *English Plays of the Nineteenth Century*, 5 vols. (Oxford: Clarendon Press, 1969–76), i (1969), 151–200 (p. 160; I. ii).

[22] Donohue, *Theatre in the Age of Kean*, 68; Joseph R. Roach has demonstrated in meticulous detail how, in the 18th and 19th centuries, acting theory was not anomalous but a reflection of the latest physiological and 'psychological' theories of the emotions—see *The Player's Passion: Studies in the Science of Acting* (Newark: University of Delaware Press, 1985).

time found out as proper for this science as those at present discovered for the facilitation of the study of natural history?[23]

The kind of science Siddons/Engel had in mind was classificatory, emphasizing clarity rather than complexity. This objectification of emotion is in keeping with melodrama's communal, anti-individualistic agenda. Emotions are robbed of the unique status often accorded to them in post-Freudian culture; they do not 'belong' to the individual experiencing them but to common experience.

The emotional basis of melodrama and its compulsion to externalize emotional states largely account for the perceived excess of the genre. Leftist critics of melodrama have experienced significant discomfort with the emotional 'excess' of melodrama, often choosing to believe that melodramatic emotion is experienced ironically by its audiences. The 'ironic' theory of excess derives from a well-meaning desire not to patronize audiences of melodrama; the assumption is that working-class audiences must be too intelligent to be satisfied by emotion alone. Looked at from another perspective, however, such ironizing of excess reinforces the intellectual hierarchy in which emotional experience, to be valuable, must be thoughtful. As importantly, the 'ironic' interpretation of excess—like the notion of excess in general—negates the possibility, explored at the beginning of chapter 17 of *Oliver Twist*, that emotional excess is not in fact excessive to those immersed in passional experience.[24] To adopt a rational, analytic perspective on excessive emotional representations, as the professional critic is so often required to do, guarantees that such representations appear excessive.

It is virtually impossible to know with any certainty how nineteenth-century theatre audiences processed emotional 'excess'. What is certain, however, is that nineteenth-century melodrama is

---

[23] Henry Siddons, *Practical Illustrations of Rhetorical Gesture and Action*, 2nd edn. (London: Sherwood, Neely & Jones, 1822), 21, 25; Siddons's is a translation of a work by M. Engel. See also Gustave García, *The Actor's Art: A Practical Treatise on Stage Declamation, Public Speaking and Deportment*, 2nd edn. (London: Simpkin, Marshall, 1888), Leman Thomas Rede, *The Road to the Stage; or, The Performer's Preceptor* (London: Smith, 1827).

[24] See Chapter 5 below on this passage from *OT* and emotional excess; Jane Shattuc's ' "Having a Good Cry over The Color Purple": The Problem of Affect and Imperialism in Feminist Theory' is an excellent critique of the 'contempt' inherent in academic dismissals of emotion excess—see Bratton et al. (eds.), *Melodrama: Stage, Picture, Screen*, 147–56 (p. 151). Shattuc argues convincingly that 'all melodramas produce a double hermeneutic: a positive one which draws on the emotional power of authentic liberatory aspirations [. . .] and a negative one which recuperates the Utopian impulse in complicity with an oppressive ideology' (Bratton et al, introductory summary, *Melodrama: Stage, Picture, Screen*, 6).

not simply excessive: apparent excess always exists in a dialectical relationship with restraining mechanisms.This dialectical emotional economy informs my typology of villainy. Even monopathy, as Heilman calls it, is however a form of excess within boundaries—the boundaries provided by the conventions of characterization/stereotype and genre. The excesses of melodrama's villains are only palatable to the audience because of the rigidly schematic ethical and aesthetic framework of the parent genre which acts as a restraining mechanism. Indeed, the excess/restraint dialectic manifests itself in the aesthetics of the genre as well as in its overt ideologies. The gestural 'language of the passions', for example, as I shall show in Chapter 4, renders emotion visible and static, thereby seeming to contain it. This convention in a sense epitomizes the controlled excess of melodrama, whereby even the most violent of emotional states are objectified and momentarily contained. The use of tableaux, stock types, and predictable pictorial endings all function similarly, allowing an outlet for excess within clearly established boundaries. These boundaries are clearly established, of course, because the restraining mechanisms of melodrama are conventions of the genre. The pictorial can be interpreted as yet another means of containing, even policing, excess. Familiarity with melodramatic convention creates the conditions by which intense emotions can be experienced 'safely'.

This emotional safety is not necessarily conservative, however. Take the melodramatic happy ending: the familiar ideological critique regards the restoration of familial and communal stability that concludes most melodrama as crystallizing the conservatism of the play as a whole.[25] The logic informing such arguments assumes that the 'static', restrained moments in melodrama render the excesses of the genre irrelevant. This is not how melodrama works. The emotional economy of melodrama is best figured as a series of waves: the moment of stasis is remarkable only because it is transitory; moments of restraint signify immanent excess and vice versa. The melodramatic ending is thus both reassuring and fragile. As Simon Shepherd puts it, 'points of arrival are not necessarily points of achieved stability'.[26]

---

[25] See the introductory summary of Simon Shepherd's essay 'Pauses of Mutual Agitation' (pp. 25–37) on 'the assumed simplicity of melodrama's ethical emotions and fantasy solutions', in Bratton et al. (eds.), *Melodrama: Stage, Picture, Screen*, 2.

[26] Shepherd, 'Pauses of Mutual Agitation', 34.

This is not to deny that melodrama is formulaic, but simply to reassess some of our assumptions about formulaic cultural expressions. It is common in cultural theory to regard the formulaic emotionalism typical of mass culture as oppressive in its tendency to standardize both art and its consumers. Dwight MacDonald's 'A Theory of Mass Culture', for example, opposes 'a narcotized acceptance of Mass Culture and of the commodities it sells' to 'the unsettling and unpredictable (hence unstable) joy, tragedy, wit, change, originality and beauty of real life'. 'The masses', he surmises, 'debauched by several generations of this sort of thing, in turn come to demand trivial and comfortable cultural products.'[27] MacDonald's overtly high cultural bias is perhaps surprisingly replicated in the work of Marxist theorist Theodor Adorno, who accused the 'culture industry' of 'standardization' of its cultural products and its consumers, and of 'liquidating an individuality past saving': popular music, for example, 'mummifies the vulgarized and decaying remnants of romantic individualism'.[28] Both these views are grounded in Romantic aesthetics, assuming, first, that to be valuable, emotional experience must be unique to the individual, and second, that social improvement is a corollary of individual self-improvement. Both uphold the Romantic dichotomy between surfaces and depths, assuming that formulae are superficial but individuals are deep. The early nineteenth-century stage reversed this hierarchy, valuing intelligible over internalized feeling and developing a system of classification and objectification in order to maximize this intelligibility. Dickens's appropriation of the formulaic emotional expressions of melodrama recognizes their potential usefulness in a communal, anti-intellectual semiotics.

Formulaic expressions of emotion were partly necessitated, of course, by changes in the physical structure of the nineteenth-century theatre itself. Rowell observes in *The Victorian Theatre* that the population of London almost trebled in size between 1811 and 1851, and, in consequence, theatres often trebled in size. Actors were thus required to 'broaden' their style in order to be seen and heard.[29] 'Constructed' projections of emotion could be powerfully affective in the vast public space of such theatres. Melodramatic acting was

[27] In Bernard Rosenberg and David Manning White (eds.), *Mass Culture: The Popular Arts in America* (Glencoe, Ill.: Free Press, 1957), 59–73 (pp. 72–3).

[28] *The Culture Industry* (1941; London: Routledge, 1991), 31, 46, 48.

[29] George Rowell, *The Victorian Theatre, 1792–1914: A Survey* (London: Oxford University Press, 1956), 1.

characterized 'by vocal exaggeration and by "quick and stirring actions" growing out of an expertise in pantomime'.[30] Such conditions meant that, increasingly, actors became more important than playwrights. The 'star' system evolved on the early Victorian stage along with the tradition of the 'stock company'. Melodrama was ideal material for both star and stock company, often offering the stars highly theatrical roles on which to exert their histrionic gusto, and the stock company the security and perfectibility of a recurring set of stereotypical roles—hero, heroine, comic man, and, of course, villain. The playwright became 'handyman to the company'.[31]

The downgrading of the cultural status of the playwright, though largely economically determined, is in keeping with melodrama's anti-intellectual aspirations. The star status accorded to the company's principal actor, by contrast, is potentially subversive of its anti-individualistic tendencies and what Anastasia Nikolopoulou calls its 'artisan cultural practice'.[32] But even the elevation of the actor is from one perspective in keeping with melodrama's subordination of the 'private' self; actors after all make their living by way of self-metamorphosis. Their visible, public acts are thus what is interesting about them and these 'acts' are potentially subversive of the notion of essential, inner selfhood. Their acts are moreover pleasurable to others and, arguably, socially beneficial.

Those characters *in* melodrama who project 'false' personae are of course usually damned. As melodrama recommends a model of identity diametrically opposed to the modern psychoanalytic or intellectual subject, any character leading, or even possessing, a private, inner life is frequently a villain. So it is not surprising that the villain is normally melodrama's most individual character. Most commentators would agree with Booth that 'the basic hero is really rather stupid'. The villain, who usually desires the heroine, is the 'moving force' of melodrama, and 'in the villain the darkness and violence of melodrama are incarnate. From the point of view of ability the villain should certainly be hero.' The hero is nothing but 'the punching-bag of the villain's brain'.[33] The villain is not so interesting, however, that his character detracts from the action as it is played out visibly. In melodramatic aesthetics, types are more valuable than individuals

[30] Donohue, *Theatre in the Age of Kean*, 70.

[31] Rowell, *The Victorian Theatre*, 1.

[32] Anastasia Nikolopoulou, 'Historical Disruptions: The Walter Scott Melodramas', in Hays and Nikolopoulou (eds.), *Melodrama: The Cultural Emergence of a Genre*, 121–43 (p. 122).

[33] Booth, *English Melodrama*, 17–18.

because they speak to what is shared, or typical; they have relevance, that is, outside themselves.

Melodrama and Populism: Cultural History

The inclusive impulse behind melodramatic aesthetics is not necessarily synonymous with a democratic politics. The cultural history of melodrama illustrates the futility of attempting to reify the politics of genre. Melodrama's populist aesthetics, its popularity with lower class and artisan audiences, and its roots in the politics of the French Revolution undoubtedly attracted a writer like Dickens, committed to the principle of cultural inclusivity. But the cultural history of melodrama foregrounds the problems and paradoxes that attend any populist project, particularly at a time when the majority of the populace was denied a legitimate political voice. At the turn of the eighteenth and nineteenth centuries, melodrama was not simply an expression of the voice of the people; but neither was it simply an instrument of the political ruling class. Melodrama's emergence in fact encapsulates the struggle of the lower classes to attain agency and representation, and the attempts of some in power to prevent their empowerment. Early stage melodrama is in fact a site of struggle for cultural and political power.

The genesis of melodrama coincides with a crucial moment in the history of popular culture, a moment, in fact, when the meaning and function of the term 'culture' was radically unstable. Raymond Williams maintains that between 1780 and 1850 the word culture underwent a significant semantic shift: 'this latter use, which had usually been a culture *of* something, was changed, in the nineteenth century, to *culture* as such, a thing in itself.'[34] Isobel Armstrong argues similarly for the importance of the Victorian period in cultural history and theory because it 'begins to conceptualize the idea of culture as a category'.[35] The reification of culture as 'a thing in itself' or 'a category', confirmed by the publication in 1869 of Arnold's *Culture and Anarchy*, is undoubtedly a response to the fact that in the Victorian period a consensual idea of culture could no longer be taken for granted.

[34] Raymond Williams, *Culture and Society, 1780–1950* (London: Chatto & Windus, 1958), p. xvi.
[35] Isobel Armstrong, *Victorian Poetry: Poetry, Poetics and Politics* (London: Routledge, 1993), 3.

The emergence of melodrama in France during the revolutionary period gives an indication of the complexity of the class and cultural politics which attend the entire history of the genre. The word itself, literally meaning 'music-drama' or 'song-drama', derives from Greek but reaches our theatre by way of French. The first recorded use of 'le mélodrame' was in 1772, and Rousseau applied it to his *Pygmalion* (1775).[36] While the conservatism of 'melodrama's fundamental conventions' can be traced to the writings of Rousseau, Rousseau's overtly political interpretation of the space of the theatre itself is radical in intention.[37] In his celebrated *Lettre à d'Alembert*, he makes an extended comparison between the aristocratic mode of 'theatre' and the virtuous or republican 'fête' or festival. Proscenium arch theatre necessitates a distinction between actors and spectators which reinforces cultural divisions whereas republican festivals do not.[38] However subversive in aim, Rousseau's binary opposition between aristocratic and republican theatre—like his idealizing of 'festival'—arguably reinforces the cultural oppositions it attempts to deconstruct.

Guilbert de Pixérécourt, by contrast, the self-styled, generally acclaimed 'father of le mélodrame', wrote spectacularly popular melodramas with the anti-revolutionary intention of reinforcing the traditional social order.[39] Pixérécourt borrowed the word, the dumb show, and the music from Rousseau's *Pygmalion* and applied these methods to the peculiarly French melodrama of the Revolution. This type of melodrama thrived in the late 1790s in the theatres of the Boulevard du Temple—which later became known as the Boulevard du Crime—and were essentially 'lurid melodramas of blood'.[40] Pixérécourt's success foregrounds many of the paradoxes which attend the politics of popular culture. An educated man who bestowed the title 'Genius' upon himself, Pixérécourt declared openly: 'I am writing for those who cannot read.'[41] He developed,

---

[36] Booth (ed.), *Hiss the Villain*, 13.

[37] Disher observes 'the division of characters into black-and-white, the faith in Nature's partiality to the good, the identification of virtue with poverty and simplicity, and vice with rank and culture, as well as "the swamping of reason in emotion, the floods of tears, the complete insensibility to the absurd" '—*Blood and Thunder*, 29.

[38] See Gregory Dart, *Rousseau, Robespierre and English Romanticism*, Cambridge Studies in Romanticism, XXXII (Cambridge: Cambridge University Press, 1999), 110.

[39] Disher, *Blood and Thunder*, 62.

[40] Booth (ed.), *Hiss the Villain*, 13.

[41] Disher, *Blood and Thunder*, 62; quoted by Howarth, 'Word and Image in Pixérécourt's Melodramas', 17.

in consequence, 'a melodramatic artistry aimed entirely at an unlettered populace'.[42] If he was a cultural revolutionary, however, he was also a political conservative, consciously employing popular drama as an instrument of ideological control. His melodramas of revolution offered audiences a fantasy experience of revolution whilst reinforcing the importance of duty and social stability. As he argued in a 1795 report to the Ministry of Police which responded to concern about the theatre's influence on public opinion: 'The theatres are there so to speak to present the distillation, the essence of the virtues, either political or personal, which every citizen must profess.'[43]

It was a pirated version of Pixérécourt's *Coelina* (1800) which first brought the term 'Melo-drame' to Britain; Thomas Holcroft's *A Tale of Mystery* (13 November 1802, CG) announced itself as 'a New Melo-Drame'. Holcroft's stated aim in the preface was 'to fix the attention, rouse the passions, and hold the faculties in anxious and impatient suspense'.[44] Like Pixérécourt, Holcroft appreciated the political potential of rousing the passions whilst holding 'the faculties' in suspense. Unlike Pixérécourt, Holcroft had radical sympathies, grounding his play in 'the populist radical rhetoric which erupted in England in the aftermath of the French Revolution'.[45] The political metamorphoses which attended melodrama's journey from the pen of Rousseau to Pixérécourt to Holcroft reinforce the futility of attempts to 'fix' the politics of genre.

In Britain, the fluctuating cultural politics of the nineteenth-century theatre have origins as far back as the Licensing Act of 1737, 'arguably the most radical and far-reaching piece of theatrical legislation ever written into the statute books'.[46] The Act prohibited the acting of plays in theatres outside the city of Westminster. This meant the sustaining of a monopoly which had existed since 1660, when Charles II effectively granted Covent Garden and Drury Lane

---

[42] Booth, *English Melodrama*, 44–5.

[43] Quoted by Gabrielle Hyslop in 'Pixérécourt and the French Melodrama Debate: Instructing Boulevard Audiences', in James Redmond (ed.), *Melodrama*, Themes in Drama (Cambridge: Cambridge University Press, 1992), 61–85 (p. 63); see also Hyslop's 'Deviant and Dangerous Behaviour: Women in Melodrama', 66, and p. 25 above for evidence of Pixérécourt's conservatism.

[44] Quoted by Donohue, *Theatre in the Age of Kean*, 106 from the playbill at the Henry E. Huntington Library.

[45] Introduction to Hays and Nikolopoulou (eds.), *Melodrama: The Cultural Emergence of a Genre*, p. viii.

[46] John Russell Stephens, *The Censorship of English Drama* (Cambridge: Cambridge University Press, 1980), 5.

exclusive royal patents to present drama of the spoken word. Every other theatre in London had to confine itself to 'illegitimate drama', which should not involve the spoken word. The Act also effectively introduced full-scale censorship to the theatre, declaring that all plays had to be submitted to the Lord Chamberlain for pre-production approval. The general tendency in eighteenth-century theatre legislation towards what Foucault would call 'discipline' and 'surveillance' is exemplified by an Act of 1751, made permanent in 1755, which required the licensing of 'places of public entertainment in the cities of London and Westminster', except Drury Lane and Covent Garden. This was explicitly 'a police measure to facilitate the maintenance of law and order at public houses which offered entertainment', and licensing powers were divided between the Lord Chamberlain and local magistrates.[47] In the main, the division of playhouses into those producing 'legitimate' and 'illegitimate' drama existed—at least officially—for over a century until the Theatre Regulation Act of 1843.[48]

The overt aim of the Licensing Act was to raise and sustain standards in the theatre; legitimate drama was intended only for the elite. The subtext of the notorious Act concerned cultural exclusion and social control: the spoken word was constituted as the symbol of legitimate cultural capital. Theatrical access to the spoken word was restricted for many whose illiteracy denied them access to the written word, in the vain hope that the written word, in the form of the nation's literary drama, would revive. Though the idea of language as a tool of power is the mainstay of much contemporary critical theory, it is hard to think of a more concrete, less theoretical example of linguistic oppression than that enforced in the British theatres between 1737 and 1843. The sheer stupidity of the legislation was farcically emphasized as early as 1789, when the actor John Palmer was called a 'rogue and vagrant' for speaking prose in a performance at the Royal Circus and sent to prison.[49] Palmer was the only unlucky victim of the Act and by the nineteenth century the law was either ignored or cleverly subverted.

The fact that *A Tale of Mystery* was first performed and first achieved popularity at Covent Garden shows the total failure of the

---

[47] Rahill, *The World of Melodrama*, 135.

[48] Rahill's *The World of Melodrama* offers a more detailed account than most of this legislation and amendments and exceptions to it (p. 135).

[49] Donohue, *Theatre in the Age of Kean*, 49.

Licensing Act to immunize the patent theatres against 'low art'. In fact, Gothic melodrama ironically found a welcoming home in the 'legitimate' Covent Garden and Drury Lane;[50] these theatres needed to jump on the melodramatic bandwagon simply to survive in an emerging market culture. But Pixérécourt's mode of drama fast became the darling of the 'illegitimate' theatres, whose audiences were predominantly artisan or working-class. The statistical composition of nineteenth-century theatre audiences is notoriously difficult to determine, but Dickens's Joe Whelks is consistent with the sense garnered by theatre historians of the typical consumer of melodrama.[51]

Indeed, a nexus of 'illegitimate' theatres already existed to provide entertainment for artisans and workers even before melodrama officially entered the capital. On its entrance, the minor theatres swiftly developed their own particular brand of the drama—equestrian melodrama was perhaps the best known of these niche entertainments.[52] The insatiable appetite of Victorian theatre audiences for melodrama is admirably demonstrated by the opinion of a London costermonger, who claimed that '*Macbeth* would be better liked, if it was only the witches and the fighting'.[53] In *A London Companion to the Theatres*, Horace Foote recorded that *Richard III*, *Othello*, and *Macbeth* were the most popular legitimate dramas, for the straightforward reason that they were 'the most melodramatic'.[54]

The Licensing Act attempted to enforce the existence of two

---

[50] Booth (ed.), *Hiss the Villain*, 22.

[51] Nikolopoulou argues that, between 1810 and 1830, the theatre witnessed 'the formation of a new sector of the theatre public, comprized of artisans, middle-class radicals, and manufacturing workers'—Nikolopoulou, 'Historical Disruptions: The Walter Scott Melodramas', 121–43 (p. 121); and (with Hays) that 'there is no doubt that early artisan spectators of melodrama, the same folks who also took part in the "making of the English working class," were the readers and, on occasion, the creators of the radical literature of the time'—introduction, Hays and Nikolopoulou (eds.), *Melodrama: The Cultural Emergence of a Genre*, p. viii. Booth maintains more straightforwardly that, 'From the audience point of view, melodrama—and pantomime at Christmas—*was* the Victorian working-class theatre'—'Melodrama and the Working-Class', in MacKay (ed.), *Dramatic Dickens*, 96–109 (p. 100).

[52] See Allardyce Nicoll, *A History of Early Nineteenth-Century Drama, 1800–1850*, 2 vols. (Cambridge: Cambridge University Press, 1930), i. 217–34, for further details of individual theatres in London and the provinces and their specialities.

[53] Quoted by Henry Mayhew, *London Labour and the London Poor: A Cyclopaedia of the Condition and Earnings of Those That Will Work, Those That Cannot Work, and Those That Will Not Work*, 3 vols. (London: Morning Chronicle, 1851), i. 15.

[54] *A London Companion to the Theatres; and, A Manual of the British Drama* (London: Marsh & Miller, 1829), 111; quoted by Donohue, *Theatre in the Age of Kean*, 128.

different kinds of theatre with distinct types of audience, but this segregation proved unsustainable. The Act bears historical witness to the fact that any binary opposition between 'high' and 'low' culture must always be illusory. The artificial segregation of 'elite' from 'popular' drama proved extremely detrimental to the health of the 'legitimate' drama in particular, which was often dry, scholastic, and lacking in vitality. In the words of J. B. van Amerongen, Drury Lane and Covent Garden 'did not live by their privileges, but [. . .] they died of them'.[55] Illegitimate drama originally adhered to the terms of the Licensing Act by neglecting the spoken word. While the 'legitimate' drama was struggling, the illegitimate drama made a virtue of necessity: the illegality of the spoken word at first compelled the minor theatres to innovate, to develop non-verbal means of dramatic expression. As a result, a cluster of related forms was thriving by the time Victoria came to the throne: burlesque, extravaganza, burletta, melodrama, revue, pantomime, burlesque-pantomime, operetta, comic opera, and opera were all highly popular. All relied to differing extents on music, spectacle, and gesture for their effects. As far as the actor was concerned, his or her main medium of communication was the body. Melodrama enacts what Herbert Blau might call 'blooded abstraction' or 'metaphysics of the flesh'.[56] 'Illegitimate' drama offers a treasure trove of tools for the artist with populist and/or egalitarian aspirations. Twentieth-century commercial cinema, for example, has built on the Victorian taste for and development of spectacle— particularly dramatic special effects. Again, postmodernist fiction like that of Angela Carter inscribes (paradoxically) the non-verbal techniques of the minor theatre and appropriates its grotesque, anti-realist genres. Illegitimate drama offers a potent signifying system to both media monopolists and cultural subversives—and Dickens, no doubt, was something of both.

The history of the nineteenth-century minor theatre is one of cultural mobility or appropriation: what is interesting, however, is that along with the familiar narrative of the culturally 'legitimate' stealing from the 'illegitimate', there is also a Robin Hood element to the story of the minor theatres. The 'dumbing down' of the London

---

[55] *The Actor in Dickens: A Study of the Histrionic and Dramatic Elements in the Novelist's Life and Works* (London: Palmer, 1926), 95.

[56] *Blooded Thought: Occasions of Theatre* (New York: Performing Arts Journal Publications, 1982), p. xiii; '*Elsinore: An Analytic Scenario*', *Cream City Review*, 6 (1981), 83—quoted by Mark Fortier, *Theory/Theatre* (London: Routledge, 1997), 48.

theatres and the power of popular taste which seemed to enforce it is symbolized in traditional theatre histories by the 1809 'Old Price' riots. This long and tumultuous battle over rises in ticket prices between the management of Covent Garden and indignant spectators resulted in there being no plays for sixty-seven nights under John Kemble's management. Although, as Nicoll points out, riots were not unusual at the theatre, these protests in a patent theatre have traditionally been seen as symbolizing 'the triumph of mob rule in the English theatre'.[57] The licensing and enforced censorship of the theatre also suggest anxieties about the power and influence of the populace, anxieties which were particularly acute in the 1830s and 1840s as the Reform and the Chartist movements (melodramatically) made their marks. The idea of the triumph of populism is rarely unambiguous, however. Elaine Hadley, for example, argues convincingly that the Old Price riots represent a melodramatic protest against the burgeoning market culture from lower-class spectators with paternalistic values.[58] The voice of the people is in this case reactionary in portent though subversive in style.

There is no ambiguity, however, about the fact that polite society largely lost interest in the theatre until the second half of the century. As for writers, there were those, like Walter Scott, successful enough to feel that the theatre was worthy of nothing but contempt.[59] Some, like Edward Bulwer, attempted to gain the best of two very different worlds; realizing that kings were 'no longer Destinies' on the stage, Bulwer turned 'to the People! Among the people, then, must the tragic author invoke the genius of Modern Tragedy, and learn its springs.'[60] Unfortunately for Bulwer, 'Modern Tragedy' never really materialized until the advent of Ibsen, Strindberg, and their companions. Charles Robert Maturin expressed a sentiment typical of many aspiring dramatists, when he wrote to Elliston: 'It is useless to

[57] *A History of English Drama*, 2nd edn., 6 vols. (Cambridge: Cambridge University Press, 1952–9), iv. 10; Rowell, *The Victorian Theatre*, 3.

[58] *Melodramatic Tactics*, 34–76.

[59] Scott claimed, 'the magnitude of these theatres has occasioned them to be theatres destined to company so scandalous that persons not very nice in their taste of society, must yet exclaim against the abuse as a national nuisance' and that 'prostitutes and their admirers usually' formed 'the principle part of the audience'—'An Essay on the Drama', in *Essays on Chivalry, Romance and the Drama*, in *The Miscellaneous Prose Works of Sir Walter Scott, Bart.*, 28 vols. (Edinburgh: Cadell, 1834–6), vi (1834), 217–395 (pp. 392–3); first pub. in the Supplement to the *Encyclopaedia Britannica* (1819).

[60] *England and the English*, 2 vols. (London: Bentley, 1833), ii. 150.

hope for the success of what is called the regular drama. I must learn to adapt myself to the taste of the public.'[61] Melodrama, it appeared, was to the public's taste.

[61] Undated letter (*c.*1821), in George Raymond, *Memoirs of Robert William Elliston,* 2 vols. (New York: [n. pub.], 1969), ii. 215; quoted by Donohue, *Theatre in the Age of Kean,* 128.

2

The Villains of Stage Melodrama: Romanticism and the Politics of Character

Henry James complained of melodrama that its audiences attended the theatre 'to look and listen, to laugh and cry—not to think'.[1] As if in response to James, Eric Bentley counters powerfully:

The tears shed by the audience at a Victorian melodrama [. . .] might be called the poor man's catharsis, and as such have a better claim to be the main objective of popular melodrama than its notorious moral pretensions. [. . .]

Once we have seen that our modern antagonism to self-pity and sentiment goes far beyond the rational objections that may be found to them, we realize that even the rational objections are in some measure mere rationalization. Attacks on false emotion often mask a fear of emotion as such. Ours is, after all, a thin-lipped, thin-blooded culture.[2]

If melodramatic tears are to Bentley 'the poor man's catharsis', to James they are signs of stupidity and barbarism. In the melodramatic scheme of things, however, it is the Henry Jameses of this world who are denigrated, demonized, and marginalized: the 'civilized', self-conscious, thinking being is almost invariably a villain. Melodrama opposes itself to thin-bloodedness: immediacy, transparency, and intensity of emotional response in its characters are the norm.

Melodrama is a child of the French Revolution and, as such, it is hardly surprising that it is red-blooded. The synchronicity between melodrama's emergence and that of Romanticism helps to explain

---

[1] 'Some Notes on the Theatre', *Nation* (11 Mar. 1875), repr. in Montrose J. Moses and John Mason Brown (eds.), *The American Theatre as Seen by its Critics, 1752–1934* (New York: Norton, 1934), 122–6.

[2] *The Life of the Drama*, 198.

the premium that melodrama places on emotion. The preface to the *Lyrical Ballads*, for example, famously announces the centrality of emotion to aesthetic and 'real life' experience, and, like melodrama, it valorizes the passions of the uneducated: 'Low and rustic life', Wordsworth writes, 'was generally chosen, because in that condition the essential passions of the heart find a better soil.'[3] The impulse towards populism which characterizes the *Lyrical Ballads* does not, however, survive in later Romanticism. Wordsworth's much quoted definition of poetry as 'the spontaneous overflow of powerful emotion' hints at the movement away from cultural inclusivity which characterizes so many Romantic writings published after the *Lyrical Ballads*. At least, a full quotation from the preface illuminates the cultural exclusivity which came to dominate high Romanticism. My initial quotation from the preface is of course a familiar misquotation: Wordsworth actually argues that poetry is 'the spontaneous overflow of powerful emotion; it takes its origin from emotion recollected in tranquillity'.[4] Wordsworth's emphasis on the importance of emotion 'recollected in tranquillity' prefigures the key difference, for my purposes, in the emotional constitutions of melodrama and high Romanticism. The emphasis in high, masculine Romanticism is on thoughtful emotion, emotion as it is processed by the psychologically complex, introspective individual who is not infrequently an artist. Canonical Romanticism in many ways prefigures psychoanalysis in so far as it intellectualizes emotion. Even when democratic politics constitute the overt content of Romantic texts, as they do most obviously in the case of Shelley, the emphasis is on extraordinariness as opposed to ordinariness, and this extraordinariness very often defines itself—in people and situations—through intellectualized emotion which can preclude cultural inclusivity.

Coleridge is of course particularly important in the process by which aesthetic emotion becomes both thoughtful and exclusive. His deployment of the words 'psychological' and 'psychologist', his interest in what we would now call the subconscious workings of emotion and the psyche, and his mediation of Shakespeare to a modern audience via his 'hobby horse' 'psychology' have been deeply influential not only on Freudian psychoanalysis, but on subsequent

[3] (1802) preface to the *Lyrical Ballads*, ed. Michael Mason (London: Longman, 1992), 55–93 (p. 60).
[4] Ibid. 82.

literary study.[5] As early as 1845, for example, De Quincey, writing on Wordsworth, identified 'good psychology' as the prerequisite of 'absolute and philosophic criticism'.[6] In the 1790s, Coleridge's (disputed) contribution to the *Lyrical Ballads* suggests a belief in a kind of populism; by the end of his career, however, he was an apologist for a multi-tiered model of culture and the notion of a clerisy or cultural elite. His movement away from populism coincides with his growing interest in the psyche. Coleridge in fact epitomizes what we could call the 'turn inwards' in intellectual history which occurred during the Romantic period, an involution of focus that in some ways characterizes modernity—or what Peter Brooks would call the 'post-sacred era'.[7] This Romantic insistence on 'interiority as the true condition for any authentically human existence' is undoubtedly intellectually radical;[8] but it is also anti-theatrical and, more importantly, culturally divisive. The implication behind the Romantic valorization of what could be called subtextual emotional experience is that only certain 'cultured' individuals have the sensitivity, psychological complexity, and education to either experience or decode this subtext. Coleridge makes the elitism of such a position comically obvious in his attacks on the *Lyrical Ballads* in the *Biographia Literaria*: 'among the [uneducated] peasantry of North Wales', he argues, 'the ancient mountains [. . .] are pictures to the blind and music to the deaf.'[9] An intense emotional response to nature is thus available only to the civilized individual who is educated into an appreciation of nature. The Romantic intellectualizing of emotional experience

---

[5] See *OED* for examples of Coleridge's use of the terms 'psychological' and 'psychologist'. His cited application of the word 'psychological' to Shakespeare's work is particularly interesting for our purposes: 'Shakespeare was pursuing two Methods at once; and besides the Psychological Method, he had also to attend to the Poetical. [*Note*] We beg pardon for the use of this *insolens verbum*: but it is one of which our Language stands in great need'—*Diss. Sc. Method*, ii. 40; Coleridge describes 'psychology' as his 'hobby horse', in the fourth chapter of the *Biographia Literaria* (1817)—see *The Collected Works of Samuel Taylor Coleridge*, ed. James Engell and W. Jackson Bate, 16 vols., Bollingen Series, LXXV (London: Routledge & Kegan Paul, 1983), vii (1). 85. Coleridge's identification with Hamlet, a character he believed to contain 'a world within himself', has been particularly influential on the 'psychologizing' of literature—see his lecture on *Hamlet* (2 Jan. 1812), repr. in *Samuel Taylor Coleridge*, ed. H. J. Jackson, The Oxford Authors (Oxford: Oxford University Press, 1985), 655–9. *Hamlet* has also, of course, been a key text in relations between psychoanalysis and literature.

[6] 'On Wordsworth's Poetry', *Taits's Magazine* (Sept. 1845), repr. in *Collected Writings*, ed. David Masson, 14 vols. (London: Black, 1896–7), xi (1897), 294–325 (p. 294).

[7] *The Melodramatic Imagination*, 15.

[8] Glavin, *After Dickens*, 103.

[9] *The Collected Works of Samuel Taylor Coleridge*, ed. Engell and Bate, vii (2). 45 (chapter 17).

has the effect of internalizing reality and rendering spontaneous, immediately intelligible emotion, in Bentley's terms, 'false emotion'.

Charles Lamb's famous elevation of the experience of reading Shakespeare over that of seeing Shakespeare performed renders explicit the cultural elitism which regularly informs high Romantic aesthetics; visible 'signs' of emotion are more vulgar than its invisible workings, emotional experience unmediated by the mind is 'low', action is less interesting than motive:

> To know the internal workings and movements of a great mind, of an Othello or a Hamlet [. . .] seems to demand a reach of intellect of a vastly different extent from that which is employed upon the bare imitation of the signs of these passions in the countenance or gesture, which signs are usually observed to be most lively and emphatic in the weaker sorts of minds, and which signs can after all but indicate some passion, [. . .] anger, or grief, generally; but of the motives and grounds of the passion, wherein it differs from the same passion in low and vulgar natures, of these the actor can give no more idea by his face or gesture than the eye [. . .] can speak, or the muscles utter intelligible sounds.[10]

Intelligent people, Lamb argues, experience the same passions as 'low and vulgar natures'; what makes intelligent people more valuable than 'weaker sorts of minds' (not people) is 'the internal workings and movements' of their minds. The Romantic tendency to individuate, internalize, and intellectualize emotional experience is in part no doubt a reaction against the barbaric passions manifested by the mob during the French Revolution. The Romantics are also reacting against eighteenth-century mechanistic theories of the emotions,[11] and the more immediate mechanization which attended industrialization. Whatever its provenance, however, any hierarchy which valorizes intellectualized feeling is potentially denigratory of the uneducated.

It is arguable, in fact, that discussions of Shakespeare by Coleridge and Lamb are responses to the growing popularity of melodrama and its tendency to popularize figures like Hamlet, Macbeth, and Richard III into ranters and gibberers (as Coleridge and Lamb see it). Most telling of all is the fact that it is mainly in the 1810s that they begin to write about drama in this way—as melodrama rises to

---

[10] Lamb, 'On the Tragedies of Shakespeare, Considered with Reference to their Fitness for Stage Representation', in David Bromwich (ed.), *Romantic Critical Essays*, Cambridge English Prose Texts (Cambridge: Cambridge University Press, 1987), 56–70 (p. 57); 1st pub. in the *Reflector* (Oct.–Dec. 1811).

[11] See Roach, *The Player's Passion*, 58–92.

prominence. There is no doubt that Romantic essayists perceived melodrama as a kind of cultural threat. Leigh Hunt was explicitly dismissive of melodrama: 'As to melodrama, nobody looks for expression in the whiskered cheeks and Tamerlane gestures of a bandit: an elephant can dispense with delicacy of inspection.'[12] When an afterpiece of his was rejected by 'the public', Lamb sought solace in a club of like-minded people who subscribed to the idea that theatre audiences (the 'public, or mob') were 'senseless, illiterate savages', 'capricious ungrateful rabble'—the opposite, in fact, of the 'man of genius'.[13] Coleridge regarded melodrama as a 'modern Jacobinical drama' which subverted the 'natural order of things [. . .] by representing the qualities of liberality, refined feeling, and a nice sense of honour [. . .] in persons and in classes where experience least teaches us to expect them'; meanwhile, other contemporaries attacked its 'monstrous aesthetic configuration' and criminal audiences.[14]

It is no accident that Peter Brooks's seminal text *The Melodramatic Imagination* made melodrama acceptable to literary critics by emphasizing its Romantic beginnings and psychoanalytic significance. Brooks maintains that we must

> recognize the melodramatic mode as a central fact of the modern sensibility [. . .] in that modern art has typically felt itself to be constructed on, and over, the void, postulating meanings and symbolic systems which have no certain justification because they are backed by no theology and no universally accepted code. [. . .] There is a desperate effort to renew contact with the scattered ethical and psychic fragments of the Sacred through the representation of fallen reality, insisting that behind reality, hidden by it yet indicated within it, there is a realm where large moral forces are operative [. . .]. The melodramatic mode can be seen as an intensified, primary, and

[12] Hunt, 'Patent Theatres and Mr. Arnold' (27 Jan. 1831), in *Dramatic Criticism*, ed. Lawrence Huston Houtchens and Carolyn Washburn Houtchens (New York: Columbia University Press, 1949), 256–60 (pp. 257–8); quoted in Rodney Stenning Edgecombe, 'Dickens, Hunt and the "Dramatic Criticism" in *Great Expectations*: A Note', *Dickensian*, 88 (1992), 82–90 (p. 85).

[13] Charles Lamb, 'On the Custom of Hissing at the Theatres, with Some Accounts of a Club of Damned Authors' (1811), in *The Works of Charles and Mary Lamb*, ed. E. V. Lucas, 6 vols. (London: Methuen, 1912), i. 101–7 (p. 105). Hays and Nikolopoulou suggest that Lamb's opposition had general currency—*Melodrama: The Cultural Emergence of a Genre*, p. viii.

[14] Coleridge, 'Critique of [Maturin's] *Bertram*' (repr. from *Courier*, Aug. and Sept. 1816), in *Biographia Literaria*, chapter 23, in *The Collected Works of Samuel Taylor Coleridge*, ed. Engell and Bate, vii (2). 207–33 (p. 221); Hays and Nikolopoulou, introduction to *Melodrama: The Cultural Emergence of a Genre*, p. viii.

exemplary version of what the most ambitious art, since the beginnings of Romanticism, has been about.[15]

Brooks's famous assessment of melodrama's central place in 'the modern sensibility' has always seemed to me confused by his disregard of the popular cultural context of melodrama in its original form. Melodrama exists in a dialectical relationship to high Romanticism because it acts as a buttress to Romantic anxieties; it provides reassuring answers, that is, to Romanticism's questions. To emphasize the idea that melodrama more often functions as an antidote to 'the modern sensibility' than as its 'central fact' is, to some extent, to view modernity from the other end of Brooks's telescope. To do so is important because the inversion of Brooks's perspective illuminates the subsequent cultural subordination of the melodramatic mode. Melodrama is only infrequently seen as contributing to the 'desperate effort', the *process* of questioning the post-sacred 'void'. The activity of searching for answers—the idea of progress, indeed—is commonly attributed to high cultural modes like Romanticism. Melodrama, by contrast, is seen as offering a static, artificial model of the sacred which fosters intellectual and emotional stagnation. Melodrama is the quick fix of modernity—necessary, endemic, yet despised and marginalized.

The 'central fact of the modern sensibility' is surely more accurately located in 'the turn inwards' of high Romanticism. Indeed, Brooks concedes as much in his announcement that Romanticism is 'the genesis of the modern, of the sensibility within which we are still living'.[16] *The Melodramatic Imagination*, moreover, is happily steeped in the Romantic 'sensibility', mediating melodrama for academic consumption from the cultural high ground. Brooks's use of the word 'psychic' highlights the extent to which his work, like so much mainstream post-Romantic intellectual and cultural history, has naturalized the Romantic involution in ways of seeing. Psychoanalysis has of course been crucial in the perpetuation of the Romantic valorization of interiority. Brooks, however, argues one-sidedly that psychoanalysis 'can be read as a systematic realization of the melodramatic aesthetic, applied to the structure and dynamics of the mind'.[17] Psychoanalysis, from the analyst's perspective at least, is in fact a realization of Romantic aesthetics and an inversion of melodramatic aesthetics. It is the patient, the subordinate partner in the

[15] *The Melodramatic Imagination*, 21–2.   [16] Ibid. 21.   [17] Ibid. 201.

psychoanalytic practice, who is melodramatic. Much of Brooks's book in fact realizes melodrama through psychoanalysis, and not the other way round: characters, for example, are most interesting as 'psychic signs' and not as the social or allegorical figures they originally constituted; myth-making is 'individual, personal', and 'melodramatic good and evil are highly personalized'.[18] To reconfigure an anti-individualistic genre like melodrama as the 'melodrama of psychology' is to miss the ideological significance of the tensions and contests surrounding melodrama's marginalization of the mind.[19]

MELODRAMATIC VILLAINY

'The quintessence of melodrama lies in villainy', argues Kucich, 'in the pleasures of melodramatic violence.'[20] Despite unanimous acknowledgement by critics of melodrama that the villain is melodrama's most interesting character, surprisingly little detailed research has been conducted into the villains of nineteenth-century melodrama.[21] In fact, surprisingly little research has been carried out on the figure of the villain at all.[22] This no doubt has much to do with the realist, psychological tradition which persisted for so long in criticism of character, and the subsequent structuralist debunking of the entire notion of character. The out-and-out villain is a type before he is a character; he is defined by his moral and theatrical function as a wrong- or evildoer.[23] As a type, he has seemed to offer little to criti-

[18] *The Melodramatic Imagination*, 35, 16.

[19] Ibid. 35.

[20] *Excess and Restraint*, 47.

[21] Frank Rahill's *The World of Melodrama* is the only text I have been able to find that identifies various models of villainy on the 19th-century stage in any detail (pp. 11–15, 207–13). Booth distinguishes in *English Melodrama* between 'two main kinds of villain: the grim, determined, immensely evil; and the shifty, cowardly, half-comic' (p. 18), and between the 'black', genteel villain who is likely to be 'cool and calculating' and the 'white' villain who is less threatening (pp. 19–20). In *Hiss the Villain*, he provides a descriptive outline of the melodramatic villain, whose 'evil [. . .] can make Iago look like a mere dabbler' (pp. 10–11). While Booth's broad observations tell us little that is not readily apparent on perusal of any 19th-century melodrama, Anna Clark's 'The Politics of Seduction in English Popular Culture' is detailed and specific but does not attempt to provide models of villainy outside its chosen type of the villainous seducer.

[22] See Introduction n. 22 above.

[23] I am referring to the villain as male here because the female villain, in melodrama and in Dickens's novels, conforms to different patterns of behaviour from her male counterparts. For reasons of lucidity then, I have dealt with her separately in Chapter 8.

cism—of whatever denomination—which prioritizes hidden intellectual complexity over one-dimensional transparency.

The villains of ninenteenth-century melodrama are, however, types struggling to become individuals; and this impulse towards individuality constitutes in large measure the definition of melodramatic villainy. The villain is a villain in any genre because he poses a threat to the dominant ethical and dramaturgic order. Melodrama is an anti-intellectual genre which eschews subject-centred, psychological models of identity. In melodrama, the villain is a threat because he is individualistic, valuing self before society. It is significant, for example, that key villainous types in nineteenth-century melodrama resemble Romantic models of heroism.[24] Individualism, interiority, and intellectual complexity are of course central to Romantic aesthetics and anathema to the melodramatic vision. In melodrama, such Romantic figures must often be vanquished or socialized before the moral and social order can be re-established.

The melodramatic villain's individualism—whether Romantic or otherwise—is, true to the laws of the genre, usually passionally defined as either expressive or repressive. As melodrama as a genre advocates transparent, public models of identity, the threat posed by the repressed villain who is a social role-player should be obvious. Such villains valorize the private self against which melodrama defines itself. Less obviously perhaps, such actor-villains draw attention to the element of performance upon which melodrama, in practice, depends. The threat of the early, passionate villains only

---

[24] I have come across several brief mentions of the Romantic characteristics of the melodramatic villain: see Hadley, *Melodramatic Tactics*, 223–5, Nick Browne, 'Society and Subjectivity: On the Political Economy of Chinese Melodrama', in Bratton et al. (eds.), *Melodrama: Stage, Picture, Screen*, 167–96 (p. 168). In an essay in the same book, Daniel Gerould maintains that, in France, from 1830 onwards the villains of melodrama— 'convicts, bandits and asocial figures'—became its heroes and vice versa as melodrama became more subversive—see 'Melodrama and Revolution', 185–98 (p. 186). Gerould echoes Brooks to an extent: *The Melodramatic Imagination* claims that, in the 1830s, 'One begins to detect a contamination of melodrama by the popular themes of Romantic drama: a search for the paradox of the sympathetic villain—deriving from both the outlaw hero and the repentant sinner of earlier melodrama' (p. 87). This shift is in keeping with Brooks's better-known identification of 'decadence' in the melodrama of the 1830s (p. 88). Lothar Fietz also writes interestingly of shifting models of individuality at the beginning of the 19th century and changing reactions to these models. For him, 'under the influence of Victorian decorum', the 18th-century rake and the 'pathetic hero of tragedy' become the villain of melodrama—'On the Origins of English Melodrama in the Tradition of Bourgeois Tragedy and Sentimental Drama: Lillo, Schröder, Kotzebue, Sheridan, Thompson, Jerrold', in Hays and Nikolopoulou (eds.), *Melodrama: The Cultural Emergence of a Genre*, 83–101 (p. 98).

appears less oppositional to melodrama's dominant ethos; while the passionate villain is, like most melodramatic characters, expressive, emotional, and transparent, his emotions are selfish and antisocial, threatening traditional structures of family and community. The demonizing of the passionate villain makes visible the covert social/ ideological basis of melodrama's moral scheme, a scheme which overtly expresses itself in transcendent, metaphysical terms. More obviously perhaps, the passionate villain renders explicit the possible problems which attend the unchecked, transparent personality; he violates the selfhood of others as he violates social boundaries. That his externalized violence often results in self-violence and the fracturing of his apparently one-dimensional identity is in keeping with the threat he poses elsewhere to melodrama's elevation of the idea of unitary selfhood. In transgressing the boundaries of selfhood, the passionate villain (like his passionless brother) exposes the fragility or indeed the fiction of the purely public self on which melodrama, in fact, depends.

The battle between good and evil in melodrama thus expresses itself in culturally resonant terms: the individual is pitted against his or her society; the private world is opposed to the public; the mind is offset against the feelings; the transparent individual is contrasted with the self-conscious role-player.

VILLAINY IN GOTHIC MELODRAMA

Gothic melodrama is foreign in flavour and atmosphere, adopting continental and eastern settings, often introducing the supernatural, and generally appearing as remote from London life as possible. It was written to one of two familiar formulae: the castle-dungeon-ghost pattern or the bandit-forest-cottage constellation.[25] At its most extreme, it developed into 'monster melodrama' or 'demonic melo- drama'.[26] Booth argues that 'an essential part of the Gothic melo- dramatists' intentions' was 'the attempt to arouse horror and fear'.[27] Indeed, Fitzball planned *The Flying Dutchman; or, The Phantom Ship* (1 January 1827, Adel.) as a ' "piece of diablerie" which should not be

---

[25] Representative of the latter formula is the most famous Gothic melodrama, Isaac Pocock's *The Miller and his Men* (21 Oct. 1813, CG), of the former, M. G. Lewis's *The Castle Spectre* (14 Dec. 1797, DL).

[26] Booth (ed.), *Hiss the Villain*, 84; Disher, *Blood and Thunder*, 80.

[27] *English Melodrama*, 83.

by any means behind *Frankenstein* in horrors and blue fire'.[28] Again, Byron said of Monk Lewis:

> Even Satan's self with thee might dread to dwell,
> And in thy skull discern a deeper hell.[29]

Gothic melodramatists made the most of the latest developments in stagecraft to achieve their spectacular effects, using trap doors, lighting tricks, and even explosives for novelty and sensation. Moreover, Disher argues that Radcliffe's Gothic novel *The Mysteries of Udolpho* actually changed the meaning of the word 'sensation': 'Henceforth the word "sensation" referred, not to the operation of the senses, but to the violent emotional excitement of the literary fashion known as "the romantic and the terrible".'[30]

In keeping with this tendency towards violent emotional excitement, the villain of Gothic melodrama is the most passionate of all melodramatic villains. The Gothic villain is invariably defined by expressive emotional excess; what distinguishes this excess from that of the 'good' characters in this excessive genre is that it does not respect social rules and boundaries.[31] The Gothic villain puts personal feeling before law, family, or community and thus violates melodrama's communal ethos. His disregard of the social world creates the impression of transcendence often associated with the 'real melodramatic' villain.[32] Violent feeling is the hallmark of the Gothic villain and the intensity with which his feelings are expressed can create the impression that the villain is not human but superhuman. Eric Bentley remarks of exaggeration in melodrama:

> The exaggerations will be foolish only if they are empty of feeling. Intensity of feeling justifies formal exaggeration in art, just as intensity of feeling creates the 'exaggerated' forms of childhood fantasies and adult dreams. It is as children and dreamers [. . .] as neurotics and savages too—that we enjoy melodrama.[33]

---

[28] *Blood and Thunder*, 98.

[29] 'English Bards, and Scotch Reviewers', in *The Works of the Right Honourable Lord Byron* (Philadelphia: Thomas, 1820), 1–86 (p. 16; ll. 275–6).

[30] *Blood and Thunder*, 36.

[31] When Kucich argues of Dickens's good characters, for example, that 'melodrama allows a complete spending of the self into emotion [. . .]—a general victory over repression' (*Excess and Restraint*, 49), he fails to acknowledge the fact that 'good' characters in melodrama—whether in Dickens or the stage variety—never spend emotion in a completely uninhibited fashion.

[32] Ibid. 62; see Introduction n. 22 above.

[33] *The Life of the Drama*, 204.

'Talent in melodramatic writing', he goes on to say, 'is most readily seen in the writer's power to make his human villain seem super-human, diabolical.'[34] These comments are in a sense more appro-priate to Gothic melodrama and its villains than to any other form of the genre. Gothic villains have difficulty in controlling or repressing their passions. Perhaps the most morally monstrous villains are the most simplistic: those malefactors who relentlessly and unashamedly vent their destructive passions on others. Far from trying to disguise their true natures, these villains revel in hatred and rage. Signifi-cantly, Gothic villains are often 'Othered' in melodrama—i.e. defined as alien by race, religion, or class status.

Such an out-and-outer can be found in M. G. Lewis's *The Castle Spectre* in the misanthropic black servant Hassan. Though we are told by both Hassan and M. G. Lewis—in the afterword to the play—that Hassan's heart 'was once feeling and kind',[35] we have to take their word for this. Throughout the play, soured by his experience as a slave, Hassan indulges his feelings of hatred and resentment. His maltreatment at the hands of the Christian slave-traders is over-shadowed in the play by its after-effects. Hassan explains to Saib: 'when the last point of Africa faded from my view, [. . .] in that bitter moment did I banish humanity from my breast. I [. . .] vowed aloud endless hatred to mankind' (p. 13; i. ii). He swears his allegiance to the tyrannical Osmond simply because Osmond is possibly more passionate and villainous than he is. Hassan explains: 'I hate him! [. . .] Oh! 'tis a thought which I would not barter for empires, to know that in this world he makes others suffer, and will suffer himself for their tortures in the next!' (p. 65; iv. i). Indeed, Osmond is totally at the mercy of his own passions, and others, in turn, are at his mercy. Violence is by definition a violation and Osmond, like other Gothic villains, possesses a desire to violate others which inevitably results in self-violation. He has secretly imprisoned his elder brother for years in order to gain his wealth, accidentally murdered the sister-in-law he loves, and spends the course of the play attempting to force himself upon their daughter Angela. He recognizes that he is trapped in 'passion's mazes' (p. 24; ii. i), but renounces responsibility for his destructive impulses. He soliloquizes:

Yes, I am guilty! [. . .] Yet lies the fault with me? did my own pleasure plant in my bosom these tempestuous passions? No! they were given me at my

---

[34] *The Life of the Drama*, 201.   [35] 4th edn. (London: Bell, 1798), 101.

birth; they were sucked in with my existence! Nature formed me the slave of wild desires, and Fate, as she frowned upon my cradle, exclaimed, 'I doom this babe to be a villain and a wretch!' (p. 33; II. iii)

It is common for the passion and villainy of Gothic malefactors to be presented as innate and predetermined. Such fatalism is often used to engage the audience's sympathy for the villain. Surprisingly, considering that Gothic melodrama was the earliest and perhaps most primitive form of the drama, it was the exception rather than the rule for the villain to be presented in an entirely unsympathetic manner.

One of the most powerful models of villainy in Gothic melodrama could be labelled (in some cases anachronistically) 'Byronic'. Many of the villains of Gothic melodrama are the poor relations of Byron's heroes. These gloomy egotists crudely invoke the Romantic valorization of complex interiority. Like the passionless villains of domestic melodrama, they use repression as a tool of self-definition. Other characters in Gothic melodrama refer to the villain as if he were otherworldly, or godlike. R. C. Maturin's *Bertram; or, The Castle of St. Aldobrand* (9 May 1816, DL) provides one of the best examples.[36] A mysterious stranger, tormented by a secret passion, Bertram is described even in his disguise by Imogine in Byronic terms:

> One stood alone,—I marked him where he stood,
> His face was veiled,—faintly a light fell on him;
> But through soiled weeds his muffled form did shew
> A wild and terrible grandeur. (p. 28; II. iii)

Clotilda likewise notices 'his dark eye's stilling energy' and the 'mystery of woe about him | That strongly stirs the fancy' (p. 28; II. iii). Bertram himself talks of his 'heart's steeled pride' (p. 33; II. iii). He interestingly labels himself 'a conscious villain' (p. 51; IV. i), and indeed, much of his agony in the play results from his consciousness of his corrupted nature. The Prior sums up his satanic character accurately and succinctly: 'High-hearted man, sublime even in thy guilt; | Whose passions are thy crimes' (p. 41; III. ii). In true Byronic fashion, Bertram feels responsible for the death of Imogine, the woman he loves; he comments, 'I killed her—but—I loved her' (p. 91; V. iii). Despite his guilt, his pride prevents his repentance; he rather positively exults in his anti-Christian suicide, dying '*With a burst of wild exultation*' (p. 91; V. iii).

[36] (London: Murray, 1816).

The Gothic villain epitomizes the dialectic which exists in melodrama between excess and restraint. His antisocial indulgence in emotional freedom has a price, resulting in self-harm as well as violence towards others. His limitless self-serving energy is ultimately self-destructive. Like the passionless villain of domestic melodrama to whom he seems so opposed, he is cannibalistic. What this means of course is that he may show traces of an inner life, and indeed value this interiority more highly than the social world. In many cases, the villain's 'psychologizing' traits are presented in emotional terms—guilt, remorse, conscience, etc.—and only routinely sketched in. To know an individual inwardly, or indeed to define individuality in terms of interiority, is antithetical to the melodramatic vision. In the same way that the passionate, excessive villain invariably sees more of his own emotional innards than he does of those he wishes to violate, the audience's familiarity with the villain's insides is subjugated to its judgement of his actions. Thus sympathy and admiration for the villain often metamorphose into censure of his immorality and egotism. In Henry Siddons's *The Sicilian Romance; or, The Apparition of the Cliffs* (28 May 1794, CG), for example, Ferrand, the Marquis of Otranto, pays lip service to the idea of having a conscience, but the audience is struck far more forcefully by that 'blackest of monsters— | *Ingratitude*' and by 'the darling idol of [his] my soul—Command'.[37] Again, some malefactors in Gothic melodrama are such victims of their own warped passion that they either break down, like Joanna Baillie's De Monfort,[38] or change their ways, like W. T. Moncrieff's Gebir, in *Zoroaster; or, The Spirit of the Star* (19 April 1824, DL). In either case, they lose their claim to the title of villain.

Variations aside, however, most Gothic villains experience a passion so intense that it is beyond their control. They are bad actors, capable of lying and/or disguising their true natures only temporarily. In Pocock's *The Miller and his Men*, for example, the chief villain leads a nominal double life, as Grindoff the miller by day and Wolf the bandit leader by night. But his disguise is always flimsy and the comic man Karl is not the only character who never entirely believes in Wolf's amateurish performance. Karl muses, 'Lord, how a man may be deceived! I took you for a great rogue; but I now find

[37] (London: Barker, 1794), 17 (I. ii), 23 (II. i). Siddons's play is an adaptation of Mrs Radcliffe's *The Romance of the Forest* (1791).
[38] The protagonist of *De Monfort* (29 Apr. 1800, DL).

you are a good Christian enough, though you are a very ill-looking man.'[39] There is a strong sense of what Donohue might call 'the climactic display of the immanent' in Wolf's eventual unmasking, a sense of violent physical and emotional release.[40] The stage directions read:

[*With a violent effort of strength, the old man suddenly turns upon WOLF and tears open his vest, beneath which he appears armed. WOLF, at the same instant, dashes KELMAR from him, who impelled forward is caught by the COUNT. The COUNT draws his sword—WOLF draws pistols in each hand from his side-pockets, and his hat falls off at the same instant— appropriate music*]. (p. 69; II. iv)

The Gothic villain's forte is revelation, not deceit. He can thus resemble what Robert Heilman calls 'the more familiar evil character', who 'tends to eliminate the judicious intelligence by yielding his being to insatiable impulses'.[41]

VILLAINY IN ROMANTIC MELODRAMA?

To introduce the category of 'romantic melodrama' is perhaps inviting confusion considering the differences this book has outlined between melodrama and high Romanticism. But to ignore romantic melodrama, as contemporaries called it, would be to ignore some of the most fascinating deviants in melodrama. To clarify at the outset then, the adjective romantic (with a lower case 'r'), when paired with the word melodrama, invariably derives from the idea of 'romance' rather than from (high) Romanticism. Romance itself, of course, took numerous forms and in my definition of romantic melodrama I want to separate—artificially but usefully—'the romantic' from 'the terrible'. My class of romantic melodrama will thus include those melodramas which descend in ethos and style, if not in actuality, from the novels of Walter Scott (rather than those which descend from the Gothic 'romance'). I wish, in other words, to associate 'romance' more closely with adventure than with horror. Scott's tendency to romanticize outlaws and criminals influenced romantic melodramatists and 'Newgate' novelists like Edward Bulwer and Harrison Ainsworth, who in turn influenced the stage. These plays are not Gothic or eastern in setting, and are characterized by the

---

[39] *English Plays of the Nineteenth Century*, I (1969), 29–72 (p. 59; II. i).
[40] *Theatre in the Age of Kean*, III.
[41] *Tragedy and Melodrama*, 242.

moral ambiguity of the protagonist: he is often a highwayman or pirate by trade, of gentlemanly origin, supposedly virtuous by nature, and attractive to women. The romantic criminal ties the usually straightforward morality of melodrama into all sorts of knots.

The typical protagonist of romantic melodrama is admirably described by W. Moncrieff in his prefatory remarks to William Barrymore's *Gilderoy; or, The Bonnie Boy* (25 June 1822, Cob.):

Gilderoy, Rob Roy and Johnnie Armstrong,—are all branches of the same family; romantic in sentiment, generous in feeling, daring in enterprize, and courageous in combat; wild in excess, lawless in conduct, ingenious in plan, and triumphant in execution; protecting poverty though persecuted by power, and abounding in marvellous stratagems and hair-breadth escapes, it is not to be wondered that their exploits have ever been favourites with the million.[42]

The stereotypical romantic 'villain', as Moncrieff's description suggests, is arguably heroic. He is a criminal in the eyes of the law, but often justifies his crimes by what could be called a nineteenth-century Robin Hood ethic. He sees himself as the scourge of the oppressors of society and feels justified in rejecting the laws of a society which rejects its poor. The romantic criminal is a stranger to his Gothic cousin's evil frenzy in the blood; although he is also passionate about his crimes and his women, his lawless lifestyle can start with a political objection to his society. The romantic protagonist's role as the voice of the socially oppressed, combined with the rebelliousness he exudes, goes some way towards accounting for the admiration he is accorded in so many romantic melodramas. In many ways, the romantic mongrel exists in a unique relationship to the melodramatic world; in an anti-individualistic genre, he epitomizes an entrepreneurial kind of individualism which is at least in part glamorized. The unrivalled popularity of such figures suggests that the new theatre audience of artisans and workers engaged powerfully with these types.

Barrymore's Gilderoy exhibits many typical traits. The highland outlaw establishes in the first scene of the play the reasons for his criminal crusade, telling Jessy that he has vowed to avenge himself against the 'fierce foes of Southern climes' (pp. 13–14; I. i) who killed his father and destroyed his home. Although Gilderoy is fiercely passionate about his lawlessness, his passion has become an ordering point of principle, a moral stricture, in his life. Gilderoy is as

[42] *Richardson Minor*, 2 (London: Richardson, [1829]), p. v.

courageous and exultant in his crime as a Gothic villain or a Renaissance revenger, but he differs sharply from them in his intelligence, sensitivity, and ingenuity. He has no relish for violence or killing, but when it is necessary he is able to justify his deeds morally. After killing Sergeant Skewerem, for instance, he muses: 'it almost went against me, but in slaying him, I've saved the life of one whose value would outweigh an hundred such' (p. 22; I. iii).

As the play progresses, Gilderoy's romantic sentiments for his sweetheart gain ascendancy over his violent passion for plunder and revenge. Eventually Gilderoy is ready to tell Jessy with honesty, 'to call thee mine, for ever I would quit the Riever's life' (p. 39; III. iii). Gilderoy subjugates his desire for revenge to his immediate human impulse to protect the lives of Jessy and her father, even though both abide by society's laws and regard Gilderoy's actions as a 'vile perversion of charity's true maxim' (p. 13; I. i). He himself eventually comes to regard his crimes as unjustifiable, rejecting his former Robin Hood ethos. When he finds Jessy alive, he effuses: 'oh, bounteous heaven! to thee I owe inexplicable bliss, deign then to pardon all my errors past, and for this act of gracious mercy, henceforward I become sweet virtue's convert, I'll quit the paths of crime, I'll err and sin no more' (p. 42; II. v). Eventually then, Gilderoy accepts society's concept of 'virtue' as adherence to society's laws. He proves himself to be, in the words of John Howie the farmer, 'a strange mixture of a man' (p. 44; II. v). After spending most of his life defending rebellion according to principles in which he passionately believes, he performs a perfunctory moral U-turn. To some this might seem fickle, or perhaps hypocritical, but within the context of the play, it is presented as admirable.

It is tempting to argue that the impulse behind romantic melodrama is ultimately conservative. In *Blood and Thunder*, for example, Disher argues that the outlaw of romantic melodrama was not 'virtuous because of his robberies. [. . .] He was virtuous despite his robberies.'[43] The sub-genre was, however, not perceived as conservative in the Romantic and Victorian periods. The so-called Newgate controversy, for example, analysed in Chapter 5, is itself a melodramatic demonstration of the threat this kind of drama was felt to pose to nothing less than the political and social stability of the nation.[44] When the crimes of *The Newgate Calendar* (1773) were

---

[43] p. 121.
[44] For a full analysis of the Newgate controversy—particularly the Newgate novels—see

dramatized on the Victorian stage, they were often romanticized. The possible influence of these plays on juvenile delinquents in particular and 'the masses' in general was of major concern throughout their stage history. The notorious murder in 1840 of Lord William Russell by his valet, B. F. Courvoisier, transformed concern into censorship.[45] As a direct result of a report in *The Times* which suggested that Courvoisier's crime had been inspired by seeing J. T. Haines's production of Ainsworth's *Jack Sheppard* (1839, Surrey), licensing of further adaptations of the novel was prohibited and existing performances discouraged.[46] After 1840, many 'Newgate' plays were banned and versions of *Oliver Twist* were policed with as much rigour as adaptions of *Jack Sheppard*: when John Oxenford's *Oliver Twist* was performed at the Queen's Theatre (11 April 1868), it was the first licensed production in nearly ten years.[47]

Thus if the romantic criminal got away with his crimes onstage, he was a villain in the eyes of the theatrical establishment. The 1840s was of course a time of particular social unrest and the Chartist movement became the objective correlative of fears about working-class revolt. In the Newgate controversy, however, anxieties about political power were inextricable from anxieties about cultural ownership. Part of the problem was that 'the people' seemed out of control; Newgate drama, for example, was rumoured to be popular in unlicensed places of entertainment. The discourse of the censors is commonly a strange mixture of the defensive and paternalistic. William Donne, the Examiner of Plays, for example, was particularly concerned about the 'influence' of *Oliver Twist* on vulnerable—and hence dangerous—members of society. 'It is highly objectionable in its moral', he argued, 'more especially as it is performed at Theatres where the Gallery is the main resort, and the greater portion of its frequenters consists of apprentices and young persons of either sex.'[48]

The censorship of stage adaptations of Newgate novels undoubtedly had an impact on the content and ideological portent of later productions. Where an early adaptation like Gilbert Abbott À Beckett's *Oliver Twist* (26 Mar. 1838, St J.) included scenes like

my introduction to *Cult Criminals: The Newgate Novels, 1830–1847*, 6 vols. (London: Routledge, 1998), i, pp. v–lxi.

[45] See Stephens's *The Censorship of English Drama*, 61–77 for a fine account of the censorship of Newgate drama.

[46] Ibid. 65.

[47] Ibid. 67, 73; LC 53066U.

[48] LC 1: 83 (2 Jan. 1860); quoted by Stephens, *The Censorship of English Drama*, 77.

Oliver's lessons in pickpocketing, later productions suppressed them.[49] An anonymous 1855 MS intended for production at the Standard Theatre, for example, not only omitted scenes of 'festive' villainy and those depicting the corruption of innocence; it announced itself as 'An Entire New Version of Mr Charles Dickens's Tale of Oliver Twist, [. . .] Carefully Avoiding All the Repulsive Matter of the Tale [. . .] to Point a Moral'.[50] Again, where À Beckett's version depicts onstage shooting, in post-censorship productions, Nancy tends to be shot offstage.[51] However, the fact that in the novel Nancy is not shot but bludgeoned to death (albeit partly with a pistol) suggests that even the early adaptations are less sensationalist than the censors imply. But it is ultimately difficult to generalize without access to these plays in performance. Even on the basis of textual evidence, Newgate drama shows considerable ideological variation from play to play. The main traces of apparent conservatism manifest themselves in the habitual 'gentility' of the romantic criminal. Even if the romantic wrongdoer did not discover that he was from a genteel background, he was usually presented as possessing a 'natural' gentility. This gentility was invariably regarded as a sign of innate virtue even in one who had spent most of his life crusading against the genteel classes.

In G. Dibdin Pitt's adaptation of *Rookwood*, for example, the moral and social messages are typically confused.[52] Cocking his pistol at Lady Rookwood, Dick Turpin 'gently' persuades her to be silent.

I am naturally polite, and have been accounted the best-bred man on the road by every female I've had the honour of addressing, and I should be very sorry to sully my well-earned reputation by anything like rudeness. I must use force of the gentlest kind. (p. 5; I. iii)

Again, later in the same play, Turpin distinguishes between 'cold-blooded murder', which is 'altogether out of [his] line', and 'a shot or two in self-defence' (p. 9; II. i). The emphasis is on Dick's romantic gallantry and chivalry, rather than on his readiness to commit a serious crime. The Victorian idea was that the romantic villain/hero was *genteel* despite his robberies. In Buckstone's famous adaptation of

---

[49] LC Add. MS 42945, fos. 683–707b.
[50] LC Add. MS 52, 955 H.
[51] See, for example, Shepherd and Creswick's adaptation (5 May 1868, Surrey)—LC 53068 F; an anonymous version at the Garrick (21 Apr. 1868)—LC 53067 P; and the Standard Theatre version discussed above.
[52] *Rookwood!* (24 Feb. 1840, SW), *Dicks*, [no.] 307 (London: Dicks, [1882?]).

Jack Sheppard (28 October 1839, Adel.), Jack's appearance is that of a man of taste and fashion:

JACK *stands laughing in the centre—his coat is of brown flowered velvet, laced with silver—a waistcoat of white satin, richly embroidered—smart boots with red heels—a muslin cravat, or steenkirk, edged with pointed lace—a hat smartly cocked and edged with feathers.*[53]

His fine clothes potentially emasculate him and certainly downplay the physicality which enabled his famous escapes. The fact that, in Buckstone's version, Mrs Keeley made the part of Jack her own arguably further distances Jack from the spectre of aggressive working-class masculinity that the censors feared he embodied.

The idea of the genteel status of the romantic criminal was so familiar to playwrights and audiences alike that romantic stage protagonists often committed crimes *in order to become genteel.* The idea that one must become a criminal in order to become genteel is arguably subversive rather than conservative in its implications. In Fitzball's musical adaptation of Edward Bulwer's 'Newgate' novel *Paul Clifford* (1830), for example, Clifford claims that his 'errors' have been 'of the head, not of the heart'; he becomes a highwayman in order to become a 'gentleman' and eventually—as befits the true son of an unlikely parental combination, an aristocratic father and an aristocratic mother-turned-robber—he reforms and conforms.[54] The villain of Fitzball's *Jonathan Bradford; or, The Murder at the Roadside Inn* (12 June 1833, Surrey) almost parodies the emergence in romantic melodrama of the unprincipled rogue who poses as a gentleman. Macraisy's mother's last advice to him is, 'beg, borrow and stale [i.e. steal], if you wish to be respectable'.[55] Although Macraisy, in the tradition of romantic criminality, begs pardon in an attempt to show his essential virtue, we have moved full circle from Gilderoy.

From one perspective, virtue is identified with gentility; from another perspective, gentility is crime. Romantic melodrama typifies the ambiguity expressed in Victorian literature generally towards gentility; it is untypical, however, of the anti-aristocratic impulse of most melodrama. It is also potentially subversive of the transparent models of identity advocated in melodrama generally. The romantic criminal's desire to appear genteel makes it necessary for him to

    [53] *Acting Nat. Drama*, 7 (London: Chapman & Hall, [1840?]), 37 (III. i).
    [54] *Paul Clifford* (28 Oct. 1835, CG), *Dicks*, [no.] 367 (London: Dicks, [1883?]), 18 (III. iv), 4 (I. i).
    [55] *Dicks*, [no.] 370 (London: Dicks, [1883?]), 5 (I. ii).

become a master at manipulating his presentation of self. The romantic criminal is thus significant in melodrama in that he is the first among melodramatic malefactors to develop a consciousness of his abilities as an actor. Indeed, Paul Clifford—in Bulwer's novel and Fitzball's adaptation—originally thought of pursuing a career as an actor, but employed his theatrical talents in the service of crime instead. The romantic criminal is conscious and even proud of his theatrical talent. Moreover, genteel society often accepts the criminal's social performances and disregards his immorality. Fitzball's *Paul Clifford* and *Jonathan Bradford* expose society's complicity in criminality, its elevation of manners over morals.

The romantic criminal, like other melodramatic malefactors, thus possesses traces of a 'private' life which is potentially threatening to the melodramatic vision. What distinguishes him from his 'out-and-out' siblings is that his inner life is usually constructed as generous and virtuous; it is appearances which are against him, and not the other way around. Likewise his role-playing is often at least partially justified by concern for social justice. The dynamics of the genre demand, however, that his innate virtue must eventually reveal itself and this means that he must eschew performativity in favour of transparency—or adopt an expressive rather than repressive theatricality. The genteel manners and theatrical awareness which are part of the romantic criminal's make-up are presented in a far more sinister light when they appear in the villain of domestic melodrama.

VILLAINY IN DOMESTIC MELODRAMA

Domestic melodrama is at the other end of the melodramatic spectrum from the Gothic variety, dramatizing various social and family problems only too familiar to its working-class audience like industrialization, urbanization, alcoholism, the disintegration of the family, and the seduction of lowly maidens by their social superiors. In 'Melodrama and the Working-Class', Booth says of domestic melodrama: 'for the first time in English drama, the working-class appeared in serious plays, not always as comic characters, in a recognisable domestic environment'.[56] Domestic melodrama is strongly anti-aristocratic in feeling, and the ruling-class villain is often seen as the symbol of various social evils. The villain of domestic melo-

---

[56] p. 103.

drama (apart from the admonitory variety) is melodrama's most unambiguous villain. In human terms, he poses a threat to the melodramatic vision in every conceivable way: he is passionless, secretive, selfish, and calculating. Viewed symbolically, he is the spectre of melodrama's inversion: he paradoxically personifies a world of pure surface. In a genre where most excesses are restrained, his restraint is excessive. His individualistic valorization of his own interiority is presented as clearly detrimental to his society.

In domestic melodrama, of all melodramatic sub-genres, the social implications of the passional constitution of the villain are overtly insisted upon. In John Walker's *The Factory Lad* (15 October 1832, Surrey), for example, the Squire is the oppressive tyrant who unfeelingly makes his workers redundant in the name of industrial progress. In Watts Phillips's *Lost in London* (16 March 1867, Adel.), Gilbert Featherstone, the owner of a Yorkshire mine, is guilty first of seducing the wife of one of the miners, and second, of taking her to the metropolis. As in most domestic melodramas dealing with the same subject, an antithesis is created between corruption in the city and innocence in the country. *Lost in London* has marked affinities with the Emily/Steerforth plot in Dickens's *David Copperfield*; Job Armroyd's search for his much younger, fallen wife, especially, strongly resembles Daniel Peggotty's search for Emily. Indeed, Dickens's novels existed in a circular relationship to domestic melodrama, both adopting its themes and conventions and providing perfect raw material for the adapters. Booth in fact uses Dickens as surety for the integrity and social relevance of—particularly domestic—melodrama:

> To those who have claimed [. . .] that [. . .] melodrama [. . .] has no relevance to the social realities of life—the charge makes just as much sense levelled at Dickens—one can reply by asking them to examine without prejudice and with some care the melodramas that treat of the life of the drunkard, the factory worker, the poor and the destitute.[57]

In *The Factory Lad*, Hatfield defines 'a true English gentleman' as 'he who feels for another'.[58] In domestic melodrama, however, the hallmark of gentility is lack of humane feeling for others; gentility is usually synonymous with villainy. Whether the villain of the piece is wicked seducer, oppressive landlord, or superficial dandy, he is nearly always presented as devoid of emotion. Of course, definitions

---

[57] 'Melodrama and the Working-Class', 107.
[58] Booth (ed.), *English Plays of the Nineteenth Century*, i (1969), 201–33 (p. 219; i. v).

of what constituted the gentleman differed greatly in the Victorian period, as the middle classes grew in number and in wealth. Again, if one wanted to be pedantic, one could argue that it was impossible to be a gentleman villain—for if one was a villain, one could not be a true gentleman. It goes without saying therefore that the villains of domestic melodrama are not gentlemen in the strictest sense of the word. Chapter 6 examines the problem of defining gentility in some detail, but for the purposes of this chapter, my selection of villainous gentlemen shall include 'gentlemen' of the old and the new schools, aristocrats, dandies, and self-made men.[59]

Whatever the particular breed, most villainous gentlemen are untypical of melodramatic characters generally. A class-based dichotomy is regularly created in domestic melodrama; calculating intellect and emotional emptiness are associated with the ruling class, whilst honesty and passionate intensity are associated with the working class. Emotional openness is presented here as a positive moral virtue; the villain is all art and no heart. Among representatives of the working class in domestic melodrama, the common feeling is that the genteel classes imitate or feign humane emotions which they do not possess; whatever their specific crimes, gentlemen are universally distrusted as creatures of the surface. In Watts Phillips's *Lost in London*, for instance, Gilbert Featherstone, seducer and mine owner, is described by his servant Blinker in the following terms:

Featherstone's no 'art—never had. To hear him speak when he's got on his company manners, you'd think butter wouldn't melt in his mouth. These hoily, insinuating chaps, they twists and they winds like corkscrews, till once they've got a *hold* and then—pop!—(*imitates drawing cork*)—who likes may 'av the hempty bottle. (p. 242; ii. iii)

Blinker's point is that Featherstone imitates virtues in order to serve his own selfish ends. Although at the end of the play Featherstone— unusually for domestic melodrama—offers to atone for his sins, Job Armroyd's description of him as 'a base, cold-hearted villain' (p. 267; iii. i) dominates the vision of the upper classes offered in *Lost in London*.

In *The Factory Lad*, the cold-heartedness of genteel villain Squire Westwood is symbolized by his choosing to use steam instead of manpower at his factory. For the twenty-first-century reader, the personal tragedies and redundancies caused by industrialization may be a

[59] Of course, the situation of the theatre and the time that the play was produced made a difference to the exact species of 'genteel' villainy presented.

familiar theme, but Walker's play has all the urgency of spontaneous protest. The most interesting aspect of the play is the fact that for the factory workers the Squire is both villainous in himself, and a hated symbol of industrialization and the class system. Westwood answers the complaints of his unemployed workers with effusive generalizations about this system. He wonders that his men dare 'to violate the laws, well framed to subject them to obedience' (pp. 217–18; I. iv); he asks 'is England's proud aristocracy to tremble when brawling fools mouth and question? No, the hangman shall be their answer' (p. 218; I. iv). Westwood is incapable of recognizing that the members of the working class are human beings with emotional lives—not to mention families. His lack of humane feeling is contrasted throughout the play with the intense passion of the outcast Rushton, who ironically is a villain according to laws that defend aristocratic power. In the eyes of the playwright, Rushton is a hero. He is at first distrusted by the factory workers for his anarchic ways—'While I have my liberty, or power, or strength, I will live as well as the best of 'em' (p. 210; I. ii.)—but the unemployed men soon realize that they too are now social outcasts. Allen tells the landlord to allow Rushton into the pub—'he may wear as honest a heart as many who wear a better garment; [. . .] let him in. The outcast should sojourn with the outcast' (p. 221; I. v)—expressing the underlying sentiment of domestic melodrama, that honesty of heart is more important than social respectability.

In the light of social changes like industrialization and the shifting of the rural population to the cities, it is easy to see why 'gentlemen', in domestic melodrama, became symbols of heartlessness and corruption. The ruling classes, in the opinion of the working-class characters in domestic melodrama—and probably working-class audiences too—cared more about machines, the law, money, fine clothes, or hedonistic pleasure than they did about the lives of other human beings. Montagu Slater, in his introduction to the crime melodrama *Maria Marten*, claims that

in the 1830s and 1840s, whenever an aristocrat—that is an actor in a silk hat and gloves—appeared on the stage of the City of London, Whitechapel Road, or the Pavilion Theatre, Mile End, there was immediately a howl. There was no choice but to make him the villain.[60]

Tom Taylor's adaptation of *A Tale of Two Cities* (30 January 1860,

---

[60]   *Maria Marten; or, The Murder in the Red Barn*, ed. Montagu Slater (London: Heinemann, 1971; repr. 1973), p. x. *Maria Marten* cannot be attributed to any single author.

Lyc.) thus simplifies the ambiguous class attitudes expressed in Dickens's original novel, by making his play more straightforwardly anti-aristocratic. In many domestic melodramas, the imagery of coldness, deadness, or specifically of machinery, is applied by workers to their social oppressors. In Walker's *The Factory Lad*, for example, Hatfield says of Squire Westwood, 'You cannot expect iron to have feelings' (p. 209; I. i). In William Bayle Bernard's *The Farmer's Story* (13 June 1836, Lyc.), Lockwood the farmer resents working so that Mortlake the gentleman landlord will reap the rewards of his labour: 'And all this, whilst a rascal with a heart like a harrow—a lump of clayey earth, in which not a thought will vegetate—may roll in riches, ride in his carriage—aye, and splash poor barefoot honesty, who happens to be walking.'[61] In John Thomas Haines's *The Factory Boy; or, The Love Sacrifice* (8 June 1840, Surrey), Eve Allison says of the rich mill owner, Magnus Mule, that 'he would suck the heart's blood of his poorer fellow-worm, then crush its weakness for his sport'.[62] Again, when Blereau, the overlooker of Mule's factory, reveals that Barbara knows 'a secret of life and death', Mule describes his shock in unusual terms: 'A bolt of ice seemed rushing through my blood' (p. 18; III. ii). And Blereau himself, ultimately more unpleasant than his repentant master, muses, 'Bah! what has *feeling* to do with business?— and honour—pshaw! another pretty bye-word' (p. 20; III. iii).

The familiarity of the character of the villainous gentleman is effectively exploited by Douglas Jerrold in *The Rent Day* (25 January 1832, DL). Old Crumbs, the steward of Squire Grantley's estate, manipulates the prejudices of the rural population about the aristocracy to his own advantage, by claiming that it is the absent Squire who demands so much money from them when actually Old Crumbs himself is their oppressor. The country tenants are only too eager to believe in the stereotype of the villainous Squire. Ironically, Grantley is a good man, while Crumbs is exploiting the tenants. The twist in the tale, however, is that Old Crumbs has not been motivated by sheer greed, but by a desire to revenge himself on both Grantley in particular, and the class system in general. He reveals to the Squire: 'I took ten guineas from a rich usurer, and was condemned for Tyburn. Your father took the wife of my bosom, and lived a wealthy, charitable gentleman.'[63]

---

[61] *Dicks*, [no.] 434 (London: Dicks, [1883?]), 4 (I. i).
[62] *Dicks*, [no.] 641 (London: Dicks, [1885]), 5 (I. i).
[63] (London: Chapple, 1832), 63; II. iv.

Though not a melodrama, the light-hearted comedy by Edward Bulwer *Not so Bad as We Seem; or, Many Sides to a Character* (16 May 1851, Devonshire House)[64] also illuminatingly questions the common association, on the nineteenth-century stage, of gentility with villainy. In *Not so Bad as We Seem*—a play in which Dickens acted many times—the plot revolves around the competition between the aristocrat Lord Wilmot (played by Dickens), and the self-made man Hardman (played by Forster). Lord Wilmot is actually a virtuous character who ironically feigns immorality in order to enhance his reputation as a fashionable gentleman; Hardman feigns honesty and simplicity in order to gain social advancement. The latter's belief that 'the world's something more than a stage', a battle between the 'darlings of fortune' and the 'stern sons of labour',[65] is a succinct summation of the message of domestic melodrama. Those who view the world as 'theatrum mundi', usually gentlemen, are regarded with intense distrust and hatred; those who possess 'deep feelings', usually members of the working class, are treated with admiration.

Lord Wilmot is, on the other hand, perhaps more similar—in appearance if not in immorality—to the villains who became increasingly popular in the second half of the century, the so-called 'West End villains'. These differed from their predecessors in so far as they were created not for a working-class audience, but for middle-class spectators who had returned to the theatre after years of absence. Booth describes the West End villain as 'a polished and urbane villain of faultless dress'; these malefactors were 'well-bred [. . .] with suave and courtly manners, impeccable taste in clothes and jewellery, and devilish fine black moustaches'.[66] One such villain, according to Booth,[67] is Chateau Renaud, from Alexander Dumas's *The Corsican Brothers* (1845), who, in the words of the adaptation by E. Grangé and Xavier de Montépin, 'treats a woman's reputation as the merest trifle in the world'.[68] The fact that what is said about Chateau Renaud is said about most old-style aristocratic seducers emphasizes the difficulty of segregating the old and the new types of villain. Gilbert

[64] This play was originally performed in front of the Queen and Prince and a large audience for the Guild of Literature and Art. There then followed many performances in Hanover Square rooms, London, and in various parts of the country at intervals during 1851 and 1852. See Forster's *Life*, 517.

[65] (London: Chapman & Hall, 1851), 44; II. i.

[66] *English Melodrama*, 145, 163.

[67] *English Plays of the Nineteenth Century*, ii (1969), 5.

[68] (10 Aug. 1850, Théâtre Historique, Paris), trans. Charles Webb, *Cumberland*, 47 (London: Music-Publishing, [1860?]), 23 (II. i).

Featherstone, to give another example of the difficulty, is both a refined man-about-town and a mine owner who oppresses the poor. Perhaps the main point of differentiation between the old and the new is that in the representation of the West End villain, elegance of dress and manner was emphasized to a far greater extreme than previously. This was in keeping with the tendency of melodrama in the second half of the century towards increased splendour of setting, character, and costume. The West End villain was often what Carlyle would have called a dandy, 'a Man whose trade, office and existence consists in the wearing of Clothes'.[69] Dickens himself, as Chapter 6 of this book demonstrates, was intrigued by the dandy-villain, the man of heartless elegance, often suggesting similarities between dandy-villains and old-style villainous peers and squires. What intrigued Dickens was the repression or negation of emotion which accompanied the dandy pose; the dandy's selfishness and passionlessness had much in common with that of the villainous squire, whatever the differences in their fashion taste.

Not all 'villains' in domestic melodrama are passionless, however. In admonitory domestic melodrama—that highly moralistic branch of the domestic which warns its audience against evils of modern living like alcohol or gambling—the central malefactor is always passionate and often a member of the working class. T. P. Taylor's *The Bottle* (1 October 1847, CL) is a classic example of the genre and William Bayle Bernard's *The Farmer's Story* interestingly combines protest against the ruling classes with warnings against the evils of alcohol. The protagonists in both melodramas morally deteriorate at a remarkably rapid rate—after taking a drink, in the case of Taylor's Thornley, and winning the lottery, in the case of Bernard's Lockwood. Douglas Jerrold's Vernon, in *Fifteen Years of a Drunkard's Life* (24 November 1828, Cob.), is passionate about the effects of alcohol on a gentleman. All three protagonists are, however, presented as victims as well as villains—victims of a passion beyond their control. Often, the real villain is presented as that 'one absorbing passion' (Taylor, *The Bottle*, 19; I. v) which is symptomatic of the addiction that alcohol or gambling can represent.

Temperance melodramas and gambling melodramas are not then so fundamentally different from other domestic melodramas as they at first appear. The real problem in admonitory domestic melodrama

---

[69] *Sartor Resartus* (1833–4), ed. Kerry McSweeney and Peter Sabor (Oxford: Oxford University Press, 1987; repr. 1991), 207.

is the dissolving of the close familial and communal ties which allow people to live happily and healthily together—the fragmentation of a caring society. Domestic melodrama in general is a drama of protest—against industrialization, urbanization, social oppression, the seduction of simple girls, the disintegration of the family, and the evils of the city. Above all, it is a protest against dehumanizing forces at work in both society and the self.

POSTSCRIPT: VILLAINY IN CRIME MELODRAMA

Crime melodrama used topical news stories and accounts of lurid and sensational murders as the basis to attract greater audiences. In *Hiss the Villain*, Booth explains how 'the growth of the mass circulation newspaper' in the nineteenth century gave melodramatists 'a treasure trove of plots in police court news and crime reporting'; 'the more sensational the crime the more versions of it'.[70] The most popular crime melodramas of the day were taken from the story of the killing of Maria Marten by the 'gentleman' William Corder. It is particularly difficult to generalize about villainy in crime melodrama, as crime melodrama itself takes several different forms. Roughly speaking, crime melodramas can be divided into three different categories; first, there were topical dramas like *Maria Marten* and *Sweeney Todd* which exploited sensational real-life murders for melodramatic effect;[71] second, there were plays such as Moncrieff's *The Scamps of London; or, The Cross Roads of Life* (13 November 1843, SW) and Charles Selby's *London by Night* (12 May 1845, Strand) which, influenced by Eugène Sue's *Les Mystères de Paris* (1842–3) and Pierce Egan's *Life in London* (1820–1), represented not one dramatic crime, but a quasi-realistic, panoramic view of the underworld in the metropolis. The third type of crime melodrama was unusual; a play like Leopold Lewis's *The Bells* (25 November 1871, Lyc.) could be described as a psychological suspense story, focusing as it does on the tortured conscience of the criminal. In its concentration on inner psychology and its almost sympathetic view of the villain, Leopold Lewis's *The Bells* seems to defy categorization as melodrama, but its overall moralistic conclusion and its use of elaborate scenic devices for sensational effect are 'truly melodramatic'.[72]

[70] p. 18.
[71] The date of the Lord Chamberlain's MS for G. Dibdin Pitt's *Sweeney Todd: The Demon Barber of Fleet Street* is 22 Feb. 1847.   [72] Booth (ed.), *Hiss the Villain*, 29.

The Bells mixes realism with melodrama, but this time in a combination fatal to the ailing constitution of melodrama. On the first entrance of the play's villain, Mathias, there seems nothing unusual about this melodramatic villain; he appears, whip in hand, accompanied by musical chord and scenic tableau.[73] Before long, however, the psyche becomes the main site and subject of the drama, and melodramatic methods of musical and scenic symbolism are being used to dramatize Mathias's inner life. Mental action replaces, or perhaps becomes, physical action. At the end of the first act and scene, for instance, Mathias's imaginative reliving of his killing of the Jew is enacted on stage (pp. 358–9), and at the climax of the play, Mathias's dream, the dream which kills him, becomes the play's reality (pp. 374–81; III). Mathias dreams that his crime will be discovered before a jury when a mesmerist hypnotizes him; in his dream, he is found guilty and sentenced to hang; in reality, he is discovered dead the next morning with his hands around his throat (p. 382; III). *The Bells* seems more Dostoevsky than nineteenth-century stage melodrama. It is typical yet untypical of melodrama; inner moral and psychological conflict is faithfully externalized, dramatized in visual terms; but melodrama is a genre of simplification and idealization which does not usually foreground inner conflict.

If 1871 is the year of *The Bells*, it also marks the acme of the classic realist novel, the publication of George Eliot's *Middlemarch*. With the novel in the cultural ascendant and Dickens in his grave, it is little wonder that melodrama turned inwards.

[73] Booth (ed.), *Hiss the Villain*, 343–82 (p. 355; I. i).

3

Dickens, Acting, and Ambivalence:
Periodical Passions

'GREAT crimes are commonly produced either out of a cold intensity
of selfishness, or out of a hot intensity of passion.'[1] Thus reads 'A
Criminal Trial', the opening article in *Household Words*, on 21 June
1856. Though the contributors' book attributes this article to Henry
Morley,[2] Morley's view, like all those expressed in *Household Words*, is
in keeping with Dickens's own.[3] Dickens's thoughts on villainy are in
no way simplistically schematic, or even consistent; but throughout
his journalistic commentary on contemporary criminals, his writings
on the theatre, and, of course, his novels, the dialectic between
passionate and passionless villainy anchors Dickens's perceptions of
deviance.

Though models of villainy throughout literary history tend to
veer towards one or other of the extremes identified by Morley,
Dickens's understanding of this familiar pairing appears to have been
immediately influenced by contemporary influences, in particular his
crime reporting and theatre-going. George Augustus Sala observed
of Dickens that 'what he liked to talk about was the latest new piece
at the theatres, the latest exciting trial or police case, the latest social
craze or social swindle, and especially the latest murder and the
newest thing in ghosts'.[4] There has been only limited appreciation in
Dickens criticism of the extent to which Dickens's novelistic villains
are shaped by the confluence of his great interest in these two topics,
crime and the theatre. As Chapter 2 made clear, for example, the

---

[1] *HW* 13 (21 June 1856), 529–34 (p. 529).
[2] See Anne Lohrli (comp.), *Household Words: A Weekly Journal, 1850–1859, Conducted by Charles Dickens: Table of Contents, List of Contributors and their Contributions Based on the 'Household Words' Office Book* (Toronto: University of Toronto Press, 1973). Lohrli's book is based on the *HW* office book, which is kept in The Morris L. Parrish Collection of Victorian Novelists, Princeton University Library.
[3] See p. 91–2 below.
[4] *Things I Have Seen and People I Have Known*, 2 vols. (London: Cassell, 1894), i. 76; quoted by Philip Collins, *Dickens and Crime*, 2nd edn. (London: Macmillan, 1965), 1.

dialectic between passionate and passionless villainy informs the two main models of villainy in stage melodrama—the villains of Gothic and domestic melodrama. Dickens's fascination with crime is obviously consistent with his well-documented imaginative engagement with deviance; but it is also explicable in terms of the theatricality which so often attends criminal behaviour and its cultural mediation. This chapter juxtaposes the observations made in Dickens's journals on the criminals of the day with his commentary on the contemporary stage and its villains in order to explore the anxieties shadowing Dickens's ideal vision of the melodramatic mode. For the impulse towards cultural inclusivity underlying Dickens's deployment of melodrama is invariably inseparable, in his writings, from questions about the moral and political significance of perfomativity in both criminal and everyday behaviour, and about the social and ethical implications of stylized, melodramatic representations of villainy.

ACTING PASSIONLESS

The generic differences between Dickens's journals and his novels mean that in his journalism, Dickens's anxieties about theatricality in its various modes are explicitly voiced. Whereas, in his novels, ideologies are often implicitly dramatized, the journals are melodramatic and populist in the sense that they express their moral and political messages passionately and even simplistically. Paradoxically, what is clear from Dickens's periodicals is that though the theatre, for Dickens, is ideally a tool of social cohesion, once theatrical instruments and strategies leave the playhouse, they are open to abuse. Social role-playing, of course, holds a particular fascination for Dickens; it represents at once a form of acting—an activity which Dickens enjoyed—and a form of deceit, an activity which Dickens claimed to deplore. Not all social performance is inherently deceitful, however, and in Dickens's journalism, it is possible to distinguish two main models of perfomativity: the deviant or repressive and the expressive or histrionic. Repressive criminality is often presented as passionless while expressive deviance is usually figured as passionate. Performativity which exacerbates the split between the 'private' and the public individual, subordinating the latter, is a deviant misappropriation of the theatrical, an inversion of its proper social function. It corrupts both self and society, increasing rather than eroding social barriers in a fashion antithetical to Dickens's professed beliefs about the theatre and the individual.

Dickens's anxieties about the divisive potential of social performance is focused in the journals on criminal behaviour. The criminals who receive most attention are, perhaps unsurprisingly, repressive criminals who violate or ignore the boundaries between the aesthetic and the social, using their chameleonic talents to deceive and manipulate. The criminal characterized by a 'cold intensity of selfishness' is the melodramatic incarnation of the (for Dickens) antisocial individual. I use the word 'melodramatic' here deliberately, as coldly selfish criminals in Dickens's journals are generally constructed as villains—hence the occasional slippage in this chapter between the terms 'villain' and 'criminal'. Any complexity a 'cold' criminal may possess is made secondary to an unambiguous emphasis on his immoral nature.

Henry Morley's 'A Criminal Trial', for example, and Dickens's 'The Demeanour of Murderers'[5] both turn William Palmer (1824–56), the famous Rugeley poisoner, into an out-and-out villain. Both articles aim to counter the tendency of newspaper reports of Palmer's trial to make the criminal fascinatingly complex. In keeping with the impression Dickens wanted to create in his journals of their expressing a single voice, the articles are uncannily alike in subject, ideas, and style.[6] Not only do they both establish and develop a dichotomy between passionate and passionless villainy; they also express a conviction that passionless villainy is more dangerous than the passionate variety. For instance, in 'A Criminal Trial', Morley argues that:

The visible ferocity, the glare of envy or wild hatred in the criminal who slays his enemy—foul and detestable as it must ever be—is not so loathsome as the *tranquil good-humour* of the wretch utterly lost in *self-content*, ready without a particle of malice or compunction to pluck neighbours' lives, as fruit, for his *material* refreshment. [. . .] Such a being would [. . .] feel kindly as men usually do towards their own *possessions*. He might be inclined most amiably—after his *selfish and proprietorial* way—towards his wife whilst he was slowly putting her to a slow and painful death by poison. (p. 529; italics mine)

Whatever emotions Palmer does possess are either for himself or for material things.[7] The dislocation of personality suggested by Palmer's

<hr/>

[5] *HW* 13 (14 June 1856), 505–7.
[6] See p. 91–2 below.
[7] In this, he resembles Kucich's 'bourgeois' villain whose performances of trans-

ability to separate his public persona from his private self is, Morley suggests, inevitably socially destructive.

The article is thus most troubled by Palmer's ability to project a false persona—in other words, to act. Like Morley's, Dickens's piece also warns the public not to be taken in either by the cool and glamorous façade of the poisoner or by newspaper descriptions of his manner:

> The public has read from day to day of the murderer's complete self-possession, of his constant coolness, of his profound composure, of his perfect equanimity. Some describers have gone so far as to represent him, occasionally rather amused than otherwise by the proceedings; and all the accounts we have seen, concur in more or less suggesting that there is something admirable, and difficult to reconcile with guilt, in the bearing so elaborately set forth. (p. 505)

The emphasis in both articles is on the poisoner's autonomy, an autonomy signifying to Morley and Dickens a pathological emotional deficiency, yet simultaneously enabling those convincing performances of 'tranquil good-humour' which the courtroom audience admires. There is some ambiguity in *Household Words* concerning the question of what exactly is troubling about the audience's response to Palmer; the audience is either 'taken in' by his performances, associating the appearance of good humour with innocence, or, perhaps more worryingly, admires 'the bearing so elaborately set forth', regardless of innocence or guilt.

Household Words attempts to redress what it regards as the dominant journalistic tone by emphasizing the emotional emptiness which allows Palmer to appear self-possessed, rather than the appearance of self-possession itself. In 'The Demeanour of Murderers', for example, Dickens is extremely specific about Palmer's emotional deficiencies:

> Can any one, reflecting on the matter for five minutes, suppose it possible [. . .] that in the breast of this Poisoner there were surviving, in the day of his trial, any lingering traces of sensibility, or any wrecked fragment of the quality which we call sentiment? [. . .] An objection to die, and a special objection to be killed, no doubt he had [. . .]. Beyond this emotion, which any lower animal would have, with an apprehension on it of a similar fate, what was to be expected from such a creature but insensibility? (p. 529)

cendence mask materialism (*Excess and Restraint*, 80. See Introduction n. 22 above). He also typifies Kucich's repressed, libidinous individual who creates an external impression of autonomy by channelling desire inwardly—see Kucich, *Repression in Victorian Fiction: Charlotte Brontë, George Eliot, and Charles Dickens* (Berkeley and Los Angeles: University of California Press, 1987), 3–4.

The defendant lacks 'sensibility' and 'sentiment', morally charged emotions ideally betokening civility. Instead of emphasizing the poisoner's poise—suggestive of a civilized being—Dickens associates his lack of civilized emotion with the animalistic, the subhuman. Dickens does not, however, equate civilized emotion with internalized, intellectualized emotion in the tradition of high Romanticism; what we could call moralized feeling tops Dickens's emotional hierarchy. This moralized emotion is the raw material of melodrama.

Dickens's reluctance to foreground Palmer's psychological complexity is obviously a rhetorical strategy designed to counterbalance journalistic reports of the trial which intellectualize rather than moralize about murder. Beneath the loud denunciations of the poisoner's performativity reside anxieties about the social function and ethical significance of role-playing. 'The Demeanour of Murderers' contains an exploration recurrent in *Household Words* and Dickens's novels of the link between the machiavellian villain's 'cold intensity of selfishness' and his sophisticated theatrical consciousness. For instance, the poisoner's confidence that he will be acquitted, according to Dickens, stems from his consciousness that he is a consummate actor of virtuous roles. He 'kept up his place as a good fellow and a sporting character; he had made a capital friend of the coroner, [. . .] he was a great public character' (p. 506). Dickens's references to Palmer's 'character' suggest not his integrity or moral worth but the fictionality of his self-projections. The most overt recognition of the link between villainy and acting comes when Dickens compares Palmer with the prominent early nineteenth-century criminal John Thurtell (1794–1824). Besides coming from very similar genteel backgrounds, Dickens tells us that 'Thurtell's demeanour was exactly that of the Poisoner's', and Thurtell 'makes a speech in the manner of Edmund Kean' (p. 506).

In the periodicals which Dickens edits, the cold-hearted villain who is aware of his own abilities as an actor is a recurring subject of enquiry. 'A Few Pleasant French Gentleman' and 'Coolness amongst Thieves', for instance, are comparatively light-hearted examples of the villain-as-actor motif, emphasizing the well-worn theme of imposture for social mobility.[8] Attendant on this theme is invariably a concern about the loss or fictionalizing of selfhood. Postmodernism and its performative theories of identity have familiarized the idea

---

[8] [Eliza Lynn], 'A Few Pleasant French Gentlemen', *HW* 15 (18 Apr. 1857), 366–9; [George Laval Chesterton], 'Coolness amongst Thieves', *HW* 3 (17 May 1851), 189–90.

that selfhood may be a fiction, or construct, rather than a stable essence. This radical questioning of the nature of selfhood and the larger implications of role-playing is not, however, the invention of postmodernism, as the writings of Dickens and others before him make clear.

An unidentified article on the French assassin Lacenaire in *All the Year Round* takes a far from light-hearted look at the relationship between psychopath and actor, and the effects on selfhood when the individual takes literally Jaques's axiom that 'all the world's a stage' (*As You Like It*, II. vii. 139).[9] Pierre François Lacenaire (1800–36), we are told, 'ran away to Paris with the illusion that he could gain his livelihood by literature' (p. 418). This aspiring literary man, apparently 'fixed in the popular imagination as the type of the polished, methodical and lettered villain', was nevertheless 'a speculator in whose eyes a murder was merely a matter of business—a man who conceived and calculated the chances of an assassination with the coolness of a banker, and who performed the operation with the calmness of a surgeon' (p. 417). In his 'coolness' and 'calmness', in his manner of regarding murder as 'business', Lacenaire is reminiscent of Dickens's poisoner, who is always cool, even when murdering his wife, whom he feels towards 'as men usually do towards their own possessions'. Lacenaire, however, is even more conscious of his acting talent than Palmer. The narrator of 'Lacenaire' overtly explains how, in the mind of this psychopath, the two worlds of reality and stage have become one. Lacenaire 'was passionately fond of dramatic art and artists, and succeeded in making acquaintance with several of them'. He even instructs M. Albert, one of the stars of the Boulevard, on how to act: 'occasionally you exaggerate; but there is no harm in that. On the stage [. . .] you must hit hard to strike home.' Lacenaire consciously regards his appearance in court as a theatrical performance: 'He regarded the audience complacently. The gravity of his position did not extinguish his literary mania; he caused to be passed about the court a copy of verses' (p. 421). While his accomplice is being executed, Lacenaire is 'exactly like an actor waiting in the wing to go upon the stage' (p. 421).

In his fascinating article 'The Melodramatic Villain in *Little Dorrit*',

---

[9] 'Lacenaire', *AYR* 5 (27 July 1861), 417–22 Authors of articles in *AYR* are identified—where possible—in Ella Ann Oppenlander's *Dickens's 'All the Year Round': Descriptive Index and Contributor Book* (Troy, NY: Whitston, 1984).

Harvey Peter Sucksmith claims that Lacenaire is the real-life proto-type of Dickens's Rigaud Blandois.[10] Sucksmith's argument is that, far from being a carbon copy of a stereotypical melodramatic villain, Rigaud is 'Dickens's recognition of the phenomenon of life attempt-ing to imitate drama'.[11] The fact that Lacenaire was a devotee of the French Romantic theatre, which shaded into melodrama, meant that his performances could seem exaggerated. But paradoxically both Rigaud Blandois and Lacenaire give performances that are simul-taneously 'powerfully realistic' and 'artificial'. Their 'falseness is dramatically presented'. Rigaud is ultimately 'a triumphant assertion of the true and vital hollowness that lies at the core of the psycho-pathic criminal's theatrical yet authentic performance'.[12] As melodrama as a genre relies on the assumption that surfaces are synonymous with depths, Rigaud interestingly personifies the spectre of melodrama's decadence—the possibility that only hollowness lies beneath surfaces.[13]

The emergence of the kind of repressive individualism which disturbed Dickens has been theorized in various ways and is often situated at the turn of the eighteenth and nineteenth centuries. Indeed this book has examined the role of Romantic writers in con-tributing to this perceived change.[14] The extent to which Romantic styles of individuality had been naturalized in the Victorian period is evident in Kucich's definition of Victorian 'repression' as a general 'tendency to make matters of intense feeling [. . .] matters of secrecy and self-reflexiveness', and, further, as a 'controlled instrument of individuality', 'a technique for defining oneself both internally and in opposition to others'.[15] Dickens's writings suggest that repression is not constitutive of individuality but of the illusion of individuality. Repressed individuals imagine that their selfhood is enhanced by the creation of a secret interiority, but the reality is that the continuous

[10] *Dickensian*, 71 (1975), 76–83.
[11] Ibid. 82.
[12] Ibid.
[13] See Chapter 4 below for a fuller discussion of Rigaud.
[14] Hadley, for example, links the evolution of the split or 'private' individual—one whose public persona is not necessarily a projection of a private 'self'—to 'the structural shift from a patronage economy to a market economy' (and culture)—*Melodramatic Tactics*, 46. Nancy Armstrong (along with D. A. Miller—see Introduction above) has argued influentially, using Foucauldian theory, that the emerging genre of the novel was constitu-tive of the 'private' individual—see *Desire and Domestic Fiction: A Political History of the Novel* (Oxford: Oxford University Press, 1987).
[15] Kucich, *Repression in Victorian Fiction*, 3–4.

performance of identity ultimately leads to the loss of any stable sense of selfhood. Repressive, deceitful individualism is thus in Dickens's ethically framed universe a cannibalistic individualism. Identity which is performative on the outside ultimately becomes performative on the inside. Selfhood is performed rather than experienced. Attempts to control or possess one's identity by keeping it secret necessitate a loss of identity. Repression thus mechanizes rather than particularizing personality. Dickens's actor-villains prefigure and condemn a social and aesthetic environment in which the individual lacks emotion and signification is divorced from significance. The cannibalistic individualism of Dickens's emotionally dysfunctional deviants makes visible many of the implications of what Jean Baudrillard has called 'the loss of the real'.[16]

PASSION AND PROFESSIONAL PERFORMERS

If Dickens disliked cannibalistic social role-players, he was in general a great supporter of stage actors. While social performance, to Dickens, could violate the principles of transparency and communality which melodramatic models of identity uphold, stage performance, at his best, provided him with his most rewarding experiences of the melodramatic mode. The story of Dickens's involvement with the theatre has been told by so many others that it is not my aim to repeat it here.[17] John Glavin's *After Dickens* rightly questions the usual assumption that Dickens's feelings about the theatre were straightforwardly positive. Dickens did indeed have anxieties about the stage which arose from an awareness of the imperfect state of the nineteenth-century stage and of the dubious status of the theatre and its actors; he also, as this chapter seeks to establish, was conscious of the ethical problems associated with certain kinds of acting. However, while Glavin argues that Dickens was 'in not quite equal parts thrilled (less) and (more) frightened by

---

[16] See Jean Baudrillard, 'Simulacra and Simulations' (1981), repr. in Peter Brooker (ed.), *Modernism/Postmodernism* (Harlow: Longman, 1992), 151–62.

[17] In addition to texts already mentioned, see for example *Charles Dickens: The Public Readings*, ed. Philip Collins (Oxford: Clarendon Press, 1965), George Dolby, *Charles Dickens as I Knew Him: The Story of the Reading Tours in Great Britain and America, 1866–70* (London: Fisher Unwin, 1885), S. J. Adair Fitz-Gerald, *Dickens and the Drama* (London: Chapman & Hall, 1910), *The Dickens Theatrical Reader*, ed. Edgar and Eleanor Johnson (London: Gollancz, 1964).

the stage', Dickens's stage thrills always seem to me to exceed his stage fright, and indeed the two responses are arguably intimately connected.[18]

As an actor, Dickens's most satisfying experience of the power of melodrama perhaps came when he acted the role of Richard Wardour in Wilkie Collins's *The Frozen Deep* (6 January 1857, Tavistock House). Wardour is a man consumed by passion, love for a woman and bitterness because the object of his desire loves another. He has all the qualities of a melodramatic villain, but the mainspring of the play's drama is derived from Wardour's unpredictable emergence as the hero who spares his rival. On 9 January 1857, Dickens wrote about the experience of acting the part of Wardour:

> As to the Play itself; when it is made as good as my care can make it, I derive a strange feeling out of it, like writing a book in company. A satisfaction of a most singular kind, which has no exact parallel in my life. A something that I suppose to belong to a Labourer in Art, alone, and which has to me a conviction of its being actual Truth without its pain, that I never could adequately state if I were to try never so hard.[19]

The relevance of *The Frozen Deep* to Dickens's personal problems is well known. As important, however, is its relevance to Dickens's social beliefs: self-preoccupation, in Wardour's case, metamorphoses as action and self-sacrifice for the larger social good. The Byronic, Romantic individual transforms himself into a melodramatic hero. The phrase 'actual Truth without its pain' is an accurate description of what for Dickens is the furthest reach of the theatre for both actor and audience: to use Dickens's own imagery, the best theatrical experiences painlessly defrost depths. Dickens's description of acting the part of Wardour—'like writing a book in company'—points to the fusion of narrative and theatre in his perception of the ideal aesthetic, a fusion at the heart of Dickens's project throughout his lifetime. As forms of unreality which openly announce their fictional status, stories and acting both allow 'honest' deceit. The idea of 'writing a book in company', partially realized by Dickens's public readings of his novels, implies a communal form of storytelling. It is a pity that Dickens the playwright comes no closer to representing 'actual truth' on the stage than the hacks he so unrelentingly mocks.[20]

---

[18] p. 11.

[19] *Letters* (Pilgrim), viii. 256.

[20] Jules Obenreizer, for instance, the passionate villain of *No Thoroughfare* (New Royal Adel., 26 Dec. 1867) originally played by Fechter, would have been an easy target for the

Dickens's most rewarding experiences of melodrama, on the stage, are generally connected with actors—in particular, with Frédérick Lemaître and Charles Fechter, both generally associated with the passionate or melodramatic school of acting.[21] The role of villain seems to have been crucial in the career of both, as well as in the development of melodramatic acting styles. According to Disher, after Edmund Kean's interpretation of Shakespeare's villains as exultant fiends, there developed in the nineteenth century an 'evil spirit in acting'; before Kean, 'human villains are maudlin. They did not become exultant until actors had exhibited Shylock, Iago and Richard III as fiends incarnate.'[22] Rahill's chapter on 'The Villain and Melodramatic Acting' confirms the importance of villainous roles—and their actors—in the development of acting styles (and vice versa), and indeed their role in ensuring the continued popularity of melodrama and melodramatic acting.[23]

Dickens's commentaries on the acting of his friends Lemaître and Fechter marvel at their ability to project a metaphysical sense of transcendence beyond the material world. Fechter's performance in *Pauline* (July 1848, Théâtre Historique, Paris) by Grangé and de Montépin—which Disher argues 'displayed Fechter as the most admirable of villains in the style of crime exultant'[24]—was typical of the passionate performances in villainous roles which won him respect from many, including Dickens. Lemaître followed in the tradition of Kean, yet differed from him in one important respect; Lemaître was 'an actor who made passion exult, not in tragedy but melodrama'.[25] Dickens's admiration for Lemaître's emphasis on passion in acting is captured in his description of Lemaître's perform- ance as melodramatic villain in Ducange and Dinaux's *Trente Ans; ou, La Vie d'un joueur* (19 June 1827, le Théâtre de la Porte

satire of Dickens the journalist, who could not have resisted conventional revelations like 'you are a fool! I have drugged you! Doubly a fool, for I am the thief and forger' *Complete Plays and Selected Poems of Charles Dickens* (London: Vision Press, 1970), 171–222 (p. 214; IV. iii). In *The Village Coquettes* (6 Dec. 1836, St J.), Mr Sparkins Flam is Dickens's attempt to embody the dandyish aristocratic seducer, a villain who cares for nothing but his clothes and his own ego. Flam is a possible prototype of John Chester in *Barnaby Rudge*. As befits a stage villain, he is defeated, and his humiliation is carefully directed towards his one sensi- tive point, his appearance. But the appearance of the vanquished Flam, his clothes torn and face disfigured, is the closest the play comes to seriousness or subtlety.

[21] See Chapters 1 and 4 for further material on melodramatic acting.
[22] *Blood and Thunder*, 113.
[23] *The World of Melodrama*, 207–13 (p. 207). See also p. 100.
[24] Disher, *Blood and Thunder*, 196.
[25] Ibid. 160.

Saint-Martin). In a letter dated [13–14?] February 1855, Dickens wrote to Forster from Paris:

Incomparably the finest acting I ever saw, I saw last night at the Ambigu. [. . .] Old Lemaître plays his favourite character, and never did I see anything, in art, so exaltedly horrible and awful. [. . .] He did the finest things, I really believe, that are within the power of acting.[26]

Lemaître's repertoire was dominated by the role of villain.[27] In one performance, Lemaître told the leader of the orchestra that he had no need of the help of music to strike fear into the audience: 'your violins are worse than useless. I need a very simple accompaniment. The tune is [. . .] myself.'[28] Lemaître was able to transform even the poorest melodramatic role into an affecting representation of human passion. In Dickens's childhood favourite *The Dog of Montargis*, for example, Lemaître took the part of the passionate villain Robert Macaire. With Lemaître as Macaire, Lewes argued, 'A common melodrama without novelty or point became [. . .] a grandiose symbolical caricature'.[29]

Lewes's description of Lemaître's acting in many ways captures what for Dickens was the furthest reach of melodrama. Daniel Gerould's description of Lemaître as a 'truly revolutionary actor' hints at qualities beyond the ability, central in melodramatic acting, to express passion movingly.[30] Albert Bermel describes how Lemaître reinvented the role of Macaire by treating the play *The Inn of the Adrets* as a farce, without changing any of the dialogue. The play was so successful performed in this way that its sequel, *Robert Macaire*, 'became one of the smash hits—if not the biggest—in the French theater of the nineteenth century'.[31] Dickens's admiration of Lemaître's acting suggests, then, that he was not averse to self-consciousness, or even what we may call 'camp', in the acting of passionate roles. Indeed, Lemaître's distancing of himself from the role of Macaire mirrors the self-reflexive screens of various kinds that Dickens erects around extreme representations of passion in his own work. It is important to a convincing and sophisticated deployment

---

[26] *Letters* (Pilgrim), vii. 536.

[27] See Disher, *Blood and Thunder*, 170–1.

[28] Ibid. 170.

[29] *On Actors and the Art of Acting*, (1875), Evergreen, LXI (New York: Grove Press, 1957), 72.

[30] 'Melodrama and Revolution', 187. According to Gerould, Lemaître transformed 'conventional moral melodramas into socially inflammatory plays'.

[31] 'Where Melodrama Meets Farce', in Daniel Gerould (ed.), *Melodrama, New York Literary Forum*, 7 (1980), 173–8 (pp. 176–7).

of melodrama that the purity or extremity of passionate experience represented is maintained, but it must also be distanced. Indeed, melodrama as a genre offers a surreal fusion of a simple, often essentialist conception of identity combined with a camply stylized mode of representation reminiscent of postmodernism's festive artificiality.

Thus if the dominant conception of identity suggested by melodrama is a monopathic one, its anti-naturalistic mode of signification suggests a dislocation between identity and its projections which is potentially subversive of the illusion of transparency which melodrama seeks to create.[32] One effect of this dislocation on an audience, however, is paradoxically to intensify and simplify the passions and personalities on stage; artificial, larger-than-life aesthetic representations, that is, can construct a more convincing illusion of 'reality' than the more muted representations of realism and naturalism. Alternatively, melodrama's stylized mode of representation can be seen as pre-empting postmodernism in its telegraphing of its own artificiality. In either case, the fact that *actors* of melodrama embody the ideal draws attention to the fabrication on which melodrama depends—albeit an 'honest' form of fabrication.

George Henry Lewes's *On Actors and the Art of Acting*, published in 1875, demonstrates the persistence in the Victorian period of the Romantic idea that emotion is the 'root' of art and identity. Two passages in particular capture the centrality of this aesthetic to Lewes's ideas about both the theatre and society. It is Lewes's major premiss that

he [the actor] also loses all power over his art in proportion to his deadness to emotion. If he really feel, he cannot act, but he cannot act unless he feel. [. . .] It is wholly impossible for him to express what he has never felt, to be an impassioned actor with a cold nature.[33]

Lewes's logic does not allow for a creature like Lacenaire, who feels more for the stage than he does for his fellow human beings, and whose performances are simultaneously convincing and inauthentic. Lewes never questions the sincerity of extra-theatrical emotion,

---

[32] Robert L. Patten comments interestingly on the tensions between the static and multifaceted conceptions of character in Dickens's work, and on the importance of acting (specifically that of Jingle) in undermining monopathic versions of identity—see ' "I Thought of Mr. Pickwick, and Wrote the First Number": Dickens and the Evolution of Character', *Dickens Quarterly*, 3 (1986), 18–25. Unlike Patten, I see these two models of character and identity as existing in a dialectical rather than a hierarchical relationship with each other.

[33] p. 93.

regarding it as the unpolluted raw material from which the actor shapes his art. It is for this reason that he is clearly shocked by the implications of Charles Mathews's interpretation of the role of melo-dramatic villain.[34] The part offered an opportunity, according to Lewes:

unique in his [Mathews's] varied career, [. . .] of portraying a melodramatic villain. [. . .] Imagine a Count D'Orsay destitute alike of principle and of feeling, the incarnation of heartless elegance, cool yet agreeable, admirable in all the externals which make men admired in society, and hateful in all the qualities tested by the serious trials of life; such was the Count presented by Charles Mathews. Instead of 'looking the villain,' he looked like the man to whom all drawing-rooms would be flung open. [. . .] No critic capable of ridding himself of conventional prepossession would see such a bit of action and forget it.[35]

Lewes's shock at a melodramatic villain not unlike the Rugeley poisoner arises from the fact that Mathews's villain inverts Lewes's 'conventional', organic 'prepossession[s]' about identity and art. On one level, Lewes assumes that social identity is normally and properly consonant with one's 'private' identity; Mathews's villain thus violates all that Lewes, like Dickens, holds sacred. On a second level, Lewes is surprised to find such a radical and sophisticated character, as he sees it, in a melodrama.

What Lewes seems to like about Mathews's villain is the realism informing the acting of both Mathews and the villain role-player he represents. In terms of presentation, melodrama is generally highly stylized—particularly in its representation of passion—promoting transparent, almost naive models of identity and emotional expression whilst drawing attention to their artificiality. Dickens is invariably fascinated and troubled by this combination of innocence and artifice; he thinks the unthinkable, that emotion can be constructed—and effectively so. Dickens the populist is torn between the promotion of 'transparent' models of identity which further the cause of communality and the consciousness of the unreality of these melo-dramatic models.

---

[34] Mathews was of course one of Dickens's personal heroes.
[35] *On Actors and the Art of Acting*, 64.

ACTING PASSIONATE

In Dickens's journals, the passionate villain is a focus for his ambivalence about melodramatic aesthetics. The villain characterized by a 'hot intensity of passion' draws attention to the fact that transparent personalities, where they exist, can be antisocial. They problematize any suggestion that the antidote to repressive individualism is emotional exhibitionism. What seems more troubling to Dickens, however, is the unreality of the passionate melodramatic villain. It is notable, for example, that 'hot' villains are nearly always, in Dickens's periodicals, characters in plays—a fact which perhaps suggests the constructedness or fictionality of such types, their unusualness in a social context which in actuality demands an acceptance of a certain level of disguise or repression. That hot-headed villains are presented as less threatening in the journals than their cooler counterparts is no doubt largely to do with the theatrical environment they inhabit; the passionless performer, by contrast, is predominantly presented in a social setting as a 'real', social threat. Melodrama as it is presented by Dickens arguably acts as a partial protection from the reality of deviance, a function which constitutes both its strength and its limitation.

It is highly probable that Dickens had some knowledge of most of the melodramas discussed in Chapter 2. However, this chapter will examine a selection of specific references in Dickens's writings to melodramas and stage villains with whom, according to documentary evidence, he was familiar. Actual quotations from Dickens's comments on melodrama and its villains, like the examination of the context of theatrical allusion, have the advantage of capturing his tone, a factor all-important in my later analysis. Dickens's familiarity with stage villains motivated by 'a hot intensity of passion' came early. Pocock's *The Miller and his Men*, for example, and its villain Grindoff, discussed in Chapter 2, are mentioned numerous times in his writings.[36] Moreover, according to Forster, it was one of the primary childhood influences on Dickens's love of the theatre, and 'Dickens's after taste for theatricals might have had its origin in these affairs'.[37] Dickens's childhood experience of passionate villainy, however, neither started nor stopped with *The Miller*; *Tales of the Genii* and

---

[36] See Ley's note on Dickens's lifelong interest in *The Miller and his Men*, in Forster's *Life*, 51. Ley holds that the play 'retained a fascination for Dickens all his life'.

[37] Ibid.

The Arabian Nights were earlier yet lasting influences on him, as the numerous references to them in his novels prove.[38] Although these eastern stories were not originally written for the theatre, the young Dickens showed his disregard for strict generic boundaries when he based his first play, a tragedy entitled *Misnar, the Sultan of India*, on one of the *Tales of the Genii*.[39] Early comic irreverence towards theatrical tales of passionate villainy is shown in a description of a production of *The Dog of Montargis*[40] set up by Dickens, his schoolfriends, and their mice at the Wellington Academy:

The boys trained the mice, much better than the masters trained the boys. We recall one white mouse, who lived in the cover of a Latin dictionary, who ran up ladders, drew Roman chariots, shouldered muskets, turned wheels, and even made a very creditable appearance on the stage as the Dog of Montargis. He might have achieved great things, but for having the misfortune to mistake his way in a triumphal procession to the Capitol, when he fell into a deep inkstand, and was dyed black and drowned.[41]

A later reference to *The Dog of Montargis* in *Dombey and Son* retains the comic tone of the earlier description. When Diogenes 'comes straight away at Mr Toots's legs', he 'tumbles over himself in the desperation with which he makes at him, like a very dog of Montargis' (chapter 41, p. 555).

The fact that Dickens both laughs at *The Dog of Montargis* and refers to it in his mature fiction focuses Dickens's paradoxical and complex attitude to both melodrama and its villains. There is plenty of material to contradict Booth's argument that Dickens's 'main purpose in going to see and writing about melodrama was to laugh at it',[42] yet when we examine Dickens's written accounts of the contemporary theatre and its productions, laughter is often the keynote.

[38] The following are just a sample of references in Dickens's fiction to *Tales of the Genii* and *The Arabian Nights*: in *MC*, chapter 5, p. 71, *DC*, chapter 4, p. 48, *GE*, vol. ii, chapter 19, p. 30, *OMF*, book 1, chapter 3, p. 20, 'A Christmas Carol' (1843), in *CB*, pp. 1–76 (stave 2, p. 28), 'The Haunted Man' (1848), in *CB*, pp. 314–99 (chapter 1, p. 319).

[39] Forster, *Life*, 6.

[40] William Barrymore's translation of Pixérécourt's original (*The Forest of Bondy; or, The Dog of Montargis*) was first performed on 30 Sept. 1814, CG. See Hodgson's Juvenile Drama (London: Hodgson, *c*.1825). The original melodrama tells the story of the rivalry between two soldiers, Aubri and Macaire. Aubri achieves promotion and Macaire is so full of the passion of jealousy that he murders his rival in the forest. The real murderer is only discovered because of the detective skill of the dog of Montargis.

See p. 80 above for an analysis of the acting of Dickens's friend Lemaître in the role of Macaire, a role he made his own.

[41] Quoted by *The Dickens Theatrical Reader*, ed. Johnson and Johnson, 9.

[42] Booth, *English Melodrama*, 178.

The tone of that laughter is, however, all-important: it is always affectionate and often, crucially, nostalgic. It is as if the simplicity and transparency symbolized by the passionate villain are to Dickens unreal and of the past—more perhaps of his personal past and childhood imagination than of a pre-nineteenth-century mode of selfhood. The one-dimensionality of the passionate male villain, in Dickens's journalism, seems to override his immorality, hence rendering him a 'safe' creature of his theatrical context. By contrast, Dickens's wilful construction of social performers like Palmer as one-dimensional is motivated by a concern that readers register the sheer wickedness of such individuals. In 'Greenwich Fair' from *Sketches by Boz*, for instance, Dickens ridicules the villain's elaborate expressions of passion, in the following terms. The villain, or wrongful heir:

comes in to two bars of quick music (technically called 'a hurry'), and goes on in the most shocking manner, throwing the young lady about as if she was nobody, and calling the rightful heir 'Ar-recreant—ar-wretch!' in a very loud voice, which answers the double purpose of *displaying his passion*, and preventing the sound being deadened by the sawdust. (p. 116; italics mine)

In both Dickens's articles in *Household Words* entitled 'The Amusements of the People', hot-headed villains are affectionately mocked. In the first, the chief villain can be recognized immediately by 'his boots, which, being very high and wide, and apparently made of sticking-plaister, justified the worst theatrical suspicions to his disadvantage' (p. 14). In the later article, though there is a coldly selfish villain in the shape of Geoffrey Thornley the Younger, it is the fiery Wilbert the Hunchback who provides the most laughs. The hero of the piece, a young sailor called Walter More, rescues Wilbert from rough treatment, but 'This misguided person, in return, immediately fell to abusing his preserver in round terms, giving him to understand that he (the preserved) hated "manerkind, wither two eckerceptions"' (p. 59). Extreme passion evidently calls for extreme pronunciation.

Indeed, the comic tone of Dickens's commentary on melodrama derives largely from an awareness of the highly stylized nature of melodramatic aesthetics. One of the most absurd manifestations of melodrama's dominant—and comforting—equation of inner with outer nature is its habit of dressing the passionate villain in high boots, which Dickens continuously mocks. In 'Two Views of a Cheap

Theatre', for instance, the villain is referred to as 'Wickedness in boots':

Virtue never looked so beautiful or Vice so deformed as when we paused, sandwich in hand, to consider what would come of that resolution of Wickedness in boots, to sever Innocence in flowered chintz from Honest Industry in striped stockings.[43]

In 'Strollers at Dumbledowndeary', the narrator surmises that the stroller wearing boots must be playing the part of the Emperor of Russia, on the grounds that 'these boots seem to oppress their wearer with a deep and awful sense of the responsibility they involve'.[44] Another extreme example of melodrama's correlation of inner moral fibre and external appearance or gesture is ridiculed in 'Mr. Whelks Over the Water', where:

It was to be expected that [the villain] Hongree would turn out badly, for his first entrance was over a bridge. (Attentive students of the British drama must have observed that the villains enter over bridges or down steps, while the virtuous characters come in modestly at the sides).[45]

In the novels, perhaps Dickens's classic exposure of melodrama's representation of passion is contained in his depiction of the Crummleses' savage in the rehearsal for *The Indian Savage and the Maiden*:

the savage, becoming ferocious, made a slide towards the maiden; [. . .] after a little more ferocity and chasing of the maiden into corners, he began to relent, and stroked his face several times with his right thumb and four fingers, thereby intimating that he was struck with admiration of the maiden's beauty. Acting upon the impulse of this passion, he (the savage) began to hit himself several thumps in the chest, and to exhibit other indications of being desperately in love, which being rather a prosy proceeding, was very likely the cause of the maiden's falling asleep. (*Nicholas Nickleby*, chapter 23, p. 289)

Interestingly, Dickens often focuses on the representation of passionate deviants to draw attention to the stylized nature of melodramatic passion—a fact which no doubt has much to do with the influence of actors of villainous roles on passionate melodramatic acting. In *The Old Curiosity Shop*, for example, so strange are the conventions of acting in Astley's theatre to little Jacob that he has greater

[43] p. 34.
[44] [George A. Sala], *HW* 9 (3 June 1854), 374–80 (p. 378).
[45] [Andrew Halliday], *AYR* 15 (30 June 1866), 589–92 (p. 590).

belief in the reality of the horses than in that of characters like 'the tyrant':

> Then the play itself! the horses which little Jacob believed from the first to be alive, and the ladies and gentleman of whose reality he could be by no means persuaded, having never seen or heard anything at all like them. (chapter 39, p. 304)

In *Great Expectations*, Mr Wopsle's rendering of Collins's *Ode on the Passions*, and particularly his representation of Revenge—'throwing his blood-stain'd sword in thunder down, and taking the War denouncing trumpet with a withering look'—is 'venerated' by the young Pip, but mocked by the older narrator (Volume i, chapter 7, p. 45); in later life, he 'fell into the society of the Passions, and compared them with Collins and Wopsle, rather to the disadvantage of both gentlemen'.[46] The loss of innocence here symbolized by Pip's adult disbelief in melodramatic representation is as wistful as it is inevitable and typifies the general movement and tone of the novel—as well as Dickens's mixed attitudes to melodrama.

The narratorial time scheme in *Great Expectations* allows Dickens to invoke a double perspective which cherishes innocence and simplicity whilst aware that both are unrealistic constructions of a childlike vision. In Dickens's non-fiction, comedy is often the instrument of the double perspective with which Dickens regards melodrama. The wistful sense of loss which frequently permeates his laughter is more often nostalgic than patronizing (though there is a thin line between the two); to patronize is to belittle or devalue, but nostalgia involves a keen, even intensified sense of the value of what has been lost. Though Dickens is conscious of the 'unrealistic' nature of melodramatic representations, this consciousness does not always lead to a sense of the inadequacy of melodrama but as often to an awareness of the paucity and corruption of the 'real' world. Instead Dickens vacillates in his attitudes to both ideal and 'real' representations. If melodrama is unrealistic, for example, it is often 'reality'

---

[46] Angus Calder, in a note in his Penguin edition of *GE*, argues that Wopsle seems to have best displayed his gifts in the following passage from Collins's *Ode on the Passions*:

> Revenge impatient rose,
>   He threw his blood-stain'd Sword in Thunder down,
>   And with a with'ring Look,
>   The War-denouncing Trumpet took,
>   Were ne'er Prophetic Sounds so full of Woe.

(Harmondsworth: Penguin, 1965; repr. 1986), 501.

which is the loser. Melodrama can be for Dickens partly a utopian genre—unrealistic but projecting a reality preferable to the mechanized, diminished world he inhabits. From another perspective, however, melodrama's innocent tableaux are laughably simplistic approximations of 'reality'.

It would be distorting the picture, however, to claim that Dickens consistently regards melodrama and its passionate villains as laughably artificial or conventional. Intertextuality offers Dickens another vehicle for the double perspective through which he projects stage melodrama. Though 'the affecting tragedy of George Barnwell'[47] (*GE*, volume i, chapter 15, p. 116) was not originally a nineteenth-century melodrama, it was regularly performed and transformed on the minor stage. It is often referred to by Dickens throughout his works, not always mockingly. In *Great Expectations*, for example, Wopsle's melodramatic reading of the tale to Pip still has a strangely powerful effect on the hero of Dickens's novel, who identifies with George Barnwell, the villain/hero whose downfall was intense passion: 'WITH my head full of George Barnwell, *I* was at first disposed to believe that I must have had some hand in the attack upon my sister' (volume i, chapter 16, p. 119). In *Circle of Fire*, William Axton argues convincingly that George Barnwell and Pip are linked throughout *Great Expectations* by two passions, the love of a woman and the desire for gentility;[48] the minor play is thus interwoven with the moral and ideological fabric of the novel. In *David Copperfield*, when David refers to Jack Maldon as 'a modern Sinbad' (chapter 16, p. 208), this is a serious criticism of David's habit of seeing life through a screen of romance which obscures his moral perception. In *Our Mutual Friend*, Eugene Wrayburn's ejaculation 'Mysteries of Udolpho!' (book 2, chapter 15, p. 405) is a cynical yet accurate comment on Lizzie's situation as a heroine who needs protection from the unimaginable horrors around her. In *Barnaby Rudge*, when Dolly Varden asks her father about Geoffrey Haredale's mysterious affairs, Gabriel advises her to 'Read Blue Beard, and don't be too curious' (chapter 41, p. 311)—a comment which has a certain aptness, since both tales involve horror and secret murder. In chapter 5 of *Martin Chuzzlewit*, the mere sight of *The Tales of the Genii* and *Ali Baba and the Forty Thieves* in a bookshop has as great an impact on the mind

---

[47] George Lillo, *The London Merchant; or, The History of George Barnwell* (1731), ed. William H. McBurney, Regents Restoration Drama (London: Arnold, 1965).

[48] pp. 110–36.

of Tom Pinch as the texts themselves had on the mind of the youthful Dickens (p. 71).

Intertextual references often demonstrate the utopian, talismanic function of individual melodramas for Dickens's characters; they simultaneously function as a warning to readers of the gulf which often exists between the idealistic imaginings of those characters and the reality of their lives. Dickens perceived that melodrama as an art form always had the potential to be something more than an exhibition for intellectuals 'to laugh at'. He recognized that, far from being a laughable departure from reality, melodrama at its most ambitious could comprise what Peter Brooks calls 'the expressionism of the moral imagination', as well as a salve or antidote for the alienating forces of modernity.[49] He was continuously searching for the realization of his vision of melodrama as a medium through which a truly mixed audience could internalize an idealized model of society and social identity which opposed itself to cultural exclusivity. He never abandoned the nineteenth-century theatre or its dominant melodramatic mode because he was conscious of its potential relevance to the primal emotional, moral, and political life of its culturally diverse audience. This potential was not always realized, however; and Dickens's writings are alive to the possibility that the artificiality of melodramatic aesthetics could be seen as problematizing their claims to cultural inclusivity. The double perspective through which Dickens often deploys melodrama is thus a means by which Dickens can promote melodramatic models of identity 'honestly' by revealing their fictional underpinnings. Paradoxically, this honesty involves the kind of self-consciousness to which Dickens, in social behaviour, seems so opposed.

STAGING COMMUNITY

The pitfalls and paradoxes of employing melodrama as a culturally inclusive mode are starkly evident on consideration of Dickens's journalistic practice. The villains of *Household Words* and *All the Year Round* (the two journals which Dickens founded and edited) are creatures of what Elaine Hadley would call the 'melodramatic mode'[50]—inevitably perhaps, as the journals themselves are melodramatic. Dickens appropriates many of the characteristics of stage

---

[49] *The Melodramatic Imagination*, 55.   [50] See Hadley's *Melodramatic Tactics*.

melodrama in his journalism: its passionate intensity, its simplification of social and moral issues, its strong moralizing tendency, and
its theatricality. His journalism has as much in common with today's
tabloid journalism as it does with the broadsheet variety. Whereas
the melodramatic tendencies of contemporary tabloids are primarily
motivated by commercialism, however, Dickens's journalistic melodrama is, at an overt level at least, driven by a sense of ethical and
social responsibility. Like melodrama, Dickens's journalism aims to
foster a sense of community and family—the 'Preliminary Word' of
the aptly named *Household Words* announces this directly.[51] This sense
of community ideally extends to all social classes; popular appeal is
for Dickens an ethical, as well as a political, imperative.

The 'melodramatic mode' of the journals is best understood, as I
have argued, as a tactical deployment of writing which is emotionally
charged and ethically framed in order to compensate for the 'cold
intensity of selfishness' Dickens felt to be infiltrating society. In his
journalistic appropriation of melodrama, Dickens's mission seems to
be the healing of social and personal fragmentation by moralistic
writing which appeals directly to the emotions. In its 'urge to publi-
cize the private',[52] its emphasis on the primacy of passion in identity
and society, and its general assumption of continuity between the
public and private individual, melodrama seemed to provide
an ideal (if paternalistic) instrument with which to counter the
alienating, mechanizing tendencies of nineteenth-century society,
personified by the coldly selfish villain. Dickens's journals construct a
virtual family, or virtual community, as their imagined audience.
They function as a key part of Dickens's larger attempts to counter
the dissolution of communal and family ties founded on sympathy
and emotional bonds, and the upsurge of antisocial brands of individualism, through the encouragement of cultural and social inclusivity.

This utopian project is problematized, in Dickens's journalism,
however, by his methods: Dickens appropriates the flagrantly 'constructed' projections of melodrama in order to promote an 'innocent'

---

[51] The 'Preliminary Word' of *HW* announces: 'THE name that we have chosen for this
publication expresses, generally, the desire that we have in originating it. [. . .] We hope to
be the comrade and friend of many thousands of people, of both sexes, and of all ages and
conditions, on whose faces we may never look [. . .]; to bring the greater and the lesser in
degree, together, [. . .] and mutually dispose them to a better acquaintance and a kinder
understanding — is the main object of our Household Words' (p. 1).

[52] Hadley, *Melodramatic Tactics*, 70.

vision of society in which identity is transparently and 'honestly' public. While the articles on melodrama expose the artifice inherent in the genre, Dickens's melodramatic journalism often hides its own sophistication, packaging carefully composed ideological fictions as 'simple' home truths. The journals are often predicated on the assumption that self-conscious, performative writing can work for the greater, simpler good. In the name of cultural inclusivity, the fiction of transparency is imposed on a reader who is not made specifically aware of the terms of ideological engagement. The journals, that is, enact a 'dishonest' mode of performativity.

This is true not only of the content of articles but of Dickens's editorial practice. Partly to aid the fiction of communality, Dickens insisted that each issue of his journals should read as if written by a single author. The illusion of consensus was to be staged. As he wrote to Elizabeth Gaskell at the outset of his career as editor of *Household Words*: 'every paper will be published without any signature; and will seem to express the general mind and purpose of the Journal.'[53] The 'general mind and purpose of the journal', of course, meant Dickens's mind and purpose. There is indeed unusual unanimity among diverse experts on Dickens's journals about the main features of Dickens's editorial theory and practice, especially as regards *Household Words*.[54] Articles in his journals had to coincide with his own views and he even encouraged them to be written in his own style.[55] Remarkably, every number had to be submitted to him for inspection, wherever he was in the world.[56] And perhaps more importantly, Dickens edited and over-wrote many articles to such an extent that the proofs looked like 'inky fishing-net[s]', to use his own phrase, when he had finished with them.[57] In effect, Dickens's

[53] Gerald Giles Grubb, 'The Editorial Policies of Charles Dickens', *PMLA* 58 (1943), 1110–24 (p. 1111); *Letters* (Pilgrim), vi. 22 (31 Jan. 1850).

[54] See *Charles Dickens as Editor: Being Letters Written by Him to William Henry Wills his Sub-editor*, selected and ed. R. C. Lehmann (London: Smith & Elder, 1912), P. A. W. Collins, 'Dickens as Editor: Some Uncollected Fragments', *Dickensian*, 56 (1960), 85–96, Philip Collins, ' "Inky Fishing-Nets": Dickens as Editor', *Dickensian*, 61 (1965), 120–8, Gerald G. Grubb, 'Dickens's Editorial Methods', *Studies in Philology*, 40 (1943), 79–100, Grubb, 'The Editorial Policies of Charles Dickens', Lohrli's introduction to *HW* above.

[55] Anne Lohrli explains the exception to this rule, that 'when an article accepted for publication did express opinions that ran counter to Dickens's, that fact was stated'— Lohrli (comp.), *Household Words*, 12.

[56] Grubb, 'Dickens's Editorial Methods', 83. The exception was Dickens's American tour of 1868.

[57] Ibid. 79. The phrase is quoted from a letter to Forster of 22 June 1856. See *Letters* (Pilgrim), viii. 139.

editorial control meant that, in the words of Anne Lohrli: 'For all that the reader knew to the contrary, almost any article might be Dickens's own writing.'[58] Or as Gerald Giles Grubb demonstrates in an early article: 'Dickens considered himself personally responsible to the public for the truth and authenticity of every article that went into his periodicals.'[59] In other words, the impression of unanimity and 'authenticity' was created by Dickens's systematic imposition of his own values and practices on the writings of his contributors. Dickens's impulse to counter an individualism he perceived as potentially antisocial is thus, on the evidence of his editorial practice at least, more paternalistic than democratic. If the model of the family or community is applied to both the editing and the readership of the journals, Dickens himself clearly plays the role of patriarch—that is, the most important and powerful individual.

Dickens had a naively egotistical (and paradoxical) faith in his own good intentions as an externally focused, social being, as well as a sophisticated understanding of the way ideological fictions can and should be constructed to counter corrupting social forces. In the journals, Dickens's polemical purpose meant the dissolution of a double perspective on his own practice in favour of staged simplicity. The appearance of transparency or political innocence is manufactured, in other words, by repressing ideological complexity. In the novels, by contrast, Dickens spent a lifetime negotiating the question of whether the conscious deployment of melodramatic aesthetics was indeed ethical and in keeping with the idea of cultural inclusivity.

[58] Lohrli (comp.), *Household Words*, p. 12.
[59] 'The Editorial Policies of Charles Dickens', 1110.

PART II

Dickens's Novels

4
Melodramatic Poetics and the Gothic Villain: Interiority, Deviance, Emotion

The Gothic villain could be termed the 'real melodramatic villain': he is the most passionate and indeed the most stupid of all villains, and for these reasons, his importation into Dickens's novels both typifies and tests Dickens's anti-intellectual project.[1] He is also among the most difficult of Dickens's villains to rescue from critical oblivion, invoking as he does so many critical bugbears. Villains like Rudge and Rigaud Blandois are popular, melodramatic stereotypes, miserable failures by any realist aesthetic yardstick. They appear relatively transparent and lacking in complexity. This lack of complexity, intelligence, or 'interiority' undoubtedly goes some way towards explaining the barrage of hostile criticism Dickens's Gothic villains have received in a post-realist age.[2] But it is also true to say that it is Dickens's unintelligent, passionate, violent villains who have provided the vehicle for the most universally admired evocations of 'interiority' in the Dickens canon—Rudge's traumatized memories of the murder of Reuben remind us of Sikes after the murder of Nancy, and Jonas after the murder of Tigg. Though the passionate villain's traces of an inner life are secondary to his (im)moral function as a wrongdoer, the logic of melodrama's moral and emotional economy means that the externalized violence of the villain inevitably results in internalized self-violence. The glimpses of interiority which attend his habitually externalized character make the passionate villain the testing ground for many of the culturally resonant problems, paradoxes, and possibilities which permeate Dickens's melodramatic writing: principally, he foregrounds the contests between behaviouristic and psychological renderings of

---

[1] This phrase is taken from Kucich's *Excess and Restraint*, 62, though Kucich does not apply it specifically to the Gothic villain. See also Introduction n. 22 and p. 51 above.

[2] See Chapter 1 n. 1 above for examples of such criticism.

character, the possibilities and paradoxes which attend passional art, and the metamorphic relationship between surfaces and depths. From the interpolated tales of *The Pickwick Papers* to the unfinished novel *Edwin Drood*, the melodramatic, violent villain is the site through which Dickens explores the relationship between passion, interiority, and deviance, and the self-reflexive implications of this relationship for the art of the popular novelist. The Gothic villain epitomizes the fusion between the 'macabre' and the 'melodramatic' at the centre of Dickens's project.

THE NOVEL AND THE FEELINGS

While a critic like Kucich legitimately sophisticates Dickens's passionate villains—they are motiveless violators of boundaries—it is more usual for critics to damn them as 'flat' stereotypes.[3] It is viewed as such, in my opinion, that they do most to illuminate the misunderstandings that have riddled criticism of Dickens. The Gothic villain poses aesthetic problems for the novelist who, unlike the playwright, has no access to unmediated, behaviouristic renderings of character. He also poses problems for traditional character criticism grounded in psychological or analytical ways of seeing. If Dickens's melodramatic models of character are to work in a novelistic context, if they are to avoid the comic excesses of the hotheads he observed on the nineteenth-century stage, Dickens needs to find ways of rendering extreme, violent emotion credibly. As Eric Bentley puts it: 'exaggerations will be foolish only if they are empty of feeling. Intensity of feeling justifies formal exaggeration in art.' This chapter will explore the aesthetic means by which Dickens renders the intense passions upon which his melodramatic art depends, and the ideologies which attend Dickens's novelistic melodrama.

It is significant that, throughout his career, Dickens renders even 'private' emotional experience using popular melodrama's impulse towards externalization, within a narrative context. The 'conjuring technique', to quote E. M. Forster, which this technique appears to represent, is more enigmatic from a twentieth-century perspective than it would have been to Dickens's contemporaries.[4] My con-

---

[3] *Excess and Restraint*, 62–5; *Repression in Victorian Fiction*, 209–11; see Introduction n. 1 above for criticism of Dickens's 'flat' villains.

[4] Forster is describing Mr Pickwick, whom we may view 'edgeways and find him not

tention is that there is an enormous gulf between twentieth-century, high cultural theories of the novel and early nineteenth-century conceptions of the novel as a popular cultural vehicle—a gulf which has obscured understanding of Dickens's art. Twentieth-century novelistic theory in particular has largely perpetuated the involution of focus prevalent in Romanticism, realism, psychoanalysis, and modernism. This is particularly true of its treatment of emotion.

Writing in 1970, Barbara Hardy epitomizes twentieth-century—specifically pre-postmodern—responses to Dickens's representation of passion. 'From *Pickwick* to *Edwin Drood*', she argues, 'the theatrical and behaviouristic rendering' dominates Dickens's representation of passion, 'and it has certain disadvantages':

The disadvantages of the rendering of passion by passionate conduct, for which Dickens's sources are probably theatrical, are plain. The conduct, as in acting, tends to be exaggerated and extreme, and the passions tend to appear simplified and separated. Moreover certain falsities arise: it gets to look as if passions are always acted out and formulated, never inner and introverted, private and secret. [. . .] More oddly, there is no particular reason for all the passionate externals. These are not actors, this is not a stage. Dickens has access to all the novelist's means of rendering strong feeling.[5]

Hardy's analysis betrays a prejudice common to many modern writers—namely, that the novel is superior to the theatre as a genre capable of rendering and analysing human passion. Her Romantic conception of emotion, moreover, elevates 'inner and introverted, private and secret' feelings over the bold, visible variety of the same. If emotion is conceived in such a way, then the novel will obviously outstrip the theatre as an affective vehicle in any literary generic hierarchy. It is not unusual, moreover, in the twentieth century, to hear claims for the superiority of the novel to any other genre—according, seemingly, to any criteria. Even S. W. Dawson's Critical Idiom volume on *Drama and the Dramatic* describes the novel as 'a dramatic form capable of surpassing the drama of the theatre in depth and vitality'.[6] Mikhail Bakhtin establishes the novel as the darling of fictional forms, arguing: 'The novel is the only developing genre and therefore it reflects more deeply, more essentially, more sensitively

thicker than a gramophone record. But we never get the sideway view'—*Aspects of the Novel*, Pelican (Harmondsworth: Penguin, 1962), 79.

[5] 'Dickens and the Passions', *Nineteenth-Century Fiction*, 24 (1970), 449–66 (p. 452).

[6] (London: Methuen, 1970), 79.

and rapidly, reality itself in the process of its unfolding.'[7] The novel, to Bakhtin, 'is plasticity itself';[8] his theory of 'novelization' claims that the elasticity of the novel form 'infects' other genres: 'In the process of becoming the dominant genre, the novel sparks the renovation of all other genres, it infects them with its spirit of process and inconclusiveness.'[9] The novel seems to owe its twentieth-century status to its ability to render depths, plasticity, and inconclusiveness—characteristics particularly valued since the 'post-sacred' foregrounding of the psyche in intellectual history.

This sense of the novel as the ultimate genre for representing and exploring those invisible, metamorphic aspects of life is particularly apparent in twentieth-century, pre-postmodern utterances by novelists on the genre's capacity to both reflect and analyse emotion. In D. H. Lawrence's *Lady Chatterley's Lover* (1928), for instance, there is the striking analytical digression:

It is the way our sympathy flows and recoils that really determines our lives. And here lies the vast importance of the novel, properly handled. It can inform and lead into new places the flow of our sympathetic consciousness, and it can lead our sympathy away in recoil from things gone dead. Therefore, the novel, properly handled, can reveal the most secret places of life: for it is in the passional secret places of life, above all, that the tide of sensitive awareness needs to ebb and flow, cleansing and refreshing.[10]

In *Remembrance of Things Past* (1913–27), Proust appreciates the difficulty of rejecting emotional certainty and simplification; he urges the use of intelligence 'to distinguish, and with how much difficulty, the shape of that which we have felt'.[11] For Proust, as for Lawrence, 'the shape' of emotion is obscure, mysterious, inward, and perhaps most importantly, metamorphic. Stephen's analysis of the lyric, narrative, and dramatic forms in *Portrait of the Artist* (1914–15) again emphasizes the flow and fluidity of emotion in narrative and dramatic form:

The lyrical form is in fact the simplest verbal vesture of an instant of emotion [. . .]. He who utters it is more conscious of the instant of emotion than of

[7] *The Dialogic Imagination*, ed. Michael Holquist, trans. Caryl Emerson and Michael Holquist (Austin: University of Texas Press, 1981), 7.

[8] Ibid. 39.

[9] Ibid. 7.

[10] Ed. John Lyon (Harmondsworth: Penguin, 1960; repr. 1990), 105.

[11] *Time Regained*, chapter 3; quoted by Barbara Hardy, *Forms of Feeling in Victorian Fiction* (London: Owen, 1985), p. 11.

himself as feeling emotion. [. . .] The narrative is no longer purely personal. The personality of the artist passes into the narration itself, flowing round and round the persons and the action like a vital sea. [. . .] The dramatic form is reached when the vitality which has flowed and eddied round each person fills every person with such vital force that he or she assumes a proper and intangible esthetic life. The personality of the artist, at first a cry or a cadence or a mood and then a fluent and lambent narrative, finally refines itself out of existence, impersonalises itself, so to speak.[12]

However different Lawrence, Proust, and Joyce are as novelists, all emphasize the metamorphic quality of human emotion in art. All three quotations give the sense of the ideal art form as a living, mobile organism. This sense is admirably captured in the philosopher Susanne K. Langer's Romantic description of music as an 'organic' vehicle for feeling:

The essence of all composition [. . .] is the semblance of *organic* movement, the illusion of an indivisible whole. Vital organization is the frame of all feeling, because feeling exists only in living organisms; and the logic of all symbols that can express feeling is the logic of organic processes.[13]

This emphasis on fluidity, metamorphosis, and organicism in artistic representation of emotion seems a long way, however, from the 'instant' passions of the nineteenth-century stage comically mocked in Gilbert Abbott À Beckett's *The Quizziology of the British Drama*:

> The Passions, [. . .]
> Ranting, stamping, screaming, fainting,
> Faces chalking, corking, painting,
> By turns they bellow'd like the wind,
> And then to whisper had a mind,
> Till each resolved to act a part
> And give a spec'men of his art.
> All display'd in half an hour,
> A taste of their expressive power.[14]

Conceptions of the novel as a vehicle for the expression of nebulous inner passion also seem very different from theories of the novel formulated by nineteenth-century popular novelists. It is significant

[12] *A Portrait of the Artist as a Young Man*, ed. Seamus Deane (Harmondsworth: Penguin, 1992), 232–3.
[13] *Feeling and Form: A Theory of Art Developed from 'Philosophy in a New Key'* (London: Routledge & Kegan Paul, 1953), 126.
[14] (London: Punch, 1846), 1.

that, in an effort to elevate the artistic status of the developing novel form, several contemporaries of Dickens emphasize the essential similarity and equality between the novel and the established, respected drama. Modern reverence for the novel as the all-encompassing genre which can include and surpass the limits of other imaginative forms is conspicuously missing.[15] In the dedication of *Basil* (1852), for instance, Wilkie Collins justifies his use of extraordinary incidents in the following terms:

Believing that the Novel and the Play are twin-sisters in the family of Fiction; that the one is a drama narrated, as the other is a drama acted; and that all the strong and deep emotions which the Play-writer is privileged to excite, the Novel-writer is privileged to excite also, I have not thought it either politic or necessary, while adhering to realities, to adhere to everyday realities only.[16]

For Collins, the novel and the play are equally effective media through which emotion can be expressed. It is interesting, moreover, that Collins's description of emotions as 'strong and deep' conveys the impression that to him emotion is something definite, fixed, and expressible, rather than fluid, secret, and intangible. Ainsworth's introduction to *Rookwood* (1834) is relevant in this respect. Again, the novelist's subject is the similarity between the novel and the stage:

The novelist is precisely in the position of the dramatist. He has, or should have, his stage, his machinery, his actors. His representation should address itself as vividly to the reader's mental retina, as the theatrical exhibition to the spectator. The writer who is ignorant of dramatic situation and its effects, is unacquainted with the principles of his art, which requires all the adjuncts and essentials of the scenic prosopopeia. [. . .] The Romance constructed according to the rigid rules of art will, beyond doubt, eventually, if not immediately, find its way to the stage.—It is a drama, with descriptions to supply the place of scenery.[17]

The emphasis is on rigidity of form and visual exhibition; Ainsworth shows no veneration for the unseen. 'The shape of that which we have felt' should be represented in bold, near pictorial form.

[15] Indeed, Kathryn Chittick's meticulous *Dickens and the 1830s* (Cambridge: Cambridge University Press, 1990) is a much-needed reminder that *PP* and *OT* were not even originally conceived as novels. The novel form, far from topping the generic hierarchy throughout the Victorian period, was not even considered a 'literary' form in the 1830s (unlike non-fiction prose, for example).

[16] *Basil: A Story of Modern Life*, ed. Dorothy Goldman (Oxford: Oxford University Press, 1990; repr. 1992), p. xxxvii.

[17] *Rookwood: A Romance*, 4th edn. (London: Macrone, 1836), pp. xii–xiii.

In his important work *Realizations,* Martin Meisel argues convincingly that 'the nineteenth century revealed a powerful bent in whole classes of fiction to assimilate themselves with drama, while drama itself was under a compulsion to make itself over as a picture'.[18] The tendency of drama towards static pictorialism affected even the greatest actors of the late eighteenth and early nineteenth centuries. Hazlitt, for instance, described Kean's Richard III and Shylock as 'a perpetual succession of striking pictures', and acting handbooks as 'old receipt-books for the passions'.[19] Coleridge maintained that seeing Kean act was 'like reading Shakespeare by flashes of lightning'.[20] To the realist critic G. H. Lewes, Kean was 'a consummate master of passionate expression'; though Lewes criticizes Kean, like lesser actors, for being 'fond, far too fond of abrupt transitions', he argues that Kean was one of the few actors able to express '*subsiding emotion*'.[21] Lewes is objecting to what Meisel calls the 'iconography of character and emotion' which dominated the popular culture of the early and mid-Victorian period.[22] The use of devices such as tableau, tableau vivant, and situation onstage, as well as a stylized language of the passions, bears witness to this iconographic tendency.[23] In the novel, illustrations and dramatic, stylized chapter endings function similarly.

Dickens's professed views on the novel as a genre, and in particular on the relationship between the novel and the drama, do not differ greatly from those of his contemporary popular novelists. Dickens's most famous and strident statement on the question—'Every writer of fiction, although he may not adopt the dramatic form, writes, in effect, for the stage'[24]—is not random or inconsistent,

[18] *Realizations: Narrative, Pictorial and Theatrical Arts in Nineteenth-Century England* (Princeton: Princeton University Press, 1983), 64.

[19] 'A View of the English Stage; or, A Series of Dramatic Criticisms' (1814(–17)), in *Complete Works of Hazlitt,* ed. P. P. Howe, 21 vols. (London: Dent, 1930–4), v (1930), 169–379 (p. 184); 'British Institution' (1814), in *Complete Works,* ed. Howe xviii (1933), 10–16 (p. 10).

[20] *Table Talk,* 2nd edn. (1836); repr. in *The Romantics on Shakespeare,* ed. Jonathan Bate (Harmondsworth: Penguin, 1992), 160.

[21] *On Actors and the Art of Acting,* 17–19.

[22] *Realizations,* 5.

[23] See Meisel's *Realizations,* 45, 47, for definitions of the 'tableau' and 'tableau vivant'. See Edward Mayhew's *Stage Effect; or, The Principles which Command Dramatic Success in the Theatre* (London: Mitchell, 1840), for a definition of a 'situation' and its similarity to 'the conclusion of a chapter in a novel' (p. 44).

[24] This was made on 29 Mar. 1858, at the Royal General Theatrical Fund, toasting Thackeray's health; see *The Speeches of Charles Dickens: A Complete Edition,* ed. K. J. Fielding (Hemel Hempstead: Harvester Wheatsheaf, 1988), 262.

but supported entirely by writings elsewhere. In those most private of scribblings, for instance, the working plans for his novels, he would use terms which referred to the theatre. Indeed, his plans for *Hard Times* employ the language of theatre—for example, 'separation scene' and 'the great effect'—and phrases suggestive of pictorialism—for example, 'Mill Pictures', 'Wet night picture' and 'moving picture of Stephen moving away from Coketown'.[25] His advice to contributors to his periodicals is likewise drenched in a belief in the novel as theatre. To Mrs Brookfield, he writes:

you constantly hurry your narrative (and yet without getting on) *by telling it, in a sort of impetuous breathless way, in your own person, when the people should tell it and act it for themselves.* My notion always is, that when I have made the people to play out the play, it is, as it were, their business to do it, and not mine.[26]

He advises other would-be novelists:

The people do not sufficiently work out their own purposes in dialogue and dramatic action; [. . .] what you do for them, they ought to do for themselves.[27]

there is too much of the narrator in it—the narrator not being an actor. The result is, that I can *not* see the people, or the place, or believe in the fiction.[28]

Even Wilkie Collins's narrators have a 'DISSECTIVE' quality in common which, Dickens argues, is actually Collins's own. He advises Collins on *The Woman in White* (1859–60): 'my own effort would be to strike more of what is got, *that way,* out of them [the characters] by collision with one another, and by the working of the story.'[29]

Indeed, when writing his own novels, Dickens takes his own vision of novel as theatre literally. His daughter Mamie's famous description of Dickens acting out his narratives in front of a mirror is remarkable testimony to the integral relationship between novel and theatre in his conception of the creative writing process.[30] Dickens,

---

[25] Quoted by Meisel, *Realizations,* 60. See also the Clarendon edition of *LD,* pp. 813 ff. and *HT,* ed. George Ford and Sylvère Monod (New York: Norton, 1966), 234 ff. Moreover, in Forster's *Life,* the biographer analyses the qualities of Dickens's letter writing as follows: 'Unrivalled quickness of observation, the rare faculty of seizing out of a multitude of things the thing that is essential [. . .]. *Not external objects only, but feelings, reflections and thoughts, are photographed into visible forms* with the same unexampled ease' (pp. 245–6) (italics mine).

[26] *Letters* (Pilgrim), xi. 160 (20 Feb. 1866).

[27] *Letters* (Pilgrim), vii. 529 (letter to Miss King, 9 Feb. 1855).

[28] Ibid. ix. 165 (letter to Charles Collins, 19 Nov. 1859).

[29] Ibid. ix. 194–5 (7 Jan. 1860).

[30] See van Amerongen, *The Actor in Dickens,* 256.

moreover, illustrates that the novel/stage equation works both ways in his striking description of the acting experience in terms of the novel, discussed in Chapter 3. Acting in *The Frozen Deep*, to Dickens, was 'like writing a book in company; [. . .] actual truth without its pain'. Although Dickens never managed to write a book in company, his public readings are further evidence of his vision of the novel as theatre, and of the author as performer. Whether writing or acting, Dickens was convinced from the beginning to the end of his career that his duty was to perform for an audience, to fuel 'that particular relation (personally affectionate and like no other man's)' which subsisted between him and the public.[31]

MELODRAMATIC POETICS AND DEVIANT PSYCHOLOGY

Dickens's methods of characterization obviously rely heavily on the melodramatic techniques of the popular theatre. Turning to Rudge and Rigaud, both wear the dark cloak which is a familiar uniform for stage villains and both, in the best physiognomical tradition of melodrama, betray their wickedness through their ugliness. Rudge wears 'a hat flapped over his face' which hides a scarred villainous physiognomy of an ominously 'cadaverous hue' (*BR*, chapter 1, pp. 3–5). Rigaud Blandois has the 'expression of a wild beast' waiting to be fed; his eyes are tellingly 'too close together' and betray 'no depth or change;' he has a 'hook nose [. . .] too high between the eyes' and thin lips beneath a 'thick moustache' shot with red (*LD*, book 1, chapter 1, p. 5). In case their appearances are not effective enough semiotic clues to their natures, in keeping with melodrama's compulsion to externalize the inner life, both Rudge and Rigaud betray themselves with every word, look, or gesture. Rigaud's first words, for example—the first human words spoken in *Little Dorrit*—are 'To the devil with this Brigand of a Sun that never shines in here!' (*LD*, book 1, chapter 1, p. 5). This speech from Rudge is typical of his general conversational style:

'Hear me,' he replied, menacing her with his hand. 'I, that in the form of a man live the life of a hunted beast! that in the body am a spirit, a ghost upon the earth, a thing from which all creatures shrink, save those curst beings of

---

[31] Quoted by Forster, *Life*, 646 (Mar. 1858). He repeated this formulation three years later in a letter about the 1861 Readings tour (*Life*, 689). A similar phrase also appears in a letter to his publishers, 16 Mar. 1858 (*Letters* (Pilgrim), viii. 533).

another world, who will not leave me;—I am, in my desperation of this night, past all fear but that of the hell in which I exist from day to day'. (*BR*, chapter 17, p. 129)

If Dickens's melodramatic methods of characterization appear to be obvious and widely recognized, however, the melodramatic characteristics of Dickens's prose poetics have received little if any recognition. I am talking here not about Dickens's comic, parodic, or satirical prose (more accessible, perhaps, in a postmodernist age), but about Dickens's descriptive prose. The melodramatic poetics Dickens employs in his descriptive prose are crucial to a sophisticated understanding of Dickensian character—specifically to comprehension of the 'conjuring trick' which enables Dickens to explore the inner life whilst eschewing subject-centred, 'psychological' *analyses* of character. In keeping with Dickens's marginalization of the mind, interiority in his novels is expressed in terms of extreme emotional states. Because Dickens's more overtly melodramatic expressions of passion appear 'artificial' to the post-realist critic, Dickens studies has been slow to appreciate and articulate the fact that, during the experience of reading, Dickens's melodramatic presentation of violent passion is often surprisingly powerful. This is partly because Dickensian passion mediates the 'psychology' so central to perceptions of art and identity from the nineteenth century onwards. It is also because the key to Dickens's Pandora's box of the passions lies, like the key to so much else in Dickens, in the relatively unexplored terrain of his narratorial prose.

If we take *Barnaby Rudge*, for example, the internal chaos of the elder Rudge's guilty conscience is externalized in the most direct way possible. Rudge re-enacts the murder. Guilt is dramatized. Moreover, it is dramatized through heightened melodramatic gesture:

It was not the sudden change from darkness to this dreadful light [. . .] that drove the man back as though a thunderbolt had struck him. It was the Bell. If the ghastliest shape the human mind has ever pictured in its wildest dreams had risen up before him, he could not have staggered back from its touch, as he did from the first sound of that loud iron voice. With eyes that started from his head, his limbs convulsed, his face most horrible to see, he raised one arm high up into the air, and holding something visionary back and down, with his other hand, drove at it as though he held a knife and stabbed it to the heart. He clutched his hair, and stopped his ears, and travelled madly round and round; then gave a frightful cry, and with it rushed away. (*BR*, chapter 55, p. 419)

The mind, as this passage states explicitly, operates through pictures. This description of Rudge's conscience-stricken reaction to the bell at the Warren, for example, bears many similarities to Leopold Lewis's later dramatization of the same scenario in the crime melodrama *The Bells* (1871).[32] More generally, this crucial sequence in *Barnaby Rudge* borrows specifically from the stage's conventional language of the passions when the role of the murdered victim is dramatized in a flashback:

What face was that, in which a friendly smile changed to a look of half incredulous horror, which stiffened for a moment into one of pain, then changed again into an imploring glance at Heaven, and so fell idly down with upturned eyes, like the dead stags' he had often peeped at when a little child. (*BR*, chapter 55, p. 420)

The 'stiffened' nature of Reuben's passions, the abrupt change from the emotion of happiness to horror, to pain, to prayer, and then to despair, remind us of the tendencies of the nineteenth-century stage towards static pictorialism.

What is important about the melodramatic gestics enacted by both Rudge and his victim is that they are not presented in isolation, but in the context of the melodramatic substructure of Dickens's descriptive prose. The narrative environment of a Dickens novel very soon destroys our conventional, extra-novelistic expectations that the animate and inanimate, human and inhuman, worlds can be sharply differentiated. That Dickens's prose poetics are rooted in a fascination with the interaction between the animate and the inanimate, and further, between animation and mechanization, is as established a 'fact' as there is in Dickens criticism.[33] What has not been emphasized, however, is that the relationship between the animate and inanimate worlds in Dickens is rendered passionally and melodramatically. Take the following passage from *Barnaby Rudge*, for example:

What hunt of spectres could surpass that dread pursuit and flight! Had there been a legion of them on his track, he could have better borne it. *There would have had a beginning and an end, but here all space was full.* The one pursuing voice was everywhere: it sounded in the earth, the air; shook the long grass, and howled among the trembling trees.[. . .] It seemed to goad and urge the

---

[32] *Hiss the Villain*, 358–9. See p. 68–9 above.

[33] Stefanie Meier's *Animation and Mechanization in the Novels of Charles Dickens* provides a very useful summary of the various influences on, and interpretations of, this tendency in Dickens—Swiss Studies in English, CXI (Zurich: Francke Verlag Bern, 1982).

angry fire, and lash it into madness; everything was steeped in one prevailing red; the glow was everywhere; nature was drenched in blood: still the remorseless crying of that awful voice—the Bell, the Bell! (*BR*, chapter 55, pp. 419–20) (italics mine)

There are two simple but important points to be made about both this passage and Dickens's melodramatic poetics more generally. First, elements of the inanimate or non-human world are presented as possessing an inner emotional life. Second, this emotional life is externalized using the behaviouristic presentational methods of popular melodrama. So the bell can goad, urge, and even lash with its haunting voice, to take just one example. The conventional renderings of passion by Rudge and Reuben which frame this paragraph are thus tuned to the narrative whole, which gives their gestics force and intensity. Even the inanimate world is alive with feeling, feeling moreover which either resembles Rudge's own, or is stimulated by a reaction against the murderer. The 'trembling trees' mirror Rudge's fear, while the 'angry' fire—the product of Rudge's guilt-ridden imagination—punishes and pursues. The 'crying' of the bell could be echoing the cries of Rudge's murdered victim; it could also represent the guilty pain of the villain-victim. This transference occurs not only by fusing character with imagery or part with whole. A kind of metonymic melodrama is played out in the prose; the 'trembling' trees, the 'angry' fire, the 'crying' bell metonymically figure and transfigure the passions of the apparently monopathic Rudge.

Even at the roots of the narrative prose, then, Dickens appropriated the prevailing tendency of popular melodrama to externalize the inner life. The function of melodrama in Dickens's poetics goes beyond this, however. Various critics have noted, in different intonations, that Dickens's prose is not simply characterized by excess and externalization; rigidity, mechanization, and restraint coexist with the former in Dickens's novelistic economy.[34] The restraint, as well as the excess characteristic of Dickens's prose, is imported from stage melodrama. Though it is tempting to describe Dickens's rendering of emotion as a welding of the 'behaviouristic' onto the 'organic' conception of the novel, what we actually have in a Dickens

[34] See Kucich, 'Mechanical Style', in *Excess and Restraint*, 195–242, Patrick McCarthy, 'Dombey and Son: Language and the Roots of Meaning', *Dickens Studies Annual*, 19 (1990), 91–106, Tore Rem, 'Melodrama and Parody: A Reading that *Nicholas Nickleby* Requires?', *English Studies*, 3 (1996), 240–54.

novel is a melodramatic organism. On the surface then, we have a combination of fluidity and stasis. Dickensian prose—like Dickensian character—can achieve Brechtian alienation effects and the illusion of naturalism or fluidity, often simultaneously.

When we examine this prose 'fluidity' close up, however, it actually consists of a metonymic chain of stylized animation—an aesthetics rooted in melodrama rather than realism or naturalism but appearing to straddle the mimetic and the figural. The illusion of fluidity is created by placing 'a perpetual succession of striking pictures' in a metonymic relation to one another. Reading Dickens is (to quote Coleridge on Kean) like seeing by flashes of lightning. Stasis is thus as illusory as fluidity; the movement of the metonymic chain means that, in the process of reading, stasis can never be other than metamorphosis. An analogy with the film-making process may help here—photographic stills shown in rapid succession create the illusion of a moving image. Dickens never lets us fully immerse ourselves in fluidity, however; though his novels are more seamless than melodrama, they ultimately refuse the illusory naturalism of film.

'*There would have had a beginning and an end, but here all space was full*' (italics mine). This phrase is important to an understanding of the function of Dickens's prose in rendering interiority. The vision of Reuben's seemingly conventional rendering of despair is also a complex visual demonstration of Rudge's own guilty despair. Villain and victim are fused with one another and with their world, in a passage which at first sight could seem little more than a series of 'pictures' or 'tableaux' from the nineteenth-century stage, static representations of single emotions. Viewed more closely, however, there is a fusion— and transfusion—of symbol and significance, narrative imagery and melodramatic gesture. Rudge's passionate gesticulations are an attempt to contain his guilt as well as an expression of guilt which cannot be contained; they are synonymous with the remembered pain of his victim. He wants to stop the inner bleeding of himself and his victim, which he sees mirrored everywhere—'everything was steeped in the prevailing red; [. . .] nature was drenched in blood'. Rudge's externalization of his inner bleeding provides temporary relief, but his blood, his guilt, cannot be contained or fixed, and once it has erupted from the veins of the narrative, there is no confining it within a single finite gesture. Interestingly, Dickens offers us a fascinating insight into his conception of narrative when he explains to

Forster that Miss Wade's 'History of a Self-Tormentor', in *Little Dorrit*, will flow from 'the blood of the book'.[35]

Dickens employs the re-enactment of Rudge's murder of Reuben Haredale to show that trauma and guilt can be symbolized but not contained by a particular emotional expression—in this case by gesture. More subtly perhaps, Dickens figures (recovered) memory of trauma as melodramatic. What could be called Rudge's stream of conscience, like Satan's Hell—as Dickens constantly reminds us—is always within and without him. But Rudge, unlike Satan, is visited intermittently by flashbacks from the past which take the form of 'tableaux' from the nineteenth-century stage, 'fixing' the last passion of the victim, but perpetuating the villain's own flow of guilty emotion. Rudge's vision of the despairing Reuben is paradoxically an inversion of the familiar use of conventional stage passion. It is not finite, but infinite, perpetually visiting itself on the villain. We are reminded here of the wavelike movement of melodrama, identified in Chapter 1. The strength of Dickens's representation of emotion and character—and where he differs from popular contemporaries like Ainsworth—lies in the fact that he harnesses the overtly melo-dramatic rendering of passion to a sense of the novel as a genre in which, to echo Joyce, emotion flows 'round and round the persons of the action like a vital sea'.

It is undeniable that overt expressions of passion in Dickens's novels often resemble superficially the passionate outbursts of melo-dramatic stage prototypes. Conventional gestures, 'tableaux', and stylized language of feeling are common features of both the stage and Dickens's novels. Dickens's melodramatic renderings of passion are, however, often more powerful during the experience of reading than the critic examining these passages in isolation can begin to explain. This is because, as I have suggested, Dickens studies has failed to analyse adequately the melodramatic poetics informing Dickens's prose. The need for close analysis of Dickens's prose has been commented on from Leavis's famous essay on *Hard Times* to Brian Rosenberg's recent theorized (and much-needed) account of Dickensian 'character'.[36] Despite this, the false synonymity often assumed between close reading and liberal humanism has deterred many from embarking on a practice that seems to add nothing to

---

[35] *Letters* (Pilgrim), viii. 280 ([?9 Feb. 1857]).

[36] *Little Dorrit's Shadows: Character and Contradiction in Dickens* (Columbia: University of Missouri Press, 1996), 26: 'This is among the most overlooked aspects of Dickens's art'.

currently central debates on ideology; the historical association of criticism of the Victorian novel with all themes 'big' and social has also not helped in this respect.

Recent work by John Kucich, Tore Rem, and Patrick McCarthy suggests a growing appreciation that analysis of Dickens's prose is not just a formalist exercise.[37] Patrick McCarthy's stimulating '*Dombey and Son*: Language and the Roots of Meaning', for example, notes the role of Dickens's language in creating both Dickensian 'vitality' and a morally complex universe. His desire to attract serious critical attention to Dickens's prose means, however, that he sees the medieval morality play (psychomachia) and myth as Dickens's informing aesthetic and ethical frameworks. Melodrama is the Victorian form of the medieval morality play and impacts on Dickens's prose in all the ways McCarthy ascribes to the psychomachia. The importance of critical recognition of the distinctly melodramatic nature of Dickens's poetics is that melodrama imports more to Dickens's novels than vitality and moral complexity: the passion (largely absent in the allegorical, pre-realism psychomachia) and the distinctive presentational techniques of melodrama are formative in Dickens's anti-intellectual ideologies.

Dickens's melodramatic prose poetics have important implications, in particular, for an understanding of Dickens's much criticized and much misunderstood psychology. It is no accident, for example, that those passages which twentieth-century readers often find most passionately powerful appear to be forays into what House calls the 'morbid and near morbid psychology' of the villain—the most notable examples involve perhaps Sikes after the murder of Nancy, Fagin at his trial, and Jonas Chuzzlewit after the murder of Tigg. It is common to account for the power of these passages psychologically or biographically. House and Wilson argue in a similar, but more familiar vein, that such passages are the product of Dickens's own tortured, guilty mind.

Though these readings have interest and power in a post-Freudian age, it is also fitting that we see Dickens's 'psychological' passages in the melodramatic terms in which they express themselves. Melodrama advocates transparency over privacy, expression over repression: heightened interiority is synonymous with wickedness. The development of an inner life in passionate villains whose *modus operandi* is normally the externalization of all feeling can be explained

[37] See n. 34 above.

with recourse to melodrama's dialectical emotional economy, whereby excessive, antisocial violence or repression inevitably leads to self-violation, and, by implication, to glimmers of an inner life. Perhaps more importantly, the melodramatic poetics which inform these descriptions of deviant 'interiority' reinforce the logic of melodrama's communal ideology: self-reflexive secrecy is the height of villainy. That Dickens was obviously as drawn to depictions of 'inner' deviance as any modern reader can of course complicate this argument, as I discuss later in this chapter. What is indisputable, however, is the 'melodramatic', behaviouristic, and passional terms in which Dickens evokes so-called 'morbid psychology'. These terms are invariably 'translated' by critics from House and Wilson onwards who read Dickens as if he were George Eliot. But to ignore Dickens's melodramatic poetics is to ignore the anti-intellectual ideologies which inform them.

Kucich rightly points out that Dickensian characterization suggests a 'refractive view of the psyche' and a 'decentering psychological approach'.[38] As evidence, he points to the reliance in Dickens on character clusters, on doubles and alter egos—caricatures like Rudge and Rigaud exist not in isolation but in relation to others. My point is that Dickens decentres the psyche even more radically than Kucich appreciates—by mediating what we could now call psychology through prose poetics depicting the feelings and physical actions of the inanimate world. This mediation or decentring is a facet of Dickens's anti-intellectualism. The mind is thus explored but not valorized; its activities are 'translated' into those of the physical, emotional, and spiritual world, hence avoiding its colonization of the imaginative and ideological hierarchies which inform Dickens's art.

If Dickens decentres the psyche, however, his caricatures and stereotypes at one level tempt the reader to assume a certain centredness to identity. Dickensian characterization often appears to rely on wholeness, on a reassuring monopathy. From the Victorian period onwards, however, critics have associated this wholeness with what E. M. Forster would call 'flatness'—with a superficial, simplistic rendering of psychology. This discrepancy is partly explained by the difference between the emotional and moral terms in which Dickens's art often figures character, and the 'psychological' criteria of traditional character criticism. It would be simplifying Dickens's writing, however, to argue that emotion supplies it with its 'depth' or

[38] 'Dickens', 400.

centre. T. S. Eliot said of Shakespeare that 'words have often a network of tentacular roots reaching down to the deepest terrors and desires'.[39] In Dickens's melodramatic art, 'the deepest terrors and desires' are also the most visible. The expressionistic tendencies of melodrama assume a synonymity between surfaces and depths and subvert the Romantic notion of roots.

Even when we examine Dickens's 'internalized' passional poetics, for example, what we actually have is a metonymic chain of externalized emotional states. This constant theatricality or animation is partly explained by the fact that, to revisit Kucich, 'Dickens always conceives inwardness as inextricable from the ways in which it is consciously or unconsciously presented to others'.[40] If inwardness is constantly visible or 'presented to others', however, this begs the question of whether inwardness actually exists in Dickens in any meaningful way. This book seeks to provide a moral and ideological rationale for his habitual externalization or deferral of innerness. It has yet to investigate the implications of a world or an art form turned inside out—totally devoid, that is, of interiority.

TAKING MELODRAMA AT FACE VALUE

Melodrama is a genre in which, as I have argued, surfaces are synonymous with depths. It is, in its original manifestation at least, transparent rather than superficial: surfaces, that is, are assumed to have depths. The assignation of meaning—whether moral, emotional, or spiritual—to melodramatic semiotics rather depends, however, on the audience's willingness to believe that surfaces signify depths, and to subscribe to melodrama's ethical and spiritual framework. Melodrama's reliance on the audience's attribution of depths to surfaces leaves it vulnerable not so much to appropriation as to inversion. As melodrama is an art of the surface, it can equally suggest transcendence or meaninglessness. Much depends on one's angle of vision.

Thus if Dickens uses melodrama as a dramatic vehicle to reinforce his moral and ideological vision of the ideal society and individual, he uses the same genre—inverted—to explore his nightmare vision of

---

[39] 'Ben Jonson', in *The Sacred Wood: Essays On Poetry and Criticism*, 7th edn. (London: Methuen, 1950; repr. 1969), 104–22 (p. 115).
[40] See Introduction n. 16 above.

both. Significantly, it is melodrama's avoidance of interiority which makes it, for Dickens, an apocalyptic as well as a utopian vehicle. Though Dickens avoids the direct representation of innerness in his works, it is important to his ideals that surfaces are assumed to have meaning beyond themselves. In a late work like *Little Dorrit*, Dickens explores the possibility (constantly implied, even in his early works) that they do not. Interestingly, it is the Gothic villain Rigaud Blandois and his prose environment which foreground Dickens's exploration of a world devoid of interiority.

The opening passage of *Little Dorrit* demonstrates both Dickens's inversion of the melodramatic vision and his dependence on melodramatic aesthetics:

THIRTY years ago, Marseilles lay burning in the sun, one day. A blazing sun upon a fierce August day was no greater rarity in southern France then, than at any other time, before or since. Everything in Marseilles, and about Marseilles, had stared at the fervid sky, and been stared at in return, until a staring habit had become universal there. Strangers were stared out of countenance by staring white houses, staring white walls, staring white streets, staring tracts of arid road, staring hills from which verdure was burnt away. The only things to be seen not fixedly staring and glaring were the vines drooping under their load of grapes. These did occasionally wink a little, as the hot air barely moved their faint leaves.

Dickens's vision is melodramatic in this passage; it is exaggerated, externalized, stylized, highly emotive, even when depicting a scene which appears empty of feeling. In many ways, this description represents an extreme challenge for the melodramatic vision because, on the surface of things, there is no energy, emotion, or action. Dickens's emphasis on the word 'staring' is fascinating because staring is a human (or animal) *activity* which does not require movement or animation. The attribution of life (but not animation) to the inanimate world means, however, that the dramatic or active becomes the norm even in a piece of 'static' (or inanimate) visual description. Inactivity, in Dickens, is described in terms of activity. Even ennui is rendered melodramatically. This perpetual animation or theatricality is the essence of what some critics vaguely define as 'vitality' or 'energy' in Dickens's writing.

However, at the same time that it is melodramatic, Dickens's vision is curiously modern. Remarkably, Dickens's prose exudes its characteristic energy even in a late novel like *Little Dorrit*, whilst simultaneously suggesting that the world and its inhabitants have become dehumanized. The 'felt life' in Dickens's Marseilles is animalistic rather than human; it is violent rather than passionate. The disturbing sense of danger which the opening description exudes is that of a hollow universe where violence, the dominant form of energy, usurps passion. The atmosphere is repressed, claustrophobic, a dramatization of the dialectical relationship which can exist between violence and repression.

The motiveless Rigaud Blandois is the 'natural'—or unnatural—creature of such an environment, parading his inauthenticity as earlier 'Gothic' villains parade their passions: he is an anti-psychological 'psychopath'. Rigaud collapses any oppositions between violence and repression, passion and passionlessness, and indeed surfaces and depths. Where Rudge is a Gothic villain proper, Rigaud is a self-reflexive Gothic lookalike. Rigaud is the (dehumanized) personification of Dickens's anxieties about both melodrama and the Gothic villain. Rigaud dramatizes the consequences of a constant externalization of passion: if innerness is constantly made visible, then arguably there is nothing left inside. Innerness (and passion), that is, become meaningless. Despite the superficial resemblance between Rigaud and Rudge, the perpetual performativity of Rigaud means that in fact he has more in common with Dickens's cannibalistic individuals. That he can seem to be both excessive and repressive simultaneously is further testimony to Dickens's dialectical emotional economy, yet here the fusion of two contradictory impulses 'in'—or perhaps through—one character represents the sophistication of Dickens's melodramatic vision rather than the fulfilment of his realist tendencies.

The timing of the two novels in question, of course, is significant here, the later *Little Dorrit* brilliantly deconstructing the fictions of passion, the self, the relationship between surfaces and depths. Rigaud Blandois is flagrantly inauthentic, a Gothic involute who personifies the horror of a world where surfaces are dislocated from humane depths; the nightmarish energy he exudes stems partly from this recognition and partly from his simultaneous habitation of the mimetic and figural levels of a text which is itself an interrogation of reality. Rigaud Blandois pre-empts the stark 'realities' of modernism and deconstruction, albeit in an entertaining and theatrical way. He is the grotesque spectre of melodrama's decadence.

DEPTHS OF FEELING?

It might be useful here to invoke the Wagnerian distinction between 'effect' and 'Wirkung'. Wagner argues that 'our natural feeling can only conceive of "Wirkung" [literally "a working"] as bound up with an antecedent *cause*'; the English word 'effect', by contrast, suggests 'a Working, without a cause'.[41] 'Effect' means that, in the words of Wagner, 'the whole of Art is resolved into its mechanical integers: the externals of Art are turned into its essence',[42] whereas 'Wirkung' means that essence is expressed by means of externals.[43] Critics of popular culture's formulaic emotionalism are objecting, in Wagner's terms, to 'effect'—particularly to the effect of mechanization (in the cultural product and its consumer) which can characterize commercial, commodified experiences of pleasure. When Henry James famously argued that Dickens was 'the greatest of superficial novelists', he was essentially arguing that Dickens took the art of 'effect' to its limits.

The assumption behind criticism of Dickens's 'effect' is that Dickens was a failed realist, a lesser artist for his inability to achieve 'Wirkung'. There is no doubt that Dickens, like any writer, had his failures, and that Gothic villains like Rudge and Monks are frequently included among them. This is because excessively passionate characters for whom externalization is a compulsion test the novel to the limits. Simply speaking, such beings are theatrical rather than 'real'. In order to make them credible, the novelist needs to create a suitably theatrical novelistic environment for them to inhabit. In an attempt to redress the critical balance, this chapter has chosen to emphasize the moments when Dickens's ambitious fusions between novel and theatre succeed. There is no doubt, however, that Dickens's most 'dramatic' failures of characterization occur when he unwittingly achieves 'effect', or emotion without depth, rather than 'Wirkung', or the fusion of essence with outward show. Often this failure occurs when Dickens fails to harness overtly melodramatic techniques for rendering character with the melodramatic poetics of his prose, or indeed when behaviouristic methods of characterization are the only methods of characterization. In *Barnaby Rudge*, for

---

[41] *Opera and Drama* (1851), in *Richard Wagner's Prose Works*, trans. William Ashton Ellis, 8 vols. (London: Kegan Paul, 1893), ii. 95.

[42] Ibid. 99.

[43] Meisel, *Realizations*, 71.

example, though the passages discussed above are immensely powerful, there are also several instances involving Rudge when melodrama becomes farce: notably when the unintelligent, inarticulate
Rudge tries to articulate emotional states which, the narrative tells us,
he does not understand.[44] Then again, in *Oliver Twist*, Monks makes
several passionate speeches towards the end of the novel which fail to
convince because they have no connection with the poetics of the
novel or with any knowledge we have of a character who has
remained stagily enigmatic throughout. These failures can be read as
perfect instances of the novelist practising what he preaches—of
taking literally the idea of the novel as theatre by making characters
do the work that more fittingly belongs to the narrator. Alternatively,
they can be seen as examples of characters attempting a kind of
self-analysis which is ill at ease with the melodramatic mode of
Dickens's early novels. In any case, these partial failures of characterization are the result of struggles between the behaviouristic and
analytic possibilities of the novel, and of practical experiments with
the idea of the novel as theatre.

These early passionate villains teach Dickens a valuable lesson,
however: that the severance of inner emotional substance from
outward show can create an effect of dehumanization, which is
itself a mode of developing and sustaining character. This finding is
ironically put to good use in his representation of passionless dandy
villains, who consciously deaden their passions in order to recreate
themselves as works of art, and in his figuring of a dismaying
variety of hollow people. Dickens is evidently aware that, in art, the
divorce of surface from inner life, the resolution of essence 'into its
mechanical integers', produces the effect of lifelessness—and that he
can use that effect in order to evoke states of terror, self-alienation, or
dehumanization. Indeed, self-conscious, anti-naturalistic, even
Brechtian alienation effects are everywhere in Dickens. Dickens's
animation of 'things', his attribution of inner lives and feelings to
inanimate objects, is also a deliberate and sophisticated device, calculated to create the illusion of life where there is none.

Dickens's manipulation of the relationship between 'effect' and
'Wirkung' is more than a mode of rendering character, moreover; it
is a self-reflexive means of interrogating his own art as a novelist.
Wagner's conception of art, for example, is organic and Romantic,
assuming that depths are more substantial than surfaces. Dickens's

[44] See *BR*, chapter 62, pp. 473–4, chapter 73, p. 565.

novels, however, are consistently ambivalent about the relationship between surfaces and depths, flirting continuously with the Wildean idea that 'All art is at once surface and symbol',[45] and prefiguring modernism and postmodernism in their recognition that life itself may be literally superficial. Despite the best efforts of recent post-structuralist analyses to appropriate Dickens, Dickens never commits himself wholly to this view—though the later novels tend more towards it.[46] What is remarkable in Dickens's writing is that he manages to suggest an organic vision of art and of life at the same time as he suggests its opposite.

Dickens's use of eye imagery, for example, is a fascinating tool in his exploration of the relationship between surfaces and depths in art and in people. For Dickens, eyes are ideally the mirrors of the soul; hence one of his most disturbing yet frequent images is that of eyes that betray surface but no depth. This image suggests a severing of outward expression from inner life. It is used to describe Rigaud, whose eyes 'had no depth or change; they glittered, and they opened and shut. [. . .] A clockmaker could have made a better pair' (book 1, chapter 1, p. 5). Lifeless eyes are also, of course, used to describe corpses, or hint at death. Hence the extraordinary impact of the memory of Nancy's eyes on Bill Sikes. Isolated from all human contact, the eyes of Nancy, for Sikes, are both a reminder of his destruction of a human life, and a reminder that Nancy was the only human being who cherished any humane feelings towards him.

Dickens's eye imagery foregrounds the complex ambivalence which attends the idea of interiority in his novels. Thus far we have observed the melodramatic association of interiority with deviance which pervades Dickens novels, and is particularly acute when Dickens evokes the troubled conscience of the passionate murderer; it is as if interiority is a consequence of murder (and vice versa?). At the same time Dickens's vision of a world of surfaces—in *Little Dorrit*, in his eye imagery, etc.—is horrific if not apocalyptic. The much vaunted 'humanizing' effect of passages in Dickens depicting the guilt and fear of the murderer also problematizes any reading of his novels which maintains that they unambiguously denigrate innerness. It is after all in descriptions like that depicting Sikes's fear after the death

---

[45] 'The Preface', *The Picture of Dorian Gray* (1891), ed. Peter Ackroyd (Harmondsworth: Penguin, 1985), 21–2 (p. 22).

[46] See Introduction above and Chapter 5 below for more on post-structuralist analyses of Dickens.

of Nancy, or Rudge's trauma years after the murder of Reuben, that they become both more aware of their own emotions and, arguably, of the emotions of others. The vision of Nancy's 'widely staring eyes, so lustreless and so glassy' (chapter 48, p. 327) thus emphasizes to Sikes that where there was once some channel of emotional warmth towards him, there is now only 'a corpse endowed with the mere machinery of life' (chapter 48, p. 327).

Thus if interiority is a consequence of violence or guilt, it can also act as a kind of guarantee of humanity, in Dickens's novels. Even this formulation is not straightforward, however; as many readers have observed, Dickens's passionate villains are most human only when they become most inhuman—i.e. by committing murder. It is only then that they value what they have lost—their emotional connectedness with other human beings. The image of Nancy's eyes, for example, frightens Sikes partly because they turn him into an object. The same effect is achieved at Fagin's trial, where he is stared at by 'a firmament, all bright with gleaming eyes':

But in no one face—not even among the women, of whom there were many there—could he read the faintest sympathy with himself, or any feeling but one of all-absorbing interest that he should be condemned. [. . .] He could glean nothing from their faces; they might as well have been of stone. (chapter 52, pp. 358–9)

The key word here is 'sympathy'. Lack of sympathy from an audience or companion turns the person under scrutiny into an object—from the outside if not the inside. Thus interiority is never synonymous in Dickens with subjectivity; it is always as much a consequence of a realization of how others see or experience an individual as it is the result of the individual's unmediated perceptions of him- or herself. This is undoubtedly one of the reasons that Dickens's first person narratives seem curiously impersonal: subjectivity in Dickens expresses itself through inter-personal emotional dynamics. The subject can thus often seem 'outside' his or her own story.

Interiority is, in other words, always rendered via melodramatic aesthetics which, as we have seen, dramatize emotional states rather than analysing psychology. Innerness is, as we have seen, constantly deferred or made visible in a poetics whose defining characteristic is externalization. If interiority eschews subjectivity, then, and if it is conveyed via a 'metonymic chain of stylized animation', as I described it earlier, this begs the question (again) of how far interiority exists in Dickens's novels. In one sense, the idea of interiority has been used provisionally throughout this chapter. Wagner's idea of an 'antecedent cause' is perhaps a more accurate description of what constitutes either 'interiority' or 'depth' in Dickens's work. For when Dickens's work is examined in detail, the sense of dimensionality or meaning attributed to surfaces is invariably seen to be given by Dickens's dramatization of dynamic emotional connections between people and things. Connected feeling or a feeling of connection thus constitutes the 'antecedent cause' which gives surfaces the impression of depths.

Fagin, for example, is the archetypal passionless villain who experiences no constructive emotional connections with others either before or after his arrest. In the courtroom he sees 'one young man sketching his face in a little note-book' and 'he wondered whether it was like'. After his sentence is pronounced, Fagin seems transformed from an artist's object into an artistic object: 'he stood, like a marble figure, without the motion of a nerve' (chapter 52, pp. 359–60). The faces of the crowd that 'might as well have been of stone' have literally petrified the villain. The evocation of Fagin's responses to his arrest foreshadows Albert Camus's existentialist rendering of the mind of the prisoner in *L'Étranger*. What is remarkable is the objectivity, the lack of emotional connection between the nominal 'subject' and his surroundings. Sikes, by contrast, is humanized by his heightened awareness of his surroundings. His surroundings and his imaginings comprise, in fact, the objective correlative of his guilt and fear. In the case of Sikes, he becomes imaginative after the murder of Nancy in a way he was not before.

What is partly at stake in Dickens's remarkable dramatizations of the emotional life of villains at moments of crisis is indeed the moral and social function of the imagination. The established explanation of the unrivalled power of such passages derives from the biographical, psychoanalytic work of Wilson and House: the artist, that is, psychologically identifies with the alienation of the outsider or the criminal. Antisocial alienation as well as guilt are preconditions of imagination. Another way of explaining the imaginativeness of the murderer, however, foregrounds the notions of sympathy and connectedness. Characters like Sikes and Jonas Chuzzlewit seem after all, by common assent, most human (and least villainous) when they are most imaginative. It is only when socially sanctioned emotional connections are severed that their value is realized.

Consciousness of the self in an emotional relation to others is thus a precondition of imagination. The fact that this consciousness occurs after violent, antisocial acts is of course in keeping with the House/Wilson theory of imagination. But the idea that imagination is associated solely with criminality in Dickens is too simple. Dickens's ambivalent attitudes to imagination, as they express themselves in the Dickens canon as a whole (including, of course, *Hard Times*), are as much about the role of the imagination in forging socially constructive, emotional connections between people as they are about the antisocial properties of the imagination.

The idea of the imaginative artist as an alienated outsider is, of course, Romantic, like much that informs the theories of Wilson and House. It is undeniable, however, that Dickens's explorations of the imagination express themselves melodramatically rather than adopting the subject-centred perspective of Romantic explorations of the same. It is thus that the passionate villain is the vehicle of all the most powerful evocations of the imaginative life in Dickens's novels. The passionate villain, as we have seen, epitomizes the melodramatic vision: he is unintelligent, excessively passionate, and externalizes all. To render his emotional and imaginative life at a time of crisis thus represents a supreme challenge for the novelist. Close attention to the poetics of passages dramatizing such moments has important repercussions for Dickens studies: Dickens succeeds in exploring what has been called the 'inner life' without mediating this life through analysis of the mind or the intelligence. Imagination is thus not the sole property of the intelligent, or those educated to analyse the mind rationally. Further than this, the idea of 'interiority' is not strictly accurate to describe Dickens's perception of the mind at its most imaginative. What Dickens's melodramatic poetics actually depict is a metonymic, dramatic externalization of emotion. 'Innerness' is thus always dynamic and visible; it is continuously deferred and inferred.

Dickens's continuous deferral or mediation of interiority represents the realization of the anti-intellectual ideologies informing melodramatic aesthetics rather than a failure of the 'psychological' or analytical functions so valued in post-Romantic aesthetics. Dickens manages to give the impression of 'depths' or 'antecedent causes' without actually valorizing or reifying either. The fact that passionate villains are the site of Dickens's most forceful rendering of the imaginative life and the interiority that is presumed to attend it is telling: where Bill Sikes or the elder Rudge become imaginative at moments of crisis, for example, what is striking about the invisible life of a passionless villain like Fagin is the lack of imagination which informs the view of the courtroom. He itemizes his audience as they objectify him: factually and unimaginatively. It is in fact the sense of superficiality and materiality which attends his vision which makes it so startling. More so than in the first scene of *Little Dorrit*, surfaces are meaningless beyond themselves.

What a comparison of the dramatization of the crises of Sikes and Fagin seems to reinforce is that, in Dickens's world, emotion gives the material world meaning beyond itself or an 'antecedent cause'. Perhaps more accurately, the perception of emotional connectedness between people gives the feeling of depths or significance to the world, to individuals, or to art (whether during or after the experience of connection). Fagin is unable to feel 'sympathy', only self-eroding passions like greed. He thus remains a creature of the surface until the end; his 'evil' resides in his complete emotional disconnection from others. He dehumanizes others as they ultimately dehumanize him. Both John Carey and Dorothy van Ghent have offered lucid interpretations of the relationship between the human and the non-human world, as it is played out in Dickens's prose.[47] What I hope to add to their insights is an understanding of the emotional terms in which the relationship between the animate and the inanimate world expresses itself in Dickens's novels, and the self-reflexive relevance of these terms for his art. Connected feeling or a feeling of connection constitutes the 'antecedent cause' which gives surfaces the impression of depths—even in material things. This is not the same as arguing that emotions constitute depth in Dickens's work. Emotions are never residual or unambiguously 'essential' in Dickens's work. They are dynamic, manifesting themselves metonymically and 'superficially'. This is perhaps an inevitable trait of melodramatic, theatrical art. But when critics like Garis assume that 'theatrical art is not an appropriate mode for dealing with the inner life, nor is an artist who works in this mode likely to be

[47] In *The Violent Effigy*, John Carey writes perceptively on Dickens's use of staring eyes: 'The blank stare, not baleful but utterly impersonal, is the optic counterpart of dislocated language. It achieves no human communication. Staring eyes haunt Dickens. [. . .] They turn you into an object, because their stare acknowledges nothing human in you' (p. 103). Dorothy van Ghent relates Dickens's consciousness of the interaction between the animate and inanimate worlds to the processes of industrialization manifest at the time and to his exploration of the relationship between good and evil—see *The English Novel: Form and Function* (New York: Rinehart, 1953), 128–9.

interested in the inner life', they underestimate the complexity of Dickens's manipulation of the inner life.[48]

Theatrical art provides Dickens with a tool for interrogating and, to an extent, deconstructing the inner life. If inner life exists in Dickens, it is emotionally constituted. But feeling never resides 'in' people in Dickens; it manifests itself metamorphically through and between people and things. Dickens's novels are epistemologically radical in their questioning of how we know what we think we know about life beneath or beyond surfaces. The reality of innerness and depths is ultimately never empirically knowable. The belief in 'antecedent causes' must ultimately be emotional rather than rational, the result of our willingness to ascribe emotion to surfaces, to construct emotional fictions—that is, to view things 'sympathetically'. The significance of this in terms of my point of departure is that though Dickens's melodramatic art relies heavily on the figuring of emotion, his texts are not straightforwardly or naively emotional. In their figuring and transfiguring of emotion, Dickens's novels are neither sceptical nor Romantic. Two impulses, one towards wholeness, content, and monopathy, and the other towards fragmentation, surface, and self-consciousness, fluctuate dialectically. The novels are closer to the poetry of Browning than to the modernist or postmodernist novel: emotional experience is posited as both construct and reality, to be simultaneously believed and questioned.

The epistemological revision of the idea of interiority or 'depths' in Dickens's novels has interesting implications for Dickens's populism and his critical reputation. The accusations of superficiality which have regularly attended Dickens's novels and the popular cultural modes informing them are premissed on a binary opposition between 'high' and 'low' culture. High art, it is assumed, is characterized by what Wagner calls 'Wirkung' and 'low art' is art of effect. Dickens effectively deconstructs this binary opposition without debunking aesthetic value judgements altogether. To Dickens, all art is art of effect, but the most imaginatively and socially valuable art creates the effect of 'Wirkung'. Dickens's cultural model is thus metamorphic rather than binary. Depths are dynamic—dependent, that is, on the feeling of connection.

[48] *The Dickens Theatre*, 53.

5

Twisting the Newgate Tale:
Popular Culture, Pleasure and the
Politics of Genre

In writing of *Waverley*, Sir Walter Scott confessed: 'I am a bad hand at depicting a hero properly so called, and have an unfortunate propensity for the dubious characters of borderers, Highland robbers, and all others of a Robin Hood description.'[1] Characters 'of a Robin Hood description' proved particularly problematic for Victorian critics. Neither heroes nor villains 'properly so called', they flaunted their moral ambiguity in a manner bound to irritate latent anxieties peculiar to the Victorian age. In the 1830s and 1840s, the most notorious breed of romantic criminal was to be found in so-called 'Newgate' fiction and melodrama. William Thackeray's coy confession of admiration for the criminal heroes of the so-called 'Newgate novels' is at the same time a witty sidesweep at Victorian mores.

Mr. Long Ned, Mr. Paul Clifford, Mr. William Sykes, Mr. Fagin, Mr. John Sheppard, [. . .] and Mr. Richard Turpin [. . .] are gentlemen whom we must all admire. We could 'hug the rogues and love them,' and do—*in private*. In public, it is, however, quite wrong to avow such likings, and to be seen in such company.[2]

'Newgate' novelists Bulwer, Ainsworth, and Dickens (and their stage adapters) caused a welter of critical controversy by foregrounding criminals who were perceived to be attractive. The comparative lack of critical hostility to Scott's Robin Hood-style characters suggests that there were specific textual and contextual factors at stake in the Newgate controversy. Focusing on *Oliver Twist*, this chapter will

[1] Cited by F. W. Chandler, *The Literature of Roguery*, 2 vols. (London: Constable, 1907), ii. 342.
[2] William Makepeace Thackeray, 'Horae Catnachianae', *Fraser's Magazine*, 19 (Apr. 1839), 407–24 (p. 408).

argue that the controversial cult status achieved by Newgate texts and protagonists had very little to do with the ethics of character in the novel, and very much to do with anxieties about power—in particular the power of popular culture at the dawn of a 'modern' age.

But to begin with some simple definitions. The term 'Newgate', of course, refers both to the famous prison destroyed by fire in 1780, and to *The Newgate Calendar; or, The Malefactors' Bloody Register*, a popular collection of criminal biographies published in 1773. In his comprehensive work *The Newgate Novel*, Keith Hollingsworth explains that, as a literary critical term, the 'Newgate' tag is nothing but a convenient historical label. In practice, it was used insultingly by contemporary commentators about a series of novels published between 1830 and 1847 which had 'criminals as prominent characters'. According to Hollingsworth, 'a book was not likely to be damned with the accusing name unless it seemed to arouse an unfitting sympathy for the criminal'.[3] The texts which aroused such concern included, most famously, *Paul Clifford* (1830), *Eugene Aram* (1832), and *Lucretia* (1846) by Edward Bulwer, and *Rookwood* (1834) and *Jack Sheppard* (1839–40) by William Harrison Ainsworth.[4] All were, in the words of John Sutherland, 'sensationally popular'.[5] It is difficult now to imagine the cultural phenomenon that the Newgate novel represented; in 1840, the murderer B. F. Courvoisier is rumoured to have blamed his crime on his having seen *Jack Sheppard*, with the result that further stage adaptations of the novel were (unofficially) prohibited;[6] and in 1852, juvenile delinquents told a House of Commons Select Committee on Criminal and Destitute Juveniles that Jack Sheppard had influenced their crimes.[7]

As *Oliver Twist* was published in serial form between 1837 and 1839 in *Bentley's Miscellany*—the same journal that published the 'Newgate' novels of Ainsworth—it was in some ways inevitable that it would be labelled a Newgate novel. Indeed, the fact that Dickens chose to write *Oliver Twist*, with its veritable rogues' gallery, despite critical

---

[3] *The Newgate Novel, 1830–1847: Bulwer, Ainsworth, Dickens, and Thackeray* (Detroit: Wayne State University Press, 1963), 14–15.

[4] These novels are included in John (ed.), *Cult Criminals*, which also includes Bulwer's *Night and Morning* (1841).

[5] John Sutherland, *The Longman Companion to Victorian Fiction* (Harlow: Longman, 1988), 462.

[6] Hollingsworth, *The Newgate Novel*, 145–8, 160; Stephens, *The Censorship of English Drama*, 66. See p. 58 above.

[7] Hollingsworth, *The Newgate Novel*, 221–2.

antipathy to books about criminals, shows a typical Dickensian blend of courage and opportunism—that is, controversy sells. At first glance, however, it seems surprising that *Oliver Twist*—a novel whose protagonist represents, Dickens tells us, 'the principle of Good surviving through every adverse circumstance' (p. lxii)—should be tarred with the same critical brush as novels featuring 'heroes' like Paul Clifford or Dick Turpin, the daring highwaymen. Villains like Sikes, Fagin, and Monks, however changed by subsequent musical metamorphoses, are not overtly glamorous. The closest Dickens gets to the seemingly innocent attractiveness of some of the Newgate heroes is the children Charley Bates and the Artful Dodger (to whom I shall return), who seem to play at the margins of the text.

So why did critics object to *Oliver Twist*—strongly enough for Dickens to feel the need to add a preface to the 1841 edition of the novel vigorously defending the novel against charges of immorality? In the vanguard of the attacks on the Newgate novel was *Fraser's Magazine*, a radical, Tory, aggressively middle-class publication, which made an enemy of Bulwer in particular—partly because of the personal animosity he inspired in its editor William Maginn and major contributor William Makepeace Thackeray. The objections to *Oliver Twist*, however, are out of step with other reviews of the novel, which were largely favourable when the first edition was published in book form.[8] In his contribution to a series of articles published in *Fraser's* protesting against the fictional romanticizing of crime, Thackeray groups Dickens with the Newgate novelists on the grounds that his portrayal of low-life villainy is caricatured and therefore unrealistic:

We (that is, the middling classes) have been favoured of late with a great number of descriptions of our betters, and of the society which they keep; and have had also, from one or two popular authors, many facetious accounts of the ways of life of our inferiors. There is in some of these histories more fun—in all, more fancy and romance—than are ordinarily found in humble life; and we recommend the admirer of such scenes, if he would have an accurate notion of them, to obtain his knowledge at the fountain-head, and trust more to the people's description of themselves, than to Bulwer's ingenious inconsistencies, and Dickens's startling, pleasing, unnatural caricatures.[9]

[8] Hollingsworth, *The Newgate Novel*, 126; Chittick, *Dickens and the 1830s*, 127. See also Kathryn Chittick, *The Critical Reception of Charles Dickens, 1833–1841* (New York: Garland, 1989).
[9] 'Horae Catnachianae', 407.

The rationale behind Thackeray's criticisms of *Oliver Twist* seems to be that because Dickens's criminals are unrealistic (in style and conception), they are therefore immoral. Dickens's preface to the third edition of *Oliver Twist* shows that he had taken such criticisms very much to heart; here he stresses the fidelity and 'truth' of his representation of low life, pitting his own writing against 'Romance' in a manner unusual for Dickens.[10] We are after all talking about the author of *Hard Times*, the writer whose style constantly evokes 'the romantic side of familiar things' (to quote the preface to *Bleak House* (1852–3), p. xiv); from the epigraph to *Sketches by Boz* to the late essay 'The Spirit of Fiction',[11] Dickens demonstrates a sophisticated awareness of the relationship between reality and fiction, evincing indeed a (pre-) 'postmodernist' consciousness that reality itself can be a fictional construct.

The preface is best understood as a piece of literary propaganda in a local critical debate. Newgate novelists and critics alike were grappling semi-consciously with the phantasmic concept that was to become 'realism' before the term was current in literary criticism, opposing it to the term 'romance'. On the most obvious level, the critical obsession with the relationship between the romantic and the real which surfaced in the 1830s and continued unabated for much of the period is an aesthetic debate, an attempt to define and delineate the powerful new genre, the novel.[12] The fact that controversy surrounded the Newgate novels at all is perhaps surprising when one considers that critics on all sides seemed to adhere to Thackeray's aesthetic rationale; put simply, that realistic fictional representations are 'good' while romantic representations are 'bad'. The obvious conclusion, therefore, is that while most writers at the time agreed that reality in the novel was a good thing, there was severe disagreement about the nature of reality itself. This is perhaps unsurprising considering the shockwaves that were still being felt from the French Revolution and the war with France (1793–1815) and the radical social and political changes which occurred in the 1830s—changes in

---

[10] See Introduction and Chapter 2 above for more on Dickens's attitude to 'romance' and high Romanticism.

[11] *AYR* 18 (27 July 1867), 118–20 (p. 119).

[12] See Lyn Pykett's article 'The Real versus the Ideal: Theories of Fiction in Periodicals, 1850–1870', *Victorian Periodicals Review*, 15 (1982), 63–74, for a well-researched account of the critical debate between realists and idealists at the mid-century; Pykett argues correctly that their views were much more complex and less oppositional than literary history has subsequently assumed.

the legal system which transformed Britain from a punitive to a 'disciplined' society, to use Foucauldian terminology, the Chartist movement, and of course the 1832 Reform Bill. 'Modernity', it can be argued, had begun.[13]

In 1837, the year that *Oliver Twist* appeared and Victoria came to the throne, the country was also in the midst of a cultural revolution quieter perhaps than the political and industrial revolutions afoot, but no less formative in the development of a 'modern' state. Literacy was increasing and developments in the publishing trade meant that books and newspapers were expanding their readership, moving further down the social ladder in the early Victorian period than ever before so that they 'began to reach the same class which the Reform Bill enfranchised'.[14] The availability of cheap fiction imprints, the dramatic proliferation in the number of cheaper literary journals in circulation, and the increasing tendency to serialize novels in periodical form (which surprisingly worked out cheaper for the 'consumer')[15] meant that 'the democratization of politics was not only reported but reflected in the press',[16] in the words of Kathryn Chittick. The popularity of penny dreadfuls, cheap weeklies, and the practice of 'extracting' and serialization in newspapers all played their part in forcing book prices down, leading to a broader readership, a trend which continued until 1850. Dickens's novels were, of course, formed by, and formative in, these crucial changes in the distribution of cultural capital. Though serialization in newspapers

[13] Michel Foucault's work sees the 'modern' period as rooted in the Enlightenment but actually arising from a self-consciously critical questioning of enlightenment values first performed by Kant in his essay 'Was ist Aufklärung?' (1784). Rejecting a positivist view of history, Foucault often refers to the modern period in necessarily vague terms as encompassing the last two centuries and originating at the turn of the 18th and 19th centuries. He is more precise when dating 'modernity'; Kant's 'Was ist Aufklärung?' is for Foucault 'a point of departure: the outline of what one might call the attitude of modernity'; 'modernity', he defines 'rather as an attitude than as a period of history', an attitude encapsulated by the 19th-century writer Baudelaire. See Foucault, 'What is Enlightenment?', in *The Foucault Reader*, ed. Paul Rabinow (Harmondsworth: Penguin, 1984), 32–50 (pp. 38–9).

Like Foucault, Isobel Armstrong identifies the 'modern' period with the emergence of a particular attitude rather than with specific historical events (although of course the two are related). For Armstrong, Victorian poets were the first writers to think of themselves as 'modern' and 'to be "new", or "modern" or "post-Romantic" was to confront and self-consciously to conceptualise *as* new elements that are still perceived as constitutive forms of our own condition'—*Victorian Poetry*, 3.

[14] Elliott Engell and Margaret F. King, *The Victorian Novel before Victoria: British Fiction during the Reign of William IV, 1830–37* (London: Macmillan, 1984), 5.

[15] Ibid. 29–33.

[16] Chittick, *Dickens and the 1830s*, 24.

was never as prominent in Britain as in France, many of Dickens's *Sketches by Boz* were originally published (and almost simultaneously 'extracted') in newspapers (1834–5) and, with his later novels, played a major role in the popularizing of fiction and newspapers.

These profound changes in communication systems and cultural ownership caused as many anxieties in the early Victorian period as the revolution in information technology has caused in our own. Indeed, in an eerie echo of now-common complaints about the power of the press, Edward Bulwer complains in 'A Word to the Public' (1847), 'The essential characteristic of this age and land is *publicity*.'[17] Victorians were encountering ideological and ethical problems which the modern mass media has made all too familiar; arguably, they were witnessing the beginnings of that very mass media. The story of the Newgate novel is inextricably entangled with the history of the mass media because the stories it related were 'sensationally popular' at a crucial juncture in the history of popular culture. It could no longer be assumed that popular culture was an uncomplicated expression of the tastes and values of the populace as the machinery and capitalist economic dynamics of modern 'mass culture' were emerging.

Bulwer's attack on the press on which he depended for his popularity suggests his own deep ambivalence about his popularity and, more importantly, the ambiguous literary status of the novel at a time when the Newgate controversy gave it such cultural centrality. The fact that the rise of the novel as a genre shadows the political and economic rise of the middle class has been securely established by Ian Watt and, more recently, Nancy Armstrong.[18] It is worth reminding ourselves, however, that neither the novel nor the middle class was as established when Dickens began *Oliver Twist* as blanket accounts of literary history sometimes lead us to believe. In the early 1830s, for example, reviews of biography, criticism, and non-fiction prose (not to mention the usual suspects, poetry and drama) were all included in the 'Literature' columns of newspapers, while fiction was all included under the headings 'Magazine Day' or 'Miscellaneous'.[19] Indeed, Chittick makes the valuable point that *The Pickwick Papers* (1836–7)

[17] Repr. in *Lucretia* (1846), in John (ed.), *Cult Criminals*, 297–334 (p. 314).
[18] Ian Watt, *The Rise of the Novel: Studies in Defoe, Richardson and Fielding* (Berkeley and Los Angeles: University of California Press, 1957), Armstrong, *Desire and Domestic Fiction*. Armstrong's work discusses the novel and the middle class in terms of the discourse of sexuality.
[19] Chittick, *Dickens and the 1830s*, p. x.

and *Oliver Twist* were not originally conceived as novels, but as a 'periodical' in the case of the former, and a 'serial' in the case of the latter.[20]

The immense popularity of the Newgate novels and the burgeoning media which allowed them to reach a wider audience than ever before no doubt helps to account for the revolutionary rise of the novel genre up the literary hierarchy. Popularity alone, however, would not be enough to alter the generic status quo in this way, as the history of the early Victorian theatre makes clear. Stage melodrama, for example, was also hugely popular and undoubtedly increased the cultural impact of Newgate stories with its many adaptations of Newgate fiction for literate and illiterate alike.[21] The popularity of these plays did nothing to rescue the reputation of the theatre; it rather aroused anxieties ostensibly about the 'quality' and moral influence of these plays. In reality, however, the fact that melodramas in working-class theatres could not be properly policed was of major concern. Though much theatre criticism emphasizes the conservatism of the melodrama which was so popular at this time, the very presence of the working classes in the theatres in unprecedented numbers to watch plays which were often overtly political was a cause of real anxiety for elements of the political and theatrical establishments. In the end, the 'legitimate' theatres survived by incorporating melodrama into their programmes. It is possible to see this U-turn on the part of the legitimate theatres as either a conservative act of cultural appropriation by the bourgeoisie or an instance of subversive upward mobility on the part of the working class's favoured mode of entertainment, melodrama. Indeed, if we consider the cultural history and dissemination of the Newgate biographies of criminals like Dick Turpin, Eugene Aram, and Jack Sheppard, it is again possible to trace either a pattern of appropriation whereby oral narratives are eventually incorporated—via 'street literature' and *The Newgate Calendar*—into the bourgeois Victorian novel, or a process by which street culture forces itself, radically and subversively, into the Victorian drawing-room.

A genuinely popular art form which aims to educate the literati and layperson alike is obviously a formidable tool of power. Indeed, in many ways, the Newgate controversy is all about power—in

---

[20] Chittick, *Dickens and the 1830s*, 64, 87.
[21] See Chapter 2 above. Hollingsworth's *The Newgate Novel* contains details of dramatizations of all the Newgate novels.

particular, the power of fictional representations of reality and, perhaps more importantly, popular culture. This fact was not lost on the participants who had none of the coyness of the modern liberal in a television age about the 'power' of literature. The Newgate controversy brought home the power of the novel with such force that the Newgate novelists were fully conscious of the power at their disposal—none more so than Dickens.

Oliver Twist is alone among the Newgate novels in analysing the role of the storyteller, entertainer, or purveyor of fictions in the power dynamics of 1830s Britain. For *Oliver Twist* offers a sustained self-reflexive exploration of both Newgate fiction and the function of the entertainer in social structures of oppression.[22] Crucial in this investigation is the relationship between 'reality' and fiction, and the role of each in the construction of the other. Contrary to the propagandist 1841 preface, the 'realism' of the novel (in the sense of its photographic truth-to-life) is largely irrelevant to Dickens's ideological and moral scheme in *Oliver Twist*. The most sophisticated layer of commentary depends, not on its exact representation of life, but on its self-referential, textual investigation of the ideological and moral complexity of the relationship between life and fiction.

Fagin is central to this critique in so far as he possesses an acute understanding of this complexity and of the way fictions can be manipulated to achieve one's purposes—i.e. to achieve power. Fagin's cynical deconstruction of life/fiction boundaries is compelling precisely because his construction as a character derives from a similarly sophisticated play with the same boundaries. Though based on real-life prototype Ikey Solomons, the character of Fagin obviously borrows heavily from the stereotype of the stage Jew and the reader's response to Fagin relies on his or her recognition of, and openness to, well-worn theatrical, literary (and racist) conventions.[23] Thus, to reapply Roland Barthes's term, the 'reality effect' created by the character/caricature of Fagin is highly dependent on the reader's knowledge of the medium of fiction from the beginning.[24]

[22] Joseph Litvak's 'Bad Scene: *Oliver Twist* and the Pathology of Entertainment', *Dickens Studies Annual*, 26 (1998), 33–49, is one of the few critical attempts I have encountered to analyse both Dickens's ambivalence about entertainment and the ideological implications of the way that entertainment is figured in the novels.

[23] See for example M. J. Landa, *The Jew in Drama* (London: King, 1926), Lauriat Lane Jr., 'Dickens's Archetypal Jew', *PMLA* 73 (1958), 94–100. See also Litvak's 'Bad Scene' on Dickens's anti-Semitism.

[24] Barthes's essay 'The Reality Effect' is reprinted in Furst (ed.), *Realism*, 135–41, from

It is through Fagin's relationship with the Artful Dodger and Charley Bates, above all, that Dickens answers the accusations that were to be levelled at him in the Newgate debate. The Artful Dodger and Charley Bates can be seen as fictional representations of the kind of boys investigated in the 1852 House of Commons inquiry into 'the situation of Criminal and Destitute Juveniles' who blamed their corruption on stage adaptations of Newgate novels. Bates and the Dodger are also the only characters in *Oliver Twist* who appear to be *overtly* attractive criminals in the same way as Robin Hood or the protagonists of the contemporary Newgate novels. They are thus crucial to Dickens in his textualized critique of Newgate fiction on two basic levels.

But to return to Fagin. Fagin is conscious from the outset that fiction, drama, and comic entertainment have the power to corrupt. There are six instances that I wish to examine of Fagin playing a key role in Dickens's self-reflexive analysis of the Newgate controversy. First, in chapter 9, he 'directs' a dramatic representation of pickpocketing, an inverted morality play performed by the Artful Dodger and Charley Bates, which Oliver perceives as 'a very curious and uncommon game' (p. 54). In chapter 18, he watches behind the scenes as the Dodger, beer and tobacco in hand—believing himself to be the incarnation of 'romance and enthusiasm' (p. 116)—uses the capitalist vocabulary of self-help to persuade Oliver of the greatness of the life of the thief: 'Why, where's your spirit? Don't you take any pride out of yourself? Would you go and be dependent on your friends?' Then the young criminals enact two 'pantomimic represen-tation[s]', one of 'a handful of shillings and halfpence', signifying a 'jolly life', and the other, Master Bates's party piece, of the gibbet. Money is thus made to seem attractive and immediate, while death by hanging is presented comically, thereby anaesthetizing its force as a real threat to life. The Dodger finally attempts to invert Oliver's moral values by telling him that he's been 'brought up bad' and that if he does not steal handkerchiefs and watches, 'some other cove will'. At this climactic moment, Fagin as director enters, advising Oliver to 'take the Dodger's word for it. [. . .] He understands the catechism of his trade' (chapter 18, p. 118).

When these attempts fail, Fagin tells Oliver comic tales, oral narratives about crime that make Oliver laugh 'heartily [. . .] in spite of his

Tzvetan Todorov (ed.), *French Literary Theory Today*, trans. R. Carter (New York: Cambridge University Press, 1982), 11–17.

better feelings'. They are the sugar to make the poison go down. The text makes explicit Fagin's consciousness of what we can call, literally, the arts of corruption:

In short, the wily old Jew had the boy in his toils; and, having prepared his mind, by solitude and gloom, to prefer any society to the companionship of his sad thoughts in such a dreary place, was now slowly instilling into his soul the poison which he hoped would blacken it, and change its hue for ever. (chapter 18, p. 120)

Fagin's intended master-stroke is to leave Oliver a volume which bears no accidental similarity to *The Newgate Calendar*. Fortunately and improbably, the book does not have the desired effect:

It was a history of the lives and trials of great criminals; and the pages were soiled and thumbed with use. Here he read of dreadful crimes that made the blood run cold [. . .]. The terrible descriptions were so real and vivid, that the sallow pages seemed to turn red with gore [. . .].
    In a paroxysm of fear, the boy closed the book, and thrust it from him. Then, falling upon his knees, he prayed Heaven to spare him from such deeds. (chapter 20, pp. 129–30)

The success that Fagin has had in persuading the Dodger and Bates of the 'greatness' of crime is everywhere evident, even in the Dodger's doodling; the Artful amuses himself 'by sketching a ground-plan of Newgate on the table with the piece of chalk' (chapter 25, p. 158). But perhaps the most striking illustration of Fagin's manipulation of the myth of romantic criminality comes when the Dodger is captured by the police. Bates is so distraught that his friend has been caught for stealing a snuff-box and not for something glamorous like robbing an old gentleman of his 'walables' that he comes very close to realizing that fame is rarely the lot of juvenile delinquents. What upsets him most is that the Dodger will not feature in *The Newgate Calendar.*

'Cause it isn't on the rec-ord, is it? [. . .] 'cause it won't come out in the 'dictment; 'cause nobody will ever know half of what he was. How will he stand in the Newgate Calendar? P'raps not be there at all. Oh, my eye, wot a blow it is! (chapter 43, p. 295)

Fagin persuades Charley, however, that newspaper reports of the criminal trials will make the Dodger's name, acting out the court-room scene so brilliantly that Charley eventually sees his friend's capture as 'a game! a regular game!' (chapter 43, p. 296).

When J. Hillis Miller wrote his influential essay 'The Fiction of Realism' (1971), it was important to draw attention to the self-reflexive elements of *Oliver Twist* which had hitherto been neglected by approaches to the novel which privileged 'content' over 'form' and accredited little sophistication—aesthetic or ideological—to the young Dickens. However, Miller's vision of Dickens's universe, like much deconstructive work of its era, is nihilistic and perhaps slightly narcissistic; for Miller, Dickens's texts foreground the interpretative process which underpins critical and social activity, a process which 'creates illusion out of illusion and the appearance of reality out of illusion, in a play of language without beginning, end, or extra linguistic foundation'.[25] Miller uses his findings to support his epigraph, taken from *Sketches by Boz*, 'the illusion was reality itself'.[26] His wilful blind spot is that throughout the essay he takes the word 'illusion' to mean emptiness or hollowness, whereas, in Dickens's fiction, theatrical and fictional 'illusions' are often intensely meaningful and 'real' to those engaged with them. And, perhaps more importantly, Dickens's novels present not an anarchic free play of illusions, but a careful positioning of key discourses in which fictions, both textual and 'real', inevitably exert ideological (and moral) influence and are always part of a material chain of cause and effect. In this sense, they have much in common with Bentham's theory of fictions, which emphasizes the double nature of verbal fictions, which are both illusory and real.[27] Dickens exploits both possible meanings of the epigraph of *Sketches by Boz*, 'the illusion was reality itself'.

Since Miller's pioneering work, a number of critics have tried to take his analysis of the self-reflexive elements of *Oliver Twist* further, maintaining as I do that, in Steven Connor's words, 'there are ways of taking self-reflexivity seriously without drowning every instance of it in an undifferentiated ocean of textuality'.[28] D. A. Miller, Robert Tracy, Steven Connor himself, and Stephen Bernstein, for example, all mention Newgate narratives particularly and explore Dickens's textual play with narratives and fictions more generally in their

---

[25] See p. 20 above.

[26] From 'The Drunkard's Death', *SB*, p. 493.

[27] See Bentham's *Theory of Fictions*, ed. C. K. Ogden (London: Kegan Paul, 1932); see also Isobel Armstrong's fascinating discussion of Bentham's theory in relation to Browning in *Victorian Poetry*, 146, 148–54.

[28] ' "They're All in One Story": Public and Private Narratives in *Oliver Twist*', *Dickensian*, 85 (1989), 3–16 (p. 3).

analyses of *Oliver Twist*.[29] However, none of these places this discussion within the framework of the social and cultural shifts of the
1830s, in particular the beginnings of mass culture. Historicizing the
text from this perspective brings an important textual detail into
focus. Dickens is not just interrogating the nature of narratives and
fictions in *Oliver Twist* (as some of this analysis of self-reflexivity,
inspired by post-structuralism, is inclined to suggest); he is as concerned with the power of a variety of specifically *popular* cultural
forms. When the novel self-reflexively alludes to the Newgate debate,
Newgate myths are nearly always disseminated via cultural vehicles
that are accessible to the lowbrow and highbrow alike. In the first
example discussed above, Fagin directs an inverted morality play in
which the Artful Dodger and Charley Bates attempt to teach Oliver
how to pick pockets. In the second, the two boys act out a 'pantomimic representation' of the joys of money on the one hand and the
horrors of the gibbet on the other; next, Fagin resorts to oral narrative, telling comic tales; then the Dodger sketches Newgate on a
table-cloth; and when Master Bates is on the point of realizing that
the romance of crime is a myth, Fagin draws on a variety of popular
cultural modes, acting, narrating, conjuring up the Dodger's performances in the law court (a favourite source of entertainment for
the Victorians) and the newspaper reports of the same, to convince
Master Bates of the Dodger's inevitable honour and fame.

It is conspicuous that the least visibly effective of all these attempts
to corrupt using Newgate myths is the famous instance when Oliver
is given the volume resembling *The Newgate Calendar*. When faced with
the written word in the physically substantial form of a book, Oliver
takes the book almost as a warning of its own power and falls down
on his knees to pray. When indoctrination is disguised as pleasure, or
entertainment, by contrast, Oliver is far more susceptible: he watches
the pickpocketing demonstration attentively as a 'curious and
uncommon game'. The same discourse of play is repeated when
Charley Bates, after various impersonations and narratives of the
Dodger's heroism from Fagin, also sees his friend's capture and
imminent court appearance as a game. Fagin's comic tales of crime
come closest to corrupting Oliver, making him laugh 'heartily [. . .]

---

[29] Miller, *The Novel and the Police*, Robert Tracy, ' "The Old Story" and Inside Stories:
Modish Fiction and Fictional Modes in *Oliver Twist*', *Dickens Studies Annual*, 17 (1988), 1–33,
and Robert Bernstein, '*Oliver* Twisted: Narrative and Doubling in Dickens's Second
Novel', *Victorian Newsletter*, 79 (1991), 27–34.

in spite of all his better feelings'. Even the Dodger, a cooler customer than Oliver and Bates, '*amuses* himself' (italics mine) by drawing a plan of Newgate on the table. It is true that what distresses Bates initially when the Dodger is captured is that there will not be a formal, written 'record' of his achievements in *The Newgate Calendar*; it is also true that Fagin's conviction that the newspapers will report on the trial heartens Charley. But what is significant is that it is Fagin's humour and his abilities as an actor and storyteller which move Charley from tears to laughter; what we could call the 'illegitimization' of the written word finally proves incidental.

Elaine Hadley is one critic whose analysis of *Oliver Twist*'s self-reflexivity is informed by the contemporary climate. In *Melodramatic Tactics*, she argues that Dickens harnesses the self-reflexive aspects of *Oliver Twist* to a consideration of the novel as an instrument of privatization; the novel, according to this reading, becomes 'a villainous figure' in an 'irresolvable conflict between melodrama and the novel that shapes Dickens's own larger narrative in *Oliver Twist*'.[30] Hadley's theme is a rewarding one, but the logocentric perspective of her analysis shapes the melodramatic nature of her conclusions: privacy is not simply a malign force opposed by the 'good' force of publicity. Nor can the novel and melodrama be seen as irreconcilable opposites, melodrama presumably acting as a heroic figure, to adapt Hadley's discourse. *The Newgate Calendar* incident, for example, patently does not show that 'Left to itself, such a subject is subject to everything'.[31] Oliver is notably more vulnerable in company and to 'public' cultural forms which eschew the written word. If the novel is the object of ethical and political interrogation in *Oliver Twist*, so too are communal forms of cultural exchange.

If the text is read closely, what seems to be consistently at stake is the function of emotion and pleasure as tools of power: amusement, laughter, and play are the ultimate ideological vehicles. In the context of Newgate debate, this has several repercussions. First, the genres central to the Newgate controversy were romance and melodrama, both of which (and often the two combined) relied on emotion and pleasure for their popular appeal. Second, the potentiality and dangers of the mass market for culture which was emerging in the 1830s are under scrutiny. Dickens seems to be exploring theories that had been put forward by W. J. Fox in the radical *Monthly Repository* in the 1830s, about the possibilities for emotion,

[30] pp. 117, 119. [31] *Melodramatic Tactics*, 119.

pleasure, and also drama as democratic vehicles of communication which would prevent the divorce of intellectual from mass culture.[32] Fox was the editor of the radical, Benthamite paper the *True Sun*, for which Dickens worked in his early days as a journalist.[33] The question of the function of emotion and pleasure in the dynamics of mass culture also has acute relevance, of course, to Dickens's own art, whose enduring popularity and cultural centrality have remained in many ways inscrutable to academic enquiry. The main problem critics seem to have had from the 1830s to the present is in reconciling Dickens's accessibility with his 'greatness' as a novelist.

Dickens obviously felt strongly that art should be inclusive, and that art which was pleasurable, entertaining, and emotionally engaging would achieve this—essays like 'The Amusements of the People' and a novel like *Hard Times* prove this beyond doubt. However, his dislike of the exclusivity of the literary elite and his desire to be popular do not necessarily suggest a belief in a fully democratic art of the kind W. J. Fox seeks to define. The implicit relevance of Fagin's role as 'a generalized Newgate novelist'[34] to Dickens's own art is no accident. To Dickens, the storyteller is in a position of power; the comic entertainer who can manipulate the reader's emotions and evoke pleasure is all-powerful. This power is not necessarily a bad thing *per se* as long as (a perennial problem) power does not fall into the wrong hands; in the early Victorian period, when truths and realities seemed to be up for grabs, to sell your own reality convincingly was arguably a radical and proactive act from middle-class writers who had never before had such power. If you do not put your ideological spin on the world then, to quote the Artful Dodger, 'some other cove will'. From the perspective of author–reader dynamics then, for Dickens, inclusive art is not necessarily democratic.

That Dickens analyses power and the power of narratives and fictions self-reflexively is perhaps a predictable insight given the current obsession of postmodernism and post-structuralism with self-reflexivity, narratives, and fictions. In this intellectual climate, then, it is particularly important to remind ourselves first, exactly what kind of narrative Dickens was writing in *Oliver Twist*, and second, that narrative is not Dickens's only concern. Unusually, Dickens's

---

[32] See Armstrong, *Victorian Poetry*, for discussion of Fox's ideas.
[33] Peter Ackroyd, *Dickens* (London: Guild Publishing, 1990), 136–7.
[34] Tracy, ' "The Old Story" and Inside Stories', 20.

narrator, in one of the few critical interpolations in the whole of the
Dickens canon, goes to great lengths in *Oliver Twist* to define and
defend his novelistic practice. In the famous 'streaky bacon' passage
in chapter 17, Dickens cites 'good, murderous melodramas' as the
model for his own 'craft'. (He specifically does not use the term
'narrative').

IT is the custom on the stage: in all good, murderous melodramas: to present
the tragic and the comic scenes, in as regular alternation, as the layers of red
and white in a side of streaky, well-cured bacon. The hero sinks upon his
straw bed, weighed down by fetters and misfortunes; and, in the next scene,
his faithful but unconscious squire regales the audience with a comic song.
We behold, with throbbing bosoms, the heroine in the grasp of a proud and
ruthless baron: her virtue and her life alike in danger, drawing forth her
dagger to preserve the one at the cost of the other; and, just as our expectations are wrought up to the highest pitch, a whistle is heard: and we are
straightaway transported to the great hall of the castle. [. . .]
   Such changes appear absurd; but they are not so unnatural as they would
seem at first sight. The transitions in real life from well spread boards to
death-beds, and from mourning weeds to holiday garments, are not a whit
less startling; only, there, we are busy actors, instead of passive lookers-on,
which makes a vast difference. *The actors in the mimic life of the
theatre, are blind to violent transitions and abrupt impulses of passion or feeling, which,
presented before the eyes of mere spectators, are at once condemned as outrageous and preposterous.*
   As sudden shiftings of the scene, and rapid change of time and place, are
not only sanctioned in books by long usage, but are by many considered as
the great art of authorship: an author's skill in his craft being, by such critics,
chiefly estimated with relation to the dilemmas in which he leaves his
characters at the end of every chapter: this brief introduction to the present
one may perhaps be deemed unnecessary. If so, let it be considered a delicate intimation on the part of the historian that he is going back to the town
in which Oliver Twist is born. (*Oliver Twist*, chapter 17, pp. 105–6 (italics
mine))

Dickens's conception of novelistic progression is evidently quite
different from that of a diachronic, linear chain of events, or, for that
matter, the evolutionary *Bildungsroman* that is often assumed to be
Oliver's story; neither does this passage suggest a sophisticated play
with narratives. Oliver is an allegorical pawn in a paradoxical double
novel whose anti-narrative principle is as strong as its narrative
impulse. As the 'streaky bacon' passage makes clear, 'alternation',
'changes', 'violent transitions', and 'sudden shiftings' all potentially

disruptive of narrative flow, coexist with that very desire to forge narratives (or, to echo Dickens's own terminology, histories). Crucial to Dickens's defence of his method here is an emphasis on 'abrupt impulses of passion and feeling', natural to those experiencing the emotion, anti-naturalistic to those observing. But what I am chiefly interested in here is the attempt to educate the reader into a partly Brechtian understanding of the function of emotion in life, drama, and, by implication, the novel.

The central place of popular stage melodrama and its raw material, passion, in Dickens's conception and practice of the novel is aesthetically and ideologically fascinating in its implications. Like Barthes's 'doubly perverse' subject, Dickens manages to achieve the (for Barthes) barely conceivable, to combine the 'text of pleasure' with 'the text of bliss'.[35] To Dickens, emotion as an artistic and political tool can be used to disrupt narratives that reassure, to de-familiarize, and to fragment stories. Alternatively or simultaneously, it can do just the opposite, satisfying primitive, monopathic desires for wholeness. All depends on our angle of vision, whether we are immersed in, or watching, the passions. Interestingly and characteristically, Dickens's example of those immersed in passionate experience is taken from the theatre: they are 'actors in the mimic life of the theatre', a slippage which complicates any temptation we may have to paraphrase this passage thus: 'narrative distances; drama immerses.' The generic fluidity in Dickens's conception of the novel explains the comparative ease with which he can theorize and utilize the novel as a site of pleasure *and* bliss. For Barthes, bliss is non-verbal, but somehow textual and thus by definition beyond definition;[36] for Dickens, unfettered by Barthes's post-structuralist

[35] 'Text of pleasure: the text that contents, fills, grants euphoria; the text that comes from culture and does not break with it, is linked to a *comfortable* practice of reading. Text of bliss: the text that imposes a state of loss, the text that discomforts (perhaps to the point of a certain boredom), unsettles the reader's historical, cultural, psychological assumptions, the consistency of his tastes, values, memories, brings to a crisis his relationship with language.

Now the subject who keeps the two texts in his field and in his hands the reins of pleasure and bliss is an anachronistic subject, for he simultaneously and contradictorily participates in the profound hedonism of all culture (which permeates him quietly under cover of an art de vivre shared by the old books) and in the destruction of that culture: he enjoys the consistency of his selfhood (that is his pleasure) and seeks its loss (that is his bliss). He is a subject split twice over, doubly perverse.' Roland Barthes, *The Pleasure of the Text* (1973), trans. Richard Miller (Farrar, Strauss & Giroux, 1975; Oxford: Blackwell, 1990), p. 14.

[36] Barthes argues in *The Pleasure of the Text* that 'pleasure can be expressed in words: bliss cannot' and '*criticism always deals with the texts of pleasure, never the texts of bliss*' (p. 21).

privileging of the 'textual' over the theatrical, the source of 'bliss' is less abstract—it is the theatre, a genre he subjects to a process of Bakhtinian 'novelization'.[37]

The *Twist* passage has more profound resonances perhaps in relation to Raymond Williams's concept of 'structures of feeling'.[38] Williams's attempt to extend analysis of the nature and workings of ideology from focusing on 'impersonal' systems of thought to include 'personal' experience—and indeed to examine the relationship between the two—is notoriously difficult to pin down. However, what is relevant to the *Twist* passage is the distinction Williams makes between personal emotion—which to Williams is thought experienced in the present—and 'ideological systems of fixed generality', which our thought processes experience as past, static, and fixed. So-called 'personal' feeling is so powerful, Williams argues, that ideological systems are 'relatively powerless' against it. 'The basic error' of Marxism, Williams argues, is 'the reduction of the social to fixed forms'.[39] The *Twist* passage seems to understand that in order for an author to have 'influence' over the reader, ideology must be experienced as all-encompassing emotion; if it is not experienced as such, it appears 'outrageous and preposterous' and, as Williams suggests, ineffective.

The logical implication of this is, however, that detachment on the part of the reader may enable him or her to maintain the ability to analyse the text's ideologies. Such a detached reader is not, perhaps, the ideal reader Dickens had in mind, given his emphasis on the centrality of passion in aesthetic experience. If Dickens envisaged the perfect author–reader relationship as a marriage of equals, then perhaps the ideal reader, like the ideal author, would maintain the ability to immerse him- or herself in emotional experience and to detach him- or herself from the experience simultaneously. Interestingly, Dickens's description of acting in *The Frozen Deep* echoes the doubleness of the *Twist* passage, merging drama with the written word, public with private, and immersion with detachment, to evoke the ultimate aesthetic experience.[40] Dickens's account of acting as

---

[37] Bakhtin's theory of 'novelization' claims that the elasticity of the novel form 'infects' other genres—see p. 98 above. It can also be argued, of course, that the theatre 'infects' the novel in the *Twist* passage and in Dickens's fiction generally.

[38] See Raymond Williams, *Marxism and Literature* (Oxford: Oxford University Press, 1977; repr. 1986), 128–35.

[39] Ibid. 129.

[40] See p. 78 and p. 103 for a discussion of this same key passage.

'like writing a book in company [. . .] actual Truth without its pain' is uncannily similar to Barthes's conceptualization of an aesthetic of textual pleasure (which encompasses both pleasure and bliss): Barthes concludes *The Pleasure of the Text*, 'If it were possible to imagine an aesthetic of textual pleasure, it would have to include: writing aloud. [. . .] A certain art of singing can give an idea of this vocal writing; but since melody is dead, we may find it more easily today at the cinema.'[41] For an author like Dickens who wrote novels 'in character' and performed his own work publicly, such an aesthetic of 'textual' pleasure (as Barthes persists in calling it) was not theoretical but real.[42] Tellingly, however, while Barthes's aesthetic is theorized from the viewpoint of an audience member, Dickens's is centred on the 'Labourer in Art, alone'. The audience/reader participates in Dickens's aesthetic of pleasure in only a secondary role. Ultimate pleasure and the power which attends it are the labouring artist's— though the 'labourer in art', uncannily like a benevolent patron, includes the audience (on which he depends) in the experience.

To argue that emotion is central to Dickens's popular art and indeed the mechanics of popular culture is not then to say that his novels or the responses they are designed to elicit in the reader are straightforwardly or naively emotional. In the emotional economy of a Dickens novel, excess or release is inseparable from restraint— whether the restraint takes the form of the rigidly formulaic plot structures of melodrama, or the satirical or parodic narrative voice.[43] Isobel Armstrong's definition of the Victorian 'double poem' as positing a 'content' as well as a self-reflexive critique of that content is particularly useful here; the double poem is 'an expressive model and an epistemological model simultaneously'.[44] For me, Dickens's novels are extreme examples of the 'double novel', a monopathic, melo-dramatic, childlike world of emotions and pleasures, coexisting with an inherently divided self-reflexive critique of the same. Similarly, the impulse to forge narratives, or connected chains of events, coexists in Dickens with the anti-narrative, dramatic principle which celebrates the immediate pleasures of emotion and the body. In Dickens, doubleness does not take the form (as it does in Armstrong's concep-

---

[41] *The Pleasure of the Text*, 66–7.

[42] For his daughter Mamie's famous description of Dickens acting out his novels in front of a mirror, see van Amerongen, *The Actor in Dickens*, 256.

[43] See p. 106 above.

[44] Armstrong, *Victorian Poetry*, 13–14 (p. 13).

tion of the double poem) of struggle or even dialogue, simply that of
coexistence.

Armstrong argues that the Victorian poem was able to achieve its
doubleness only because Victorian poets were conscious of their
'secondary' position in Victorian mass culture.[45] Dickens disproves
the potentially elitist assumption that profundity of insight into one's
culture depends on being outside it. On the contrary, in *Oliver Twist*,
the interrogation of the potential of popular culture as a vehicle of
power, and indeed the infiltration of 'official' culture by popular
cultural modes, is enabled not simply by abstract intellectual self-
reflexivity, or endless narratives about narratives, but by his reliance
on the variety of cultural modes he analyses. For Dickens, these
are ideological and moral vehicles, as well as objects of intellectual
analysis or cultural enquiry.

[45] Armstrong, *Victorian Poetry*, 3.

6

Dickens and Dandyism:
Masking Interiority

In the words of Thomas Carlyle's *Sartor Resartus*, 'FIRST, touching Dandies, let us consider, with some scientific strictness, what a Dandy specially is'.[1] Carlyle's text declared the dandy to be

a Clothes-wearing Man, a Man whose trade, office and existence consists in the wearing of Clothes. Every faculty of his soul, spirit, purse, and person is heroically consecrated to this one object, the wearing of Clothes wisely and well: so that as others dress to live, he lives to dress.[2]

Edward Bulwer described the hero of his fashionable novel *Pelham; or, The Adventures of a Gentleman* (1828)—for many Victorians, including Carlyle, closely associated with the idea of dandyism—as: 'a personal combination of antitheses—a fop and a philosopher, a voluptuary and a moralist—a trifler in appearance, but rather one to whom trifles are instructive, than one to whom trifles are natural.'[3] The dandy became synonymous, for readers of *Fraser's Magazine*—which conducted a crusade against the novels of Bulwer Lytton—with the pathetic fop, the 'tailor-made' as opposed to the 'natural' gentleman.[4]

On the Continent, by contrast, French writers and socialites appreciated the potential inherent in the theatricality of the dandy pose. The curious combination of power and flexibility in the pose was appropriated variously as a symbol of aristocratic, bourgeois, or intellectual defiance. Baudelaire's lines—

---

[1] p. 207.
[2] Ibid.
[3] Preface to *Pelham*, 2nd edn., 3 vols. (London: Colburn, 1828), i. 5.
[4] William Maginn, 'Mr. Edward Lytton Bulwer's Novels; and Remarks on Novel-Writing', *Fraser's Magazine*, 1 (June 1830), 509–32 (p. 516).

Éternelle supériorité du Dandy.
Qu'est-ce que le Dandy?[5]

—portray the dandy as an elevated spiritual being, whilst his writings as a whole explore the complexity of the relationship between dandyism, aestheticism and morality. In Britain, fearful respect for the dandy was implied rather than admitted until Oscar Wilde fully explored the consequences of presenting the self as a work of art— implied, that is, by the constant critical contempt poured on the apparently laughable fashion-victim. Even in the Regency period, which both spawned and celebrated the dandy, dandyism was mocked. In Pierce Egan's *Life in London*, for example, Jerry says of Dick Trifle, 'He is the completest *Dandy* I ever saw, [. . .] no use [. . .] except as a mark for RIDICULE to *shoot* at!' (book 2, chapter 5, p. 309).

Twentieth-century critics rightly recognized that the Victorians, on the whole, protested too much about the irrelevance and triviality of the dandy. Ellen Moers's definition of the type in her seminal work *The Dandy* suggests some of the characteristics which the Victorians found problematic about the type. The dandy is

a creature perfect in externals and careless of anything below the surface, a man dedicated solely to his own perfection through a ritual of taste. The epitome of selfish irresponsibility, he was ideally free of all human commitments that conflict with taste: passions, moralities, ambitions, politics or occupations.[6]

Steven Marcus, on the other hand, suggests that the dandy is 'a parody of the self as a work of art—displaying the outward form which covers an inward nullity', 'a man gone dead inside, a man wholly externalised, [. . .] a man who has split himself in two and then cut himself off from his inner being by a denial that he is anything but pure surface'.[7] For William R. Harvey, Dickens's dandies are grouped with his fops, but even so are 'characterized by ennui, restlessness, unrealized potential, and uncertainty of purpose'.[8] Robin Gilmour argues that 'the contemporary phenomenon of the

---

[5] Quoted by Ellen Moers as the epigraph for chapter 12 of *The Dandy* (London: Secker & Warburg, 1960), 271. Moers's source, Charles Asselineau's *Charles Baudelaire: sa vie et son œuvre* (Paris: Lemerre, 1869), cites Baudelaire's words as 'Supériorité du dandy. Qu'est-ce que le Dandy?' (pp. 45–6).

[6] p. 13.

[7] *Dickens: From Pickwick to Dombey*, 229, 230.

[8] 'Charles Dickens and the Byronic Hero', *Nineteenth-Century Fiction*, 24 (1969), 305–16 (p. 307).

dandy' was 'a manifestation of the continuing prestige of "exclusive" style in an age of burgeoning democracy'.[9] More recently, Jessica R. Feldman has claimed that 'as precursors of the "post-modern"', dandies project the idea of the body as 'a system of signification, a cultural construct'—to the extent that even the idea of biological sex is undermined.[10] James Eli Adams's influential *Dandies and Desert Saints: Styles of Masculinity* is more moderate, highlighting the performative nature of dominant models of masculinity and the perceived lack of manliness in intellectual labour. Interestingly for our purposes, he argues (among other things) that 'the antagonism between the hero and the dandy [. . .] operates as one of the founding symbolic oppositions of Victorian discourse'.[11]

The variety of definitions of the dandy paradoxically suggests the impossibility of definition. The dandy is crucial to this study for a variety of reasons which should by now readily suggest themselves. The dandy is the cannibalistic individual perfected. He—and the dandy is invariably male—is the paradoxical personification of passionlessness, of humanity without interiority. He values aesthetic taste above all. He flaunts the possibility that selfhood is a fictional construct, recreating himself as a work of art. The idea of a man transforming himself into an art work—and an art work, moreover, suggestive of passionlessness—has obvious self-reflexive implications for Dickens's own writing, which is fascinated not only by the interaction between people and things, but by emotional extremes.[12] Viewed as an art work, the dandy personifies the art of effect, yet an 'effect' which is culturally and socially revered.

He figures directly and prominently in nineteenth-century stage melodramas: it is not unusual that the passionless villain of domestic melodrama is a dandy, and the later 'West End villain' is characterized by his fastidiousness about his appearance. The relevance of the dandy to melodrama extends beyond his function in individual melodramas, however. The dandy is the symbol of melodrama's inversion. His self-deification is an overt affront to the notions of community or social responsibility. Where melodrama advocates

---

[9] 'Between Two Worlds: Aristocracy and Gentility in *Nicholas Nickleby*', *Dickens Quarterly*, 5 (1988), 110–18 (p. 114).

[10] *Gender on the Divide: The Dandy in Modernist Literature* (Ithaca, NY: Cornell University Press, 1993), 271, 270.

[11] (Ithaca, NY: Cornell University Press, 1995), 21.

[12] See Chapter 8 below for an analysis of the (deviant) women in Dickens who are presented, or present themselves, as works of art.

transparency of self-projection, the dandy flaunts his own super-ficiality; paradoxically, this celebration of superficiality demands a perpetual repressive performativity. He is an actor to the core who takes literally the idea of the world as a stage. His apparent freedom from emotion or interiority functions as a sign not only of autonomy but of social and cultural exclusivity antithetical to the melodramatic vision; he does not want to be understood by others, nor does he want to feel for them. He exaggerates the logic of 'civilized' society—that to be civilized, one must distance oneself from passions which partake of barbarism. Suggesting a world of pure surface and symbol, he radically problematizes not only the ethos of melodrama, but some of the founding ideologies of Victorian society and culture.

One of the most fraught ideological debates in the Victorian period concerns the idea of the gentleman. Dickens's dandies often focus his investigation of the relationship between true and false gentility, and between gentility and villainy. They centre his exploration of the dehumanizing forces at work in Victorian society and the self. Although Dickens often explores the class conflicts of domestic melodrama, far from simplistically associating gentility with villainy, Dickens's novels, along with Thackeray's, make perhaps the most important fictional contribution to the redefinition of the gentleman. Dickens looks at the question from all angles, investigating the grey area between the middle classes and the aristocracy, the relationship between 'rank' and class, the importance of money and the work ethic in the changing industrialized society, the relationship between manners and morals in a socially mobile society, and the link stressed by *Fraser's Magazine* between the criminality of the rich and the poor (discussed later in this chapter). Again, on a more abstract level, he perceived that an appearance of gentility often demanded repression of the emotional life, and, like Carlyle, he understood the potential power of clothes in a world of social role-playing.

It is not, however, the principal aim of this chapter to examine Victorian ideas about the gentleman—a task which has been admirably carried out by Robin Gilmour in *The Idea of the Gentleman in the Victorian Novel*.[13] I am interested in gentlemen, first and foremost, when they are villains, and this in itself is problematic, for in Dickens's writing, a villain cannot be a true gentleman. A gentleman stops being a gentleman, for Dickens, when the appearance of

[13] (London: Allen & Unwin, 1981).

gentility is more important than the moral elevation that should ideally characterize the gentleman; that is, a gentleman becomes a villain when gentility ceases to be an end in itself and becomes the means to attain power, status, and money—in other words, the means to gratify the self. In Dickens's novels, the figure of the dandy plays a crucial part in what could be called the de-moralizing of the term gentleman: Dickens investigates the processes by which the term gentleman becomes divorced from its original moral signification and employed in the nineteenth century largely as an indicator of social status. The dandy often sits uneasily on the cusp between villainy and gentility. Dickens's dandies are haunted by the ghost of Lord Chesterfield. They suggest that manners and morals are not always synonymous, and that a gentleman on the outside may not be a gentle man on the inside; or, to echo the words of Lord Chesterfield himself, that: 'A man of the world must, like the Chameleon, be able to take every different hue; which is by no means a criminal or abject, but a necessary complaisance; for it relates only to manners, and not to morals.'[14] The dandy is ideally a passionless person, an actor to the core, a living role. The recurrence of such figures in Dickens's fiction—where the presented forms of life imitate the stage as often as the stage mimics life—suggests both his fascination with the possibility of such a self-less human being, and his concern about the larger causes and effects of dandyism.

SOCIETY AS STAGE: VICTORIAN SELF-FASHIONING

In 'London Recreations', one of the early *Sketches by Boz*, Dickens's narrator offers the following piece of social commentary:

THE wish of persons in the humbler classes of life, to ape the manners and customs of those whom fortune has placed above them, is often the subject of remark, and not unfrequently of complaint. The inclination may, and no doubt does, exist to a great extent, among the small gentility—the would-be aristocrats—of the middle-classes. Tradesmen and clerks, with fashionable novel-reading families, and circulating-library-subscribing daughters, get up small assemblies in imitation of Almack's, and promenade the dingy 'large room' of some second-rate hotel with as much complacency as the enviable few who are privileged to exhibit their magnificence in that exclusive haunt

---

[14] *Lord Chesterfield's Letters* (1774), ed. David Roberts (Oxford: Oxford University Press, 1992), 106 (19 Oct. 1748).

of fashion and foolery. Aspiring young ladies, who read flaming accounts of some 'fancy fair in high life', suddenly grow desperately charitable [. . .] With the exception of these classes of society, however, and a few weak and insignificant persons, we do not think the attempt at imitation to which we have alluded, prevails in any great degree. (p. 92)

In this description, the narrator consciously attempts to put 'the small gentility [. . .] of the middle classes' in their place, by emphasizing that they represent just one section of society (and, of course, by using such adjectives as 'small', 'would-be', 'dingy', 'aspiring', and 'weak' to describe them). But his analysis is disingenuous because the point he is making about the upwardly mobile Victorian 'small gentility' is that the social impact of their habitual imitation is far from 'small'. The imitation which they practised for the sake of achieving a degree of social mobility was to change not just their own position but the whole fabric of society, so that as a class they had no fixed place to which the narrator of the sketch—the creature of a young, aspiring journalist—could conveniently marginalize them.[15]

In Dickens's novels, the middle classes are not relegated to the wings but usually take centre stage. The theatrical metaphor is not gratuitous here, for Dickens's fictions consistently demonstrate that an individual's powers of imitation are the most effective means of social advancement available to him or her. His writing is thus, to an extent, in tune with Victorian 'self-help' literature—epitomized by Samuel Smiles's *Self-Help* (1859)—and the 'self-culture' which generated and was generated by the literature. But there is one important difference (amongst many) between Dickens's novels and self-help literature, in that Dickens is conscious of the dangers of a society founded on imitation and regard for self. Dickens's sense of the corruption which must be inherent in a society that thinks it is a theatre is nowhere more acute than in *Nicholas Nickleby*. For the most part, the much-abused 'theatricality' of the novel is used consciously as a sophisticated tool of social and moral investigation. Crummles's theatre is integral to the scheme of the novel at all levels, acting as a mirror to the *theatrum mundi* throughout; the behaviour of the professional actors is used to parallel, parody, and echo that of the social role-players, usually to the discredit of the latter.[16]

[15] There is also another sleight of hand in this passage which is significant in relation to my later analysis of *NN*. The narrator mocks the 'small gentility' for imitating their betters, and then promptly implies that their so-called betters are in an important—moral—sense no better than those imitating them anyway; their world is one of 'fashion and foolery'.

[16] For recent accounts of the significance of theatricality in *NN*, see Glavin, *After Dickens*,

Just as Dickens's famous 'streaky bacon' passage in *Oliver Twist* (chapter 17, pp. 105–6) argues that melodrama is no more exaggerated than life, in *Nicholas Nickleby*, Dickens observes that the appearance of those on the stage of society is as absurdly 'artificial' as that of the actors in Crummles's illegitimate theatre. Here the analogy is implied through the parallel experiences of Nicholas and Kate, rather than stated by the narrator. When Nicholas sees the Crummleses in full make-up and costume, he is shocked because he has already seen how they look offstage: 'Here all the people were so much changed, that he scarcely knew them. False hair, false colour, false calves, false muscles—they had become different beings' (chapter 24, p. 302). Meanwhile, as a dressmaker, Kate is working behind the stage of society, but she still gets a rude awakening when she makes her own debut. At Ralph's party, she discovers to her consternation that the aristocrats there do not understand honest expressions of feeling, or sincerity, but assume that all behaviour is feigned. When Sir Mulberry Hawk finds her reading a book, for example, he exclaims, 'What a delightful studiousness! [. . .] Was it real, now, or only to display the eyelashes?' (chapter 19, p. 240). This is just a taste of things to come, for when Kate appeals, 'If you have one spark of gentlemanly feeling remaining, you will leave me instantly', Sir Mulberry (reminding us of Mrs Skewton) ironically replies: 'why will you keep up this appearance of excessive rigour, my sweet creature? Now, be more natural—my dear Miss Nickleby, be more natural—do' (chapter 19, p. 241). The aristocrat thus assumes that Kate's show of emotion is as artificial as the Crummleses' histrionic shows of feeling. Their exaggerated words and gestures are mocked by Dickens and Phiz's accompanying illustration—entitled 'Theatrical emotion of Mr. Crummles' (chapter 30)—when Nicholas leaves the company. The Crummleses express emotion similarly on- and offstage, but this does not necessarily mean that they are insincere. Throughout the novel, Dickens implies that it is not possible to assume that histrionic displays of emotion are less genuine than quieter expressions of feeling.

But Kate's appeal to Hawk's 'gentlemanly feeling' is obviously misplaced in a novel which is, on the surface, as absolutely anti-

98–101, Tore Rem, 'Playing around with Melodrama: The Crummles Episodes in *Nicholas Nickleby*', *Dickens Studies Annual*, 25 (1996), 267–85, and Paul Schlicke, 'Crummles Once More', *Dickensian*, 86 (1990), 2–16, who argues against the theory that the theatrical episodes in *NN* are thematically significant.

aristocratic as any domestic melodrama. The overall attitude which
seems to emerge towards the aristocracy can be summed up by the
amusing conversational exchange between Miss Petowker and Mr
Lillyvick: ' "What do you call it, when Lords break off door-knockers
and beat policemen, and play at coaches with other people's money,
and all that sort of thing?" "Aristocratic?" suggested the collector'
(chapter 15, p. 184). As a professional actress, Miss Petowker's notions
are moulded by the stage, but the novel as a whole suggests that there
is no clear-cut distinction between society and the stage. Sir
Mulberry Hawk thus apes the behaviour of the aristocratic villain of
domestic melodrama. It is therefore doubly ironic that Kate appeals
to Sir Mulberry Hawk's 'gentlemanly feeling' when she—like the
heroine from melodrama—is at the mercy of a villain she would
recognize as heartless if she were more familiar with the stereotypes
of Victorian melodrama. He is 'the systematic and calculating man of
dissipation, whose joys, regrets, pains, and pleasures, are all of self'
(*NN*, chapter 28, p. 357). The narrator explains Hawk's pursuit of
Kate, in terms relevant to this book as a whole:

the pursuit was one which could not fail to redound to his credit, and greatly
to enhance his reputation with the world. [. . .] Most men live in a world of
their own, and [. . .] in that limited circle alone are they ambitious for distinction and applause. Sir Mulberry's world was peopled with profligates
and he acted accordingly. (chapter 28, p. 357)

The word 'acted' is not used loosely, for the narrator elaborates on
his vision of the world as a theatre involving a complicit pact between
actor and audience:

Thus, cases of injustice, and oppression, and tyranny, and the most extravagant bigotry, are in constant occurrence among us every day. It is the
custom to trumpet forth much wonder and astonishment at the chief actors
therein setting at defiance so completely the opinion of the world; but there
is no greater fallacy; it is precisely because they do consult the opinion of
their own little world that such things take place at all, and strike the great
world dumb with amazement. (chapter 28, p. 357)

The main point to be made about this passage is not that Sir
Mulberry Hawk is a passionless dandy or a role-player. Although
Hawk has obvious affinities with the dandy and this passage directly
announces that he is an actor, he never achieves the absolute denial
of the human which characterizes dandyism in its purest form. The
name Hawk tells us why: Hawk never loses the violence and aggres-

sion of the animal, and indeed, from his fight with Nicholas onwards, the brutality and sensuality of his nature gradually crack his social mask of lassitude and indifference. *Nicholas Nickleby* demonstrates, however, that a society which offers such rewards to those who deny, distort, or transform the inner self is itself as corrupt as any individual villain—be it Sir Mulberry Hawk or Ralph Nickleby. As such, it is not so important that the novel is anti-aristocratic as that it is anti an entire society which exalts image over 'antecedent cause'. The ultimate symbol of the valorization of image is, of course, the dandy, but *Nicholas Nickleby* is not significant in this context for its individual dandies; it is more significant for its fictional evocation of the social conditions which encourage the separation of role from self, and of signifier from signified.

All those figures in *Nicholas Nickleby* who worship the gods of gentility or fashion are implicated in the moral corruption personified by Sir Mulberry Hawk. Thus Mr Mantalini, the Hawk-imitator with his 'agreeable weaknesses [. . .] such as gaming, wasting, idling, and a tendency to horse-flesh' (chapter 21, p. 259), is not the only, or the most prominent, member of Sir Mulberry's audience. The comic value of the Kenwigses should not blind us to the fact that they are desperate—and unsuccessful—social climbers; the hilarious antics of Mrs Nickleby and her vegetable-throwing suitor should not obscure the fact that Mrs Nickleby's false notions of gentility lace the novel like a leitmotif. Literally in the middle of this drama of social mobility is Mrs Wititterly, of Cadogan Place, a street which is

the one slight bond that joins two great extremes; it is the connecting link between the aristocratic pavements of Belgrave Square, and the barbarism of Chelsea. [. . .] Wearing as much as they can of the airs and semblances of loftiest rank, the people of Cadogan Place have the realities of middle station. It is the conductor which communicates to the inhabitants of regions beyond its limit, the shock of pride of birth and rank, which it has not within itself, but derives from a fountain-head beyond; or, like the ligament which unites the Siamese twins, it contains something of the life and essence of two distinct bodies, and yet belongs to neither. (chapter 21, pp. 264–5)

Mrs Wititterly, like Mrs Nickleby, demonstrates one of the most pernicious effects of a society obsessed with self-fashioning in that she is unable, or unwilling, to distinguish between true and false gentility; she does not, in other words, make moral distinctions. She is thus, not only, like Mrs Nickleby, taken in by Hawk and his cronies; she also partakes of his amorality.

But the significance of Mrs Wititterly is more complex than that. Like other aspirational members of the middle classes, Mrs Wititterly is always playing a role—for example, when Kate first meets her, 'She was reclining on a sofa in such a very unstudied attitude, that she might have been taken for an actress all ready for the first scene in a ballet, and only waiting for the drop curtain to go up' (chapter 21, pp. 265–6). What distinguishes Mrs Wititterly is that her ideas about gentility and fashion are taken more from books than life. For instance, when Dickens's narrator first introduces her to the reader, the satire is biting:

Now, in the ordinary course of things, and according to all authentic descriptions of high life, as set forth in books, Mrs. Wititterly ought to have been in her *boudoir*; but whether it was that Mr. Wititterly was at that moment shaving himself in the *boudoir* or what not, certain it was that Mrs. Wititterly gave audience in the drawing-room. (chapter 21, p. 265)

Again, in the same chapter (28) in which the narrator explains that Sir Mulberry Hawk is an actor who could not exist without an eagerly complicit audience, Mrs Wititterly is actually the audience for Kate's reading of the spoof 'silver fork' novel *The Lady Flabella*. This scene is a hilarious parody of fashionable novels which invariably included the figure of the dandy. But Dickens is not just engaging in literary gamesmanship here. He is making a point about self-fashioning—and the role of fiction in self-fashioning—crucial to my investigation of dandyism. In the passage discussed earlier from *Sketches by Boz*, the emphasis is on imitation as the key to social mobility. The word imitation in this context suggests imitation of others, the adoption of a different self. But throughout Dickens's writing, he demonstrates an awareness of the fact that different forms of imitation and social role-playing are possible. From one perspective, it could be said that Sir Mulberry Hawk does not imitate at all, that his type of acting involves *negation* (of self) rather than *imitation* (of others). Dickens perceives, however, that the two kinds of role-playing cannot be simplistically separated.

Negation of self can result from the attempts of individuals to imitate not only people but artistic models of identity—and indeed art works themselves. Readers like Mrs Wititterly aspire to the appearance of passionlessness they perceive as a symbol of social and cultural capital. She clearly indicates a 'popular' taste for a cultural elitism which is socially divisive; ultimately, she suggests a market for passionlessness. What aspirational imitation seeks to achieve is ultimately a denial of the human, a state of abstraction or nothingness which Dickens finally and paradoxically dramatizes in human form in the Veneering scenes in *Our Mutual Friend*. Society's obsession with genteel appearances works towards that denial of the human which is the essence (or non-essence) of dandyism. Dickens is acutely conscious of the role of art in creating and supplying a market for dandyism. He is also aware of the irony that attempts to recreate the self as a work of art assume that art is passionless. The professional actors and the professional artist—Miss La Creevy—in the novel are not implicated in society's obsession with gentility and the negation of the emotional life which is the upshot of this obsession. Both the Crummleses and Miss La Creevy are popular artists who 'imitate' for the artisan and working classes. While their work is not what Leavis would call 'great', neither is it shown to compound social problems. 'Genteel' society and its 'popular', fashionable literature, by contrast, implicitly encourages—via imitation—the separation of individuals from their emotions and from each other. That performative, popular art is not necessarily a bad thing is perhaps inevitable given the theatrical nature of Dickens's own art; that it can be, when performances of passionlessness are privileged, is a warning about both perfomativity and popular art.

ACTING THE SELF: DANGEROUS DANDIES

While Sir Mulberry Hawk can never rid himself of the violent animal beneath his dandified veneer, Montague Tigg in *Martin Chuzzlewit* is, in the eyes of most of the other characters in the novel, consummately successful at transforming himself into Tigg Montague. The narrator, however, is more circumspect:

He had a world of jet black shining hair upon his head, upon his cheeks, upon his chin, upon his upper lip. His clothes, symmetrically made, were of the newest fashion and the costliest kind. [. . .] And yet, though [. . .] turned and twisted upside down, and inside out, as great men have been sometimes known to be; though no longer Montague Tigg, but Tigg Montague; still it was Tigg: the same Satanic, gallant, military Tigg. The brass was burnished, lacquered, newly stamped; yet it was true Tigg metal notwithstanding. (chapter 27, p. 427)

The character of Tigg presents different problems from that of Sir Mulberry as the reversal of his names suggests. Before Tigg becomes Montague, he typifies 'the gent', a breed described by Ellen Moers as made up of 'young men at the very bottom of the respectable class'; 'the Gent', she maintains, 'was a second-hand, shop-worn imitation of the dandy'.[17] The dandyism of the gent is of a kind Moers recognized in Dickens himself as a 'bastard theatrical dandyism';[18] Montague Tigg, like Dick Swiveller and the young Dickens, dresses for effect, to draw attention to himself, not because the dandy pose has any symbolic significance for him. This 'bastard theatrical dandyism' is significantly different from the 'pure' form of dandyism, that passionless elegance personified by Beau Brummell; where Brummellian dandyism is repressive, the gent's dandyism is expressive, even histrionic. The gent's passion for flamboyant dress is thus motivated more by 'a naïve, almost childlike pleasure in dressing up'[19] than by a serious belief that he can appear and thus become a gentleman. It is significant that Moers describes the gent as a 'shop-worn imitation of the *dandy*' (italics mine), rather than a second-hand imitation of the gentleman, for the gent's dandyism is more about adorning and celebrating the self than it is about disguising oneself as a gentleman; the dandy's clothes would thus be more impressive to the gent than his social status. The gent as dandy is what James Kincaid would call a 'playful' rather than an 'earnest' performer.[20]

However, the supposedly playful gent Montague Tigg emphasizes the difficulty of dividing characters in such a way, by transforming himself into the 'earnest'—or more sinister—Tigg Montague. Tigg also foregrounds an ambiguity inherent in Victorian attitudes to dandyism, an ambiguity pinpointed by Bulwer, who distinguishes in *England and the English* between 'the Dandy Harmless' and 'the Dandy Venomous' or 'the drone dandy' and 'the wasp dandy'.[21] The same divided attitude to dandyism—in this case of the gent—is apparent in Albert Smith's *The Natural History of the Gent* (1847). On the one hand, the breed seems comparatively harmless. As Ellen Moers puts it:

[17] *The Dandy*, 215.

[18] Ibid. 228.

[19] Ibid. 222.

[20] 'Performance, Roles, and the Nature of the Self in Dickens', in MacKay (ed.), *Dramatic Dickens*, 11–26 (p. 12).

[21] i, pp. vi and 118. Interestingly, Bulwer seems to regard 'the drone dandy', Lord Mute, as less dangerous than 'the wasp dandy', Sir Paul Snarl. His imagery is of course echoed by Harold Skimpole and Eugene Wrayburn.

'They have a passion for all things theatrical, and their style of dress has much of the "light comedian" about it. They are very young, very gullible, very fresh and very vulgar, and they dream of falling into money.'[22] But on the other, they are the product of 'our present condition of society—that constant wearing struggle to appear something more than we in reality are, which now characterizes every body, both in their public and private phases'.[23] The gent cannot thus be regarded as an innocent and irrelevant extra in society's drama of social mobility. He is symbolically significant and suffers from the same diseased desire for an appearance of gentility as the rest of society. The potentially metamorphic relationship between 'playful' and 'earnest' dandies is summed up succinctly by Mark Tapley: 'there's ever so many Tiggs a passing this here Temple Gate any hour in the day, that only want a chance to turn out full-blown Montagues ev'ry one!' (chapter 52, p. 803). Mark's remark is more than an observation on social climbing. It suggests the possibility that, given the right conditions, apparently harmless dandy gents may emerge from the cocoon of self as powerful and as morally and socially problematic as the butterfly dandy Alfred D'Orsay.[24]

But if Dickens demonstrates, in *Martin Chuzzlewit*, that a Tigg can become a Montague, he does not solve the problem of whether a Montague can successfully destroy a Tigg. The problem of whether Tigg's transformation is just of the surface or includes the inner self is highlighted in Jonas's analysis of Tigg's change:

you were another figure when I saw you first. Ha, ha, ha! I see the rents and patches now! No false hair then, no black dye! You were another sort of joker in those days, you were! You even spoke different, then. You've acted the gentleman so seriously since, that you've taken in yourself. If he [Pecksniff] should know you, what does it matter? Such a change is proof of your success. (chapter 41, pp. 636–7)

Whereas the narrator recognizes 'the same Satanic, gallant, military Tigg' and 'true Tigg metal' below the surface of Montague (*MC*, chapter 27, p. 427), Jonas suggests that Tigg's transformation is internal as well as external. But there are ambiguities within, as well as between, these two key passages: in the narrator's analysis, although Tigg is a person turned 'inside out', he is still somehow

[22] *The Dandy*, 217.
[23] *The Natural History of the Gent* (London: Bogue, 1847), 3.
[24] See *The Dandy*, 147–63 for Moers's discussion of Victorian ambivalence towards the parasitic yet charismatic Count D'Orsay.

supposed to retain an inner self made of 'Tigg metal'—yet as Steven
Marcus suggests in his description of the dandy as 'a man wholly
externalised', it is surely impossible to turn oneself inside out, without
creating an 'inward nullity'.[25] Then again, in Jonas's account of
Tigg's metamorphosis, though he ostensibly maintains that Tigg is
an entirely different 'sort of joker' now, he also makes clear that he
can see through Tigg's 'rents and patches', 'false hair', and 'black
dye'—implying that there is a private self beneath the social costume,
a Tigg at odds with his outward Montagu persona.

Perhaps the central moment in Jonas's analysis is the claim,
'You've acted the gentleman so seriously since, that you've taken
yourself in.' Jonas describes the internalizing of the self which
Dickens strongly objects to in his journalism: Tigg has literally taken
his self in. The moral corruption and emotional dislocation which
attends this involution of self is expressed through Dickens's
word-play. The idea of 'taking oneself in' obviously suggests that
Tigg is a self-deceiver, but self-deception is a complex concept. A
self-deceiver has either taken him- or herself in so completely that no
trace of the original self exists; or she or he believes in one image of
self, while the reality is quite different (and often less flattering). This
ambiguity is never resolved in Tigg's case; either way, the process of
taking the self in is, to Dickens, a cannibalistic process which renders
the self disjointed and dysfunctional.

Dickens's methods of characterization strongly suggest, of course,
that he wants to discourage the taking of the self in, or 'the mask [. . .]
worn internally', to quote John Carey.[26] It is thus in keeping with the
externalized impulse of Dickens's novels that we are never allowed
the inside view of Tigg—or most of Dickens's other dandies. The
presence or absence of interiority is rendered implicitly. The potential problem that this creates for Dickens, however, is that he leaves
himself open to the same accusations of superficiality that attend the
dandy. While Dickens, as I have discussed, ideally aims to suggest
'antecedent causes' through surfaces, he is also able to suggest the
absence of such 'causes' through these same surfaces. One of the
reasons that images of role-playing are so prevalent in his novels is
that an interrogation of roles can offer a means of exploring the
implicit private self without separating that self from its rightfully (for
Dickens) 'public' context. His representation of Tigg is characterized

---

[25] *Dickens: From Pickwick to Dombey*, 229–30.
[26] 'Dickens and the Mask', *Studies in English Literature*, 59 (1983), 3–18 (p. 11).

by ambivalence partly because Dickens is prone to making provisional moral distinctions between expressive ('good') performativity
which turns the self inside out and repressive ('bad') performativity
which takes the self in: Tigg of course employs both kinds of theatricality. That Dickens's melodramatic art is dependent on both repressive and expressive performativity, as well as the very surfaces and
roles which the dandy holds so dear, no doubt also contributes to his
ambivalence about the type.

This ambivalence is typical, however, of larger Victorian attitudes
to the dandy. Montague Tigg celebrates the apparently harmless
'bastard theatrical dandyism' of the gent; Tigg Montague appears to
personify a more dangerous form of dandyism; he is possibly a
'perfect' dandy, 'a man gone dead inside, a man wholly externalised'.
However, the fact that Tigg does become Montague suggests that it is
not possible to accurately regard the dandy as either entirely harmful
or harmless. Ultimately, Tigg succeeds in at least appearing to be
Montague because he exists in the same Victorian society which is
depicted in *Nicholas Nickleby*, a society which accepts surface for
substance, the appearance of gentility for the reality.

But if Dickens's texts clearly portray the superficiality or moral
myopia of Victorian society, they are less straightforward in their
investigation of the mystery of the 'pure' dandy—or the question I
have already raised of whether it is possible to rid oneself of an 'inner'
or private self. Steven Marcus argues that Tigg's dream (chapter 42)
suggests the final impossibility of negating the inner life, but I would
argue that the issue remains deliberately ambiguous in *Martin
Chuzzlewit.*[27] What is certain, however, is that in a novel which
contains a character (Pecksniff) labelled a 'Great Abstraction'
(chapter 31, p. 498), Dickens is consciously exploring the possibility of
human hollowness. The analysis is in its early stages and Dickens ultimately sits Tigg precariously on a fence between theatrical dandyism
and dandyism of the inner self, between selfishness and a literal, pernicious self-lessness.

In *Bleak House*, Dickens's omniscient narrator returns to the issues
raised by Montague Tigg, in the most important, sophisticated, and
direct analysis of dandyism I have found in Dickens's works. What is
wrong, the narrator asks, with the 'brilliant and distinguished circle'
at Chesney Wold?

[27] *Dickens: From Pickwick to Dombey*, 230.

Dandyism? There is no King George the Fourth now (more's the pity!) to set the dandy fashion; there are no clear-starched jack-towel neckcloths, no short-waisted coats, no false calves, no stays. There are no caricatures, now, of effeminate Exquisites so arrayed [. . .]. There is no beau [. . .]. But is there Dandyism in the brilliant and distinguished circle notwithstanding, Dandyism of a more mischievous sort, that has got below the surface and is doing less harmless things than jack-towelling itself and stopping its own digestion, to which no rational person need particularly object?

Why, yes. [. . .] There *are*, at Chesney Wold this January week, some ladies and gentlemen of the newest fashion, who have set up a Dandyism— in Religion, for instance. Who, in mere lackadaisical want of an emotion, have agreed upon a little dandy talk about the Vulgar wanting faith in things in general [. . .].

There are also ladies and gentlemen of another fashion, not so new, but very elegant, who have agreed to put a smooth glaze on the world, and to keep down all its realities. For whom everything must be languid and pretty. [. . .] Who are to rejoice at nothing, and be sorry for nothing. Who are not to be disturbed by ideas. On whom even the Fine Arts, attending in powder and walking backward like the Lord Chamberlain, must array themselves in the milliners' and tailors' patterns of past generations, and be particularly careful not to be in earnest, or to receive any impress from the moving age. (chapter 12, pp. 159–60)

In a novel like *Bleak House*, which emphasizes the interconnectedness of individuals of all types and social classes,[28] the absoluteness of the passage's distinction between harmless Regency dandyism and the 'more mischievous' variety must be questioned. But Dickens's novels can present dandyism as an innocent piece of fun, on the one hand, and as a serious moral and social danger on the other. The vacillation in Dickens's depiction of dandyism arises partly, as we have seen, from his ambivalence about what he shares with the dandy: a reliance on surfaces and roles. It owes something, moreover, to the dandy's ability to adopt either expressive or repressive performativity. (Dickens, of course, seems often to feel less threatened by the former).[29] What generally saves Dickens from aesthetic dandyism, however, is the moral, cultural, and social mission which frames his deployment of roles and surfaces—as well as the importance he places on emotion as a medium of communication in art and in life. His novels moralize and socialize the dandy's passionlessness; a fascination with surface appearance, innocent or risible enough in itself, is

---

[28] The text specifically draws attention to this interconnection in the famous passage beginning: 'What connexion can there be [. . .]?' (chapter 16, p. 219).

[29] See Chapter 3 above.

shown to be part of an unhealthy chain of cause and effect initiated by the 'genteel' classes.

But there are several dandified individuals in Dickens's works who are shielded from guilt by a certain aura of innocence—Dick Swiveller, for example, or Mr Guppy. The energy of these characters belies their textual or thematic function and betrays an affection for the dandy which Dickens, like other prominent Victorians, never succeeded in erasing or explaining. Thus, we have the nostalgic attitude set forth to Regency dandyism in this passage, seemingly cleared of any part in the current 'dandyism of a more mischievous kind'. A similar instance is evident in the posthumous tribute to the Count D'Orsay in Dickens's *Household Words*.[30] Again, dramatically symbolic of the attraction and the danger the dandy suggested to the Victorians is D'Orsay's inclusion—with his back to the sketcher, in shadow—in Maclise's engraving of the Fraserians.[31]

The ambivalence of Victorian attitudes to the dandy was at its most acute in contemporary attitudes to D'Orsay, who was beautiful and charming—and, more worryingly, parasitic, living off the Blessingtons. It should be clear from this description that, although famously modelled on (the Romantic critic) Leigh Hunt, Dickens's Harold Skimpole has much in common with D'Orsay too. I am not suggesting that Dickens consciously used D'Orsay as a prototype—a question not particularly relevant here—but that Skimpole personifies the artistic and moral issues surrounding the elevation of beauty over ethics in *Bleak House*, rather as D'Orsay symbolized the same issues for his time. Skimpole advocates what Tolstoy feared— that the 'idea of what is beautiful' supplant 'the idea of what is right'.[32] His aestheticism looks back to that of Keats and forward to that of Wilde. Skimpole appears to have nothing in common with the 'ideal' dandy and is not beautiful; most importantly, he is shabby, and does not care about his appearance; he is possibly mercenary (like D'Orsay) and he professes to be a man of intense feeling. But Skimpole is crucial to my discussion because he intellectually

[30] The posthumous tribute to D'Orsay in *HW* reads: 'Count D'Orsay, whose name is publicly synonymous with elegant and graceful accomplishment, and who, by those who knew him well, is affectionately remembered and regretted, as a man whose great abilities might have raised him to any distinction, and whose gentle heart even a world of fashion left unspoiled'—[Leigh Hunt], 'Lounging through Kensington', *HW* 7 (6 Aug. 1853), 533–8 (p. 536).

[31] *Fraser's Magazine*, 11 (Jan. 1835); this double-page engraving was included to mark the beginning of *Fraser's* sixth year.

[32] *What is Art?*, trans. Almer Maude (Chicheley: Minet, 1971), 183.

advocates the philosophy implicit in dandyism. With disturbing social and human implications, he elevates art over life. He views life aesthetically and is always able to justify his amorality with recourse to a philosophy which maintains that human life is at its most precious when it is artistic or picturesque. Moreover, Skimpole is so successful at justifying his aestheticism—reminiscent, not accidentally, of certain strands in high Romanticism—that many characters in the novel are unable to condemn his amorality, regarding him as a unique enigma. Skimpole's intellect thus has a similar effect to D'Orsay's beauty: it anaesthetizes moral sensibilities.

Throughout the novel, for example, Skimpole is perceived by some as a harmless innocent and by others as a mercenary manipulator. At one extreme, Jarndyce's first description of Skimpole labels him 'the finest creature upon earth—a child' (chapter 6, p. 67); at the other, Bucket's verdict is, 'Whenever a person proclaims to you "In worldly matters I'm a child," you consider that that person is only a-crying off from being held accountable, and that you have got that person's number, and it's Number One' (chapter 57, p. 775). Esther's narrative fuses the two attitudes at once and is impressively effective at conveying her deep ambivalence towards Skimpole. For example, when Skimpole is first arrested for debt, Esther observes:

> It was a most singular thing that the arrest was our [hers and Richard's] embarrassment, and not Mr Skimpole's. He observed us with a genial interest; but there seemed, if I may venture on such a contradiction, nothing selfish in it. He had entirely washed his hands of the difficulty, and it had become ours. (chapter 6, p. 74)

Then again, the horrified amazement Esther feels when Skimpole recommends that the sick Jo should be turned out of doors is conveyed by her bald description: 'The amiable face with which he said it, I think I shall never forget' (chapter 31, p. 435). Skimpole intellectualizes people rather than forging emotional connections with them. Esther's habit of reporting Skimpole's speech is telling, for the words without the engaging manner of the speaker do not fail to sound hollow. In chapter 43, Esther notes crucially

> The more I saw of him, the more unlikely it seemed to me, *when he was present*, that he could design, conceal, or influence anything; and yet the less likely that appeared *when he was not present*, and the less agreeable it was to think of his having anything to do with any one for whom I cared. (pp. 596–7 (italics mine))

It is Skimpole's manner which is captivating. The key to his character is the fact that, like Steerforth (whom I will discuss in the next chapter), he has the actor's ability to charm and captivate an audience. When Skimpole is not present, however, the spell is broken and his words seem empty or inconsistent with any moral code. Skimpole's 'presence' as an actor, however, is so powerful that the reaction he stimulates in the audience is best described as an unwilling, rather than a willing, suspension of disbelief. Skimpole confirms the subversive impression suggested throughout Dickens's novels of the power of 'artificial' self-projections. Esther, unlike David Copperfield, is not infatuated with her subject, however; she wants to judge him sternly, but is ineffectual when confrontation occurs.

The mystery surrounding Skimpole is more similar to that surrounding Tigg Montague than that associated with Steerforth. While we are given glimpses of Steerforth's private self in *David Copperfield*, in *Bleak House*, we are left ignorant about the existence or composition of any inner life Skimpole claims to possess. To return to the novel's key passage on dandyism, Skimpole's lack of emotional connection with others links him with 'dandyism of a more mischievous sort, that has got below the surface'. Whereas society prima donnas like Lady Dedlock are shown to be distorted by the effort of repressing passion—a theme at the heart of Dickens's writing from *Dombey and Son* onwards—Harold Skimpole is portrayed as free from such struggles. This apparent absence of interior struggle functions as a sign of his monstrosity.

If Skimpole is an actor to his very core, so too is Mr Turveydrop, a character who seems to satirize Lord Chesterfield's obsession with dancing and decorum. Esther's initial description of Mr Turveydrop—'He was a fat old gentleman with a false complexion, false teeth, false whiskers, and a wig' (chapter 14, p. 190)—bears a marked resemblance to Dickens's narrator's description of the Crummleses in stage make-up in *Nicholas Nickleby* (chapter 24, p. 302). However, if Turveydrop's act does not deceive Esther, it deceives Turveydrop himself. As the old lady at deportment classes tells Esther, 'The airs the fellow gives himself! [. . .] He fully believes he is one of the aristocracy!' (chapter 14, p. 192). The key difference between Skimpole and Turveydrop is, as Rowland McMaster argues: 'While Turveydrop is a social phenomenon in the form of an art work, Skimpole is an aesthetician whose views have social implications.'[33]

[33] 'Dickens, the Dandy, and the Savage: A Victorian View of the Romantic', in Juliet

Thus although Skimpole is not obsessed with his own appearance—which is actually distinctly shabby—his elevation of art over life, of aesthetic considerations over moral realities, emphasizes the disturbing implications of dandyism, implications fully explored in Oscar Wilde's *The Picture of Dorian Gray* (1891).

Skimpole embodies the worrying possibility that, in the words of Wilde's Lord Henry Wotton, 'If a man treats life artistically, his brain is his heart.'[34] The result of the brain replacing the heart, in Dickens's vision, is social divisiveness of the most extreme kind. Skimpole's aestheticism openly embraces social and cultural exclusivity and hierarchy, resulting in a repellent philosophy which disregards the importance of human life. His desire to inhabit a world which includes 'no brambles of sordid realities' (chapter 6, p. 72), for example, results in the apparently harmless social philosophy: 'I take it that everybody's business in the social system is to be agreeable. It's a system of harmony, in short' (chapter 18, p. 252). His dislike of work he sees as a preference for the 'Drone philosophy' over the Bee philosophy (chapter 8, p. 93), rather than an irresponsible neglect of his family and a parasitic reliance on his friends. When Esther confronts him about the issue of responsibility, he answers, 'Responsibility is a thing that has always been above me—or below me' (chapter 61, p. 829). His divorce of social privilege from moral responsibility (which exaggerates that of many Dickensian 'gentlemen') is indeed almost fascistic in its implications. He says of slaves on American plantations, for example: 'I dare say theirs is an unpleasant experience on the whole; but, they people the landscape for me, they give it a poetry for me, and perhaps that is one of the pleasanter objects of their existence' (chapter 18, p. 253). He explains that he would be more interested in Jo as an 'illustration' of the 'misdirected energy, which has a certain amount of reason in it, and a certain amount of romance', than 'merely as a poor vagabond' (chapter 31, pp. 434–5). He even perceives his own daughters aesthetically, labelling them his 'Beauty daughter', his 'Sentiment daughter', and his 'Comedy daughter' (chapter 43, p. 595). And last but certainly not least, he consistently talks about himself as if he were another person. Esther observes on the first occasion she meets him his habit of 'speaking of himself as if he were not at all his own

and Rowland McMaster, *The Novel from Sterne to James: Essays on the Relation of Literature to Life* (London: Macmillan, 1981), 54–70 (p. 61).

[34] *The Picture of Dorian Gray*, 253.

affair, as if Skimpole were a third person' (chapter 6, p. 70). From one perspective, we could see his habit of self-objectification as similar to the actor's separation from his role; from another, we could see it as the aesthetician's view of himself as a work of art.

Despite his supposed inability to see them, the 'brambles of sordid realities' do, however, rear their ugly heads—in his parasitic scrounging, his eviction of Jo, his neglect of his family, his corruption of Richard, the bribe he takes from Vholes, and his final distortion of Jarndyce's supposed selfishness. Yet Skimpole betrays no sign of recognizing them—or himself; his mask does not reveal the slightest crack. This insensitivity coexists, interestingly for our purposes, with a constant trumpeting of his own emotional sensitivity. His protestations of sensitivity are so convincing initially that Esther remarks: 'He was so full of feeling too, and had such a delicate sentiment for what was beautiful or tender, that he would have won a heart by that alone' (chapter 6, pp. 71–2).

The problem with Skimpole is that all his fine feeling seems to be reserved for art, not human life—though the fact that we usually see him in company with human beings rather than works of art makes even his feeling for art questionable. In his professed sensitivity to art, so at odds with the insensitivity he practises towards other human beings, he resembles Wilkie Collins's Count Fosco and the historical murderer Lacenaire; there are also similarities with Oscar Wilde's Dorian Gray—who is, interestingly, markedly affected by a poem about the hand of Lacenaire.[35] If the 'sordid realities' of Skimpole's life are not as shocking as the sensational lives of Lacenaire and Dorian Gray, this is not the point; nor is it the point that Skimpole is not as perfect in externals as the 'pure' dandy. In his use of the intellect to advocate the elevation of art over life, or the divorce of art from its social consequences, Skimpole personifies the kind of art which was anathema to Dickens. He is significant because of his aesthetic philosophy, an ethos which Baudelaire, Wilde, and, before them, Dickens realized was dangerous.

If Skimpole is an aesthetician, he is not, to reuse Marcus's definition of dandyism, a 'parody of the self as a work of art'. He embodies a different phenomenon—he is a parody of the self as a human being. If he resembles Lacenaire in this respect, he also suggests the character Dickens possibly modelled on Lacenaire, Rigaud Blandois.

---

[35] *The Picture of Dorian Gray*, 197–8. The poem is from Théophile Gautier's *Émaux et camées* (1852).

All three, to echo Harvey Peter Sucksmith's description, discussed in Chapter 3, triumphantly assert their paradoxically 'true and vital hollowness', their 'theatrical yet authentic performance'. All three are not actors of the surface, but actors of the self. In the case of Rigaud Blandois, this literal self-lessness means that he emphasizes, as Hillis Miller has pointed out, the link between gentility and criminality or diabolism.[36] In the case of Skimpole, the conclusions reached by his aesthetic theorizing emphasize the pernicious consequences of high society's dandyism of the self, its negation of emotion and social reality; but Skimpole differs from Rigaud in that his character is instrumental in demonstrating the link between aestheticism and immorality rather than that between gentility and immorality.

No character in Dickens's works demonstrates the links between dandyism, gentility, and villainy better than John Chester in *Barnaby Rudge*. A parody of the arch-villain of the Victorians, Lord Chesterfield, as well as a 'parody of the self as a work of art', he is obsessed with the appearance of fashion and gentility in a way that Skimpole is not. The narrator makes clear throughout the novel that he is an actor by nature; Chester even understands the implications behind his dandyism. Viewed from one perspective, he appears to conform exactly to Kucich's description of the 'bourgeois' villain: 'In a nonviolent way, the villain deliberately strips himself of desire, or motive, in order to occupy in the eyes of the other the transcendent space of the nonhuman—that which is beyond life and death.'[37] From another perspective, he is the ultimate heartless aristocratic villain. When his son Edward claims to speak from his heart, Chester counters factually that the heart is nothing but 'an ingenious part of our formation—the centre of the blood-vessels and all that sort of thing' (chapter 32, p. 243). To Haredale, he explains:

The world is a lively place enough, in which we must accommodate ourselves to circumstances, sail with the stream as glibly as we can, be content to take froth for substance, the surface for the depth, the counterfeit for the real coin. I wonder no philosopher has ever established that our globe

[36] J. Hillis Miller, *Charles Dickens: The World of his Novels* (Cambridge, Mass.: Harvard University Press, 1958; repr. 1965), 229 n.

[37] *Excess and Restraint*, 80. Kucich's analysis of the 'bourgeois' villain adapts René Girard's concept of *askesis*: see Girard, *Deceit, Desire, and the Novel: Self and Other in Literary Structure*, trans. Yvonne Freccero (Éditions Bernard Grasset, 1961; Baltimore: Johns Hopkins University Press, 1961; repr. 1988), 153–75.

itself is hollow. It should be, if Nature is consistent in her works. (chapter 12, p. 91)

The nearest Chester comes to philosophical corroboration of his view of the world as one of surface is in his reading of Lord Chesterfield's *Letters*. 'In every page of this enlightened writer', he enthuses, 'I find some captivating hypocrisy [. . .] or some superlative piece of selfishness to which I was utterly a stranger' (chapter 33, p. 174). Dickens's narrator elaborates on Chester's paradoxically 'honest' admiration of immorality in terms similar to those used to explain Ralph Nickleby's mentality in *Nicholas Nickleby*: 'Men who are thoroughly false and hollow, seldom try to hide those vices from themselves; and yet in the very act of avowing them, they lay claim to the virtues they feign most to despise' (chapter 23, p. 174).[38]

If Chester is an 'honest' villain, he is still, like Chesterfield, an actor. Neither is an expressive actor; they are both repressive, negating any sense of self, changing hue if the occasion requires, and always maintaining a polished yet unostentatious veneer. Chester's acting involves the presentation of the self as a work of art. His appearance is characterized by 'perfect calmness' (chapter 10, p. 76), revealing 'no mark of age or passion' (chapter 40, p. 302). His perfection of the dandy pose and his view of the world as a globe with no substance means that he cannot comprehend that other human beings are themselves anything but role-players, devoid of emotional lives. He thus ironically perceives his own son, the savage, animalistic Hugh, as a mythical figure, a centaur that 'would make a very handsome preparation in Surgeons' Hall, and would benefit science extremely' (chapter 75, p. 574).

It is fascinating, however, that at key moments when Chester is unambiguously labelled an actor by the narrator, we glimpse an inner self that this 'perfect' dandy has affected to deny. The face behind the mask first appears clearly after Gabriel Varden has told him that Hugh is his son: 'As he quitted the room, Sir John's face changed; and the smile gave place to a haggard and anxious expression, like that of a weary actor jaded by the performance of a difficult part' (chapter 75, p. 582). The second occasion occurs during his final confrontation with Haredale—'now he dropped his mask, and showed his hatred in his face' (chapter 81, p. 626)—and finally, at the moment just before his death, he has 'scorn and hatred in his look'.

[38] See *NN*, chapter 44, pp. 567–8. See also Chapter 7 below for a discussion of Gowan's similar logic.

Though 'seeming to remember, even then, that this expression would distort his features after death, he tried to smile' (chapter 81, p. 627), it is too late to fool the reader. Chester is not after all the 'perfect' dandy, devoid of inner passions, nor is he an actor to the core.

HOLLOW INTERIORS, NOVEL VENEERS

Though it could be argued that the vision of the person behind the persona reveals some inconsistency in the characterization of Chester, what is important here is Dickens's—perhaps last-minute— decision to portray Chester as ultimately a social role-player, rather than a human actor or 'perfect' dandy. For shadowing this study of people presenting themselves as works of art is the question of the self-reflexive relevance of the dandy to Dickens's art—in particular, the recurring artistic problem of whether it is possible for a writer to represent a superficial person without seeming to partake of the superficiality presented. Further, is it possible to 'complicate' superficiality without diminishing the force of the dandy's villainy? In *Barnaby Rudge*, Dickens's decision to reveal a face behind the mask probably resulted from his concern to make his character humanly and artistically credible. Whether his artistic judgement was justified in so doing—or whether he should have left the issue of selfhood open-ended, as he does in the case of Skimpole, who never drops his act—is debatable. But what is certain, in the case of both characters, is that neither is presented, to echo a phrase Dickens uses elsewhere, as 'a horrible wonder apart' (*ED*, chapter 20, p. 175). Dickens does not valorize or explore the passional vacuum which paradoxically supplants the private self of the dandy, preferring instead to imply and explore this vacuum via its manifestation in social connections and contests. This can have the effect of diminishing the projected individuality of the villain while rendering his superficiality complex. None of Dickens's dandy villains are shown to be freaks of nature; all are inextricably connected with their society. The 'textual life of Dickens's characters', to borrow the title of James A. Davies's book on Dickens, in itself often explains or dramatizes the dandy's lack of passion.[39]

Dickens's manipulation of the relationship between 'text'—which

[39] (Houndmills: Macmillan, 1989).

has a semiotic thrust—and 'story'—which has a mimetic thrust—is the principal means by which he can credibly signal that a character may be that paradox, an inhuman human, rather than a lifeless fictional creation. In more direct terms, this means, as we saw in the case of Sir Mulberry Hawk, that a character can appear to be a straightforward aristocratic villain in relation to the story, or chain of narrated events, while his textual function is far more complex—he is no more a villain than the society which produced him, a society of role-players who elevate surface over substance. In the case of Chester and Skimpole, Dickens's textual investigation of the dandy is far more intricate, for embedded in both novels is something more than an exploration of the relationship between role-playing and the self, or the concept of society as theatre.

In each text, Dickens embodies his own response to certain contemporary debates about the relationship between the dandy and his society. In *Barnaby Rudge*, Dickens dramatizes several of the tenets of the anti-dandiacal *Fraser's Magazine* on the dandy's significance, not least of which is William Maginn's perception of a relationship between the criminality of high life and that of low life:

it is a favourite notion with our fashionable novelists, to sacrifice the middle-classes equally to the lowest and the highest. [. . .] There is a sort of instinct in this. The one class esteem themselves above the law, and the other are too frequently below it. They are attracted, then, by a sympathy with their mutual lawlessness. They recognise a likeness in their libertinism.[40]

It is ironic that Dickens was so regularly attacked by the anti-Newgate critics of *Fraser's Magazine* for his unrealistic representation of crime. *Barnaby Rudge* in particular cleverly analyses the inextricable links between the criminality of the aristocracy and those 'below' the law. And this analysis is not accidental, or instinctive. It takes the form of a carefully patterned dramatization of Maginn's argument. Thus we have, most obviously of all, Chester's regular meetings with his illegitimate son Hugh, as well as Lord George Gordon's weakly egotistical agitation of the masses. Chester too is an agitator, recognizing Hugh, during the riots, 'with the air of a patron' (chapter 53, p. 409). The violence of those underlings, the scum of society who meet at the Boot, is thus stirred by the supposed cream of society, men like Chester who perfume their quarters after visits from fellow human beings. Of course, the most cutting point that Dickens makes

[40] 'Mr. Edward Lytton Bulwer's Novels', 515.

on the mutual lawlessness of the genteel and the very poor is made through the revelation that Hugh is Chester's son (just as he makes the same point through the revelation that Magwitch is Pip's bene-factor in *Great Expectations*).[41] This relationship is one of which *Fraser's*—with its famous distinctions between the 'natural' and the 'tailor-made' gentleman—should have approved. One tendency of the dandy was to regard the self not as an animal, but as a gentleman; Hugh is a telling reminder to Chester of the physicality that he cannot ultimately deny.

In *Bleak House*, Dickens explores the relationship between the groups labelled in *Sartor Resartus* the 'dandiacal sect' and the 'drudge sect'. The drudges are not the criminal poor, but the poor who have been criminally neglected by society. The central ethos in the chapter of *Sartor Resartus* entitled 'The Dandiacal Body' is that the complete gulf between the dandies and the drudges will eventually destroy the country:

To the eye of the political Seer, their mutual relation, pregnant with the elements of discord and hostility, is far from consoling. These two principles of Dandiacal Self-Worship or Demon-Worship, and Poor-Slavish or Drudgical Earth-worship, or whatever that same Drudgism may be, do as yet indeed manifest themselves under distant and nowise considerable shapes: nevertheless, in their roots and subterranean ramifications, they extend through the entire structure of Society, and work unweariedly in the secret depths of English national Existence; striving to separate and isolate it into two contradictory, uncommunicating masses. [. . .]

To me it seems probable that the two Sects will one day part England between them.[42]

Skimpole's eviction of Jo in *Bleak House* is symbolic of the division of England into the privileged and the neglected, or the dandies and the drudges. The eviction is doubly ironic as Skimpole has no more pennies to rub together than Jo, and certainly has more debts, but Skimpole's cultural capital—not to mention Self-Worship—give him access to elite circles. Throughout the novel, moreover, scenes of dire poverty (in Tom-All-Alone's, for example) are juxtaposed with those depicting the lassitude of the wealthy. Although *Bleak House* empha-sizes 'connection' between classes, connection is tellingly undercut by

[41] Robin Gilmour calls *GE* 'the most complex and satisfying fictional examination of the idea of the gentleman in the Victorian period'—*The Idea of the Gentleman in the Victorian Novel*, 143.
[42] *Sartor Resartus*, 216.

lack of communication. Even when the poor are visited by outsiders, there is rarely communication; in the case of Mrs Pardiggle, for example, self-worship replaces genuine charity or understanding. But perhaps one of the best examples of social double standards in *Bleak House* is the fact that law-abiding Coavins the bailiff and his family are treated as lepers by society, whilst those 'gentlemen' who create a demand for bailiffs are regarded as blameless—as fashionable indeed.

Thus, by textually 'placing' Skimpole and Chester in contemporary social contexts, by dramatizing, through each of the novels in which they appear, contemporary attitudes to the dandy, Dickens makes clear that such characters are not mysterious, anomalous monsters; rather, they are monstrous products of their time. The implication of Dickens's critique of a polarized, unequal society is obviously to reinforce the desirability of the idea of cultural inclusivity to which dandyism is an affront. The dandy's disavowal of his social constitution does not make his connections to his society any the less real. And just as Victorian dandies were products of their social environment, Dickens's dandies can never be divorced from their novelistic environment.

By the time he wrote *Our Mutual Friend*, Dickens had discovered how to represent human beings devoid of inner selves. In *Our Mutual Friend*, insubstantial people appear as they are, as human abstractions. For this reason, by a curious logic, the novel does not contain a pure, passionless dandy; for the only substantial thing about the typical dandy is his fashionable appearance, and abstractions cannot, by definition, have a distinct appearance—an abstraction is an idea, or an airy nothing. The Veneerings, therefore, have no more substance than their name suggests, and in one way, indeed, they have less. For although the Veneerings' name implies that they are superficial people, the physical appearance of the Veneerings is not foregrounded in the novel. They represent the logic of cannibalistic individualism. They exist principally as an idea summed up by a name; they are thus more abstract than physical representations of surface human beings. They have no reality, for themselves or others, except when it is confirmed by the mirror that dominates their dinner parties; the mirror, that is, literally and symbolically looms larger than life. Where the social climbers in *Nicholas Nickleby* pretend to be something that they are not, the Veneerings pretend to be something, to be human, to be real. They paradoxically (dis)embody Baudrillard's idea of the 'loss of the real'. In the ideological and ethical context of a Dickens novel, however, their superficiality is condemned rather than celebrated or ironized.

Of course, throughout his novels, Dickens is given to dehumaniz-ing the human (and vice versa).[43] Dickens includes in his novels a 'whole race' of people that Harold Skimpole might have called ' "stuffed people",—a large collection, glassy eyed, set up in the most approved manner on their various twigs and perches, very correct, perfectly free from animation, and always in glass cases' (*BH*, chapter 37, p. 532). Dickens's race of 'stuffed people' includes not only aristocratic fossils, but also more pernicious varieties of the species, characters like Vholes who, with his 'lifeless manner' and 'inward manner of speaking' (chapter 37, p. 533), is the most cannibalistic of all Dickens's involuted individuals. Dickens, of course, is specific about Vholes's cannibalistic nature, describing his relations as 'minor cannibal chiefs', his removal of his 'close black gloves' like 'skinning his hands' and of his 'tight hat as if he were scalping himself' (chapter 39, p. 649). In *Little Dorrit*, it is not only Rigaud Blandois who is described in mechanistic terms (book 1, chapter 1, p. 5); the word 'unfeeling' is the keynote of the intro-ductory description of Mrs Merdle, who thereafter becomes virtually synonymous with her 'broad unfeeling handsome bosom' (book 1, chapter 20, p. 233); her husband Mr Merdle, 'the greatest Forger and the greatest Thief that ever cheated the gallows' (book 2, chapter 25, p. 691), is a nonentity or human vacuum at the centre of the text; and Mrs General, 'having long ago formed her own surface to such perfection that it hid whatever was below it (if anything)' (book 2, chapter 7, p. 492), exists in a world of 'papa, potatoes, poultry, prunes and prism, prunes and prism' (book 2, chapter 5, p. 462). There is, however, a slight but significant difference between the dehumaniza-tion of the human in *Our Mutual Friend*, compared with Dickens's previous novels. Before *Our Mutual Friend*, the inhumanity of human beings is presented through characterization in conjunction with appropriate imagery, metaphor, and simile; in *Our Mutual Friend*, the Veneerings are no longer humans, but images of incomplete humans or metonymic people. They both exaggerate and undermine that 'exteriority of the inward' that pervades Dickens's novels—under-

---

[43] See Chapter 4 above for further discussion of the relationship between the animate and the inanimate world as it is presented in Dickens's melodramatic prose poetics.

mine in the sense that both their exteriority and their innerness announce themselves as reflections of exteriority and innerness.[44] While Timothy Clark describes Dickens's fascination with idea of the image as 'a non-signifying materiality', the image of the Veneerings is one of non-signifying immateriality.[45]

Ironically, the dehumanization of the human is a device also used in Lord Chesterfield's *Letters*; people are not only referred to as actors; they are described as machines, or mechanisms.[46] The use of the word 'perfect' is not unusual in the *Letters* and reflects Chesterfield's belief that human beings can be programmed or moulded to perfection, like mechanisms or works of art.[47] The crucial difference between Dickens's world picture and the dandiacal or Chesterfield version, however, is that Dickens's veneers are framed by the ideology of cultural inclusivity. 'Stuffed people' and Veneerings are not the only inhabitants in the Dickens universe; they epitomize a certain malaise which Dickens's social critique, and the alternative models of identity it suggests, does its best to counter.

The Veneerings arguably demonstrate the superiority of the written word to the theatre as an instrument with which to investigate genteel society's valorization of surfaces. This is perhaps paradoxical as the theatre, particularly melodrama, is reliant— physically—on surfaces. The resources of the novel, however, allow the Veneerings to be presented directly to our imagination; it would be impossible for any Victorian stage melodramatist or director/ manager physically to represent human abstractions; this would be a contradiction worthy of Shakespeare's Bottom. On the printed page, the Veneerings take their place as a necessary part of the imagery and machinery of a novel investigating, on a literal and metaphorical plane, the relationship between the human and the non-human, real people and fictional stereotypes, passion and lack of passion, etc. The Veneerings literally disappear into the work of art. At the same time, the 'superiority' of the novel as a medium for investigating 'the loss of the real' suggests its potential for cultural divisiveness. Dickens's novelistic dandification of dandies ultimately hints at the ability of the written word literally to reduce people to intellectual abstractions.

---

[44] Timothy Clark, 'Dickens through Blanchot: The Nightmare Fascination of a World without Interiority', in Schad (ed.), *Dickens Refigured: Bodies, Desires and Other Histories*, 22–38 (p. 31).

[45] Ibid. 36.

[46] For example, see *Letters*, 186 (19 Dec. 1749), 228 (16 May 1751).

[47] Ibid. 221 (28 Feb. 1751).

That Dickens's passionless, hollow individuals are framed by melo-drama's passional economy and culturally inclusive ideology is designed to ensure, however, that the written word's potential for 'abstracting' people is analysed rather than simply utilized.

7
Byronic Baddies, Melodramatic Anxieties

The Byronic hero appears to symbolize the kind of Romantic individualism Dickens despised.[1] He is a self-destructive role-player, whose pale, aristocratic features mask a mysterious inner life. His energy is largely internalized, as the external world—excepting, perhaps, the female sex—seems to offer little for which he cares, little in fact which interests him as much as the theatre of his own ego. It is not surprising that this symbol of the involuted, antisocial, often aristocratic individual was demonized in melodrama. It is also unsurprising that the few direct comments made by Dickens on Byron and his poetry were disapproving or moralistic in tone. On 25 November 1840, Dickens wrote to S. Horrell:

It is not the province of a Poet to harp upon his own discontents, or to teach other people that they ought to be discontented. Leave Byron to his gloomy greatness, and do you

> Find tongues in trees, books in the running brooks,
> Sermons in stones, and good in everything.[2]

On 28 February 1843, Dickens confessed in significant terms to Miss Coutts that he was 'in danger of turning misanthropical, Byronic, and devilish'.[3]

If the Byronic individual acts as a threat to the overt moral and ideological scheme of melodramatic art, however, he functions more ambiguously in relation to melodramatic aesthetics. For the Byronic hero is (like the poet himself) highly theatrical, and particularly attractive to those employing melodramatic aesthetics because of the

---

[1] The apparent antithesis between the values of Dickens and Byron partly explains the disappointing omission of Dickens from Andrew Elfenbein's *Byron and the Victorians*, Cambridge Studies in Nineteenth-Century Literature and Culture, IV (Cambridge: Cambridge University Press, 1995).

[2] *Letters* (Pilgrim), ii. 155.

[3] Ibid. iii. 447.

claims he makes to a passional life. Most important, however, is the defining interiority of the Byronic individual: his inner life is in fact never visible but constantly inferred via extravagant performances of secretive selfhood. Thus Byron's strategies for the presentation of self share melodrama's avoidance of the subject-centred view of identity. Like stage melodrama, Byron's poetry relies on surfaces to imply an inner life that is emotionally constituted; like Dickens, Byron uses the visible manifestations of selfhood to interrogate the nature and reality of the passions and the invisible life. Indeed, Dan Jacobson argues that the guilty secret that most Byronic heroes seem to possess 'is their own suspicion that they are fakers'.[4] In his interrogation of the idea of the inner life as the 'root' of externalized projections, Byron has as much in common with Dickens (and with postmodern writers) as he has with Romantic predecessors like Coleridge. Both question, yet engage with, the idea of essences.

The Byronic individual thus functions as the site of a layered critique in Dickens's work. On an obvious level, he is the overt object of Dickens's exploration of the ideological and ethical implications of Romantic individualism and the art to which it is central. On a second level, Dickens uses the Byronic type as an oppositional instrument through which he can interrogate melodramatic art and its assumptions about identity. But the Byronic individual is melodramatic, as well as Romantic, as his frequent appearances as the villain in melodrama confirm. The mongrel pedigree of Dickens's Byronic individuals—which draw on both Byron's poetry and the Romantics 'in' melodrama—thus makes them the ideal site for a relative reassessment of the assumed opposition between Romantic and melodramatic art.

While we are familiar with the kind of challenges melodramatic art poses to its legitimate Romantic contemporary, the melodramatic focus of this study has necessarily silenced the challenges Romanticism poses to melodrama. Dickens uses the Byronic individual primarily to question melodrama's ethical and ideological scheme: this assumes that the moral universe is the 'first cause' which speaks through the social world, and that moral behaviour expresses itself in a universal language which transcends class. Dickens's Byronic types problematize, in particular, the melodramatic assumption that sincerity—that moral talisman of the Victorians—is an ethical

---

[4] 'What's Eating Lara? (or Lord Byron's Guiltiest Secret)', in *Adult Pleasures: Essays on Writers and Readers* (London: Deutsch, 1988), 31–9 (p. 35).

quality rather than a social construct, which expresses itself uniformly across classes through unmediated externalization of the emotions. Melodrama advocates rather than analyses transparent models of selfhood and consequently demonizes forms of role-playing which obscure the private self. While Dickens's non-fictional statements suggest his championing of a transparent model of individuality motivated by 'impassioned purposefulness' and 'the meaningfulness of effort', his novels, particularly the later ones, complicate this ideal.[5] The Byronic individuals of Dickens's novels reflect his awareness that one's chosen method of self-presentation is not necessarily an index of moral character. Dickens's Byronic characters are obsessed with sincerity and reflect Dickens's appreciation that achieving a state of sincerity is not a simple matter of externalizing or expressing one's inner thoughts and feelings. Nor is it a case of being true to oneself, as Shakespeare's Polonius misguidedly suggests:

> This above all—to thine own self be true,
> And it must follow, as the night the day,
> Thou canst not then be false to any man. (*Hamlet*, i. iii. 78–80)

—or of believing in the image of self one projects, as Erving Goffman maintains; he reserves 'the term "sincere" for individuals who believe in the impressions fostered by their own performance'.[6]

But if the Byronic individual problematizes, in Dickens's novels, the melodramatic association of sincerity with tranparency or publicity, he is also the site of Dickens's subversion of the Romantic tendency to situate sincerity *inside* the private individual. Matthew Arnold demonstrates the high cultural pervasiveness, in the Victorian period, of the Romantic idea that the authentic 'self' resides in an asocial, interior space:

> Below the surface-stream, shallow and light,
> Of what we *say* we feel—below the stream,
> As light, of what we *think* we feel—there flows
> With noiseless current strong, obscure and deep,
> The central stream of what we feel indeed.[7]

---

[5] Johnson, *Charles Dickens: His Tragedy and his Triumph*, ii. 697.
[6] *The Presentation of Self in Everyday Life*, Pelican (1959; Harmondsworth: Penguin, 1987), 28–9.
[7] From an essay entitled 'St. Paul and Protestantism', *Cornhill Magazine* (Nov. 1869); repr. in *The Poems of Matthew Arnold*, ed. Kenneth Allott (London: Longmans, 1953), 543.

The Byronic type thus foregrounds Dickens's questioning of both Romantic and melodramatic ideologies: for both assume, with different emphases, that the self can transcend social conditioning.

Operating in tandem with an interrogation of the notion of sincerity in Dickens's novels is always a consideration of the ethical and social function of various kinds of acting or role-playing. Dickens is particularly concerned with the class and power dynamics of the relationship between the conscious performer of self and his audience, or between the Romantic and the melodramatic individual. It is interesting how often Dickens, in the later novels, pairs Byronic with melodramatic characters, or at least with characters (often lower class) who possess a childlike, melodramatic belief in the transparency of surfaces—we think of Steerforth and 'Daisy' Copperfield, and Wrayburn and Headstone (or Lizzie), to name just a couple of examples. The repressive performativity so vilified in Dickens's journalism is so often the characteristic, in the novels, of the socially superior, Byronic deviant that Dickens eventually has to foreground the implications of the fact that it can spring from class conditioning as much as innate selfishness or wickedness. Viewed symbolically, these pairings dramatize the cultural hierarchy which so often underpins the relationship between the Romantic and the melodramatic mode.

A consequence of Dickens's increased emphasis on the social construction of selfhood and its ethical exhibitions is that he dilutes, or at least unmasks, his melodramatic art. Dickens appears to dress his characters as either villains or heroes whilst questioning the essentialist ethical scheme which produced them. Dickens never abandons melodramatic aesthetics: in the later novels, he plays on them. At the heart of Dickens's interrogation of the melodramatic foundations of his fiction is the function of melodramatic character types as models of social identity. Dickens, as we have witnessed, appreciated the constructedness of melodramatic character throughout his career; so in this sense the revisionism conducted through Byronic characters represents no new 'discoveries'. At issue here is the social and ethical function of art. What separates Dickens from Byron is the synonymity Dickens assumes between moral and culturally inclusive art. What attracts Dickens to melodrama is the communal nature of the models of identity and society it suggests. While Byron's heroes convey more sophisticated insights into both selfhood and society than the comparatively simplistic Byronic villains of melodrama, for example, they do not necessarily act as models of moral improvement, or as instruments of communality.

Dickens's continued reliance on melodramatic aesthetics and ideologies, even in the late novels, suggests his reluctance to let go of a vision of popular art as an instrument of social cohesion. In other words, people continue to need utopian, if unrealistic, versions of themselves and their society. But it is the unrealistic nature of his melodramatic models which visibly troubles Dickens in the late novels: to project ideal fictions on an unsuspecting public is hardly consonant with transparency or 'sincerity'; nor is the idea that the author knows best consistent with strictly egalitarian art. However, Dickens is never convinced that unmediated reality is a good thing in fiction, nor does he ever equate popular culture with democratic culture. As a result, the moralistic thrust of melodrama is not jettisoned but refined.

Dickens continues to reject the Romantic valorization of interiority, and/or any suggestion that educated analyses of the inner life *are* reality. The increasing seriousness and intensity with which the repressed, 'private' individual is regarded is thus mediated through a sustained attention to role-playing and its social conditions. Transparent, idealized character types remain integral to Dickens's vision, but he attempts to resolve the 'problem' of their unreality by highlighting their fictional status. The reader is thus given the choice of whether or not to believe in them and how to interpret them. Dickens employs melodrama, that is, with a self-consciousness that becomes more noticeable as his career nears its end. Moreover, this self-consciousness is itself problematized, as Dickens interrogates its ideological and ethical status. The two-way double perspective through which the melodramatic and the self-conscious, Byronic vision are often explored, in late Dickens, focuses his increasing sense of the difficulties attending art which aims to be both ethical and culturally inclusive.

SINCERELY STEERFORTH?

James Steerforth in *David Copperfield* is arguably the first of Dickens's non-comic, novelistic characters to be significantly influenced by the Byronic type. Indeed, commentators (employing varying moral emphases) have traditionally argued that Steerforth is the most

Byronic of all Dickens's creations.[8] Common to many descriptions of Steerforth is the idea of his autonomy or social detachment. Mario Praz set the critical tone when he described Steerforth as 'the fascinating, untrammelled aristocrat, [. . .] the symbol of the Romantic poet in the guise in which he appeared in England, in Byron particularly, and with a few allusions to Shelley as well (his death in a shipwreck during a storm)'.[9] While Steerforth certainly strikes other characters in the novel as being otherworldly, his Byronism is clearly the product of class conditioning. I am not talking here about his aristocratic status, for the point about Steerforth is that he is neither unambiguously aristocratic, nor 'untrammelled', as Praz puts it. It is the Byronic hero who is aristocratic: Steerforth plays the part of the Byronic hero for social status and power. His Byronism is not simply an act, however, nor is he a social climber. Steerforth and his Byronism are his mother's creations.

From the first, Mrs Steerforth, with her 'stateliness' of manner and 'lofty' air, has brought her son up to play a regal and heroic role which sits oddly with her choice of a minor public school like Salem House, for example, or with Steerforth's frequent choice of lower-class companions. She tells David that Salem House

> was not a fit school generally for my son, [. . .] but [. . .] my son's high spirit made it desirable that he should be placed with some man who felt its superiority, and would be content to bow himself before it; and we found such a man there. (chapter 20, p. 253)

Her emphasis on her son's 'high spirit', 'superiority', rebelliousness, and individualism—all qualities admired by the Romantics Byron and Shelley, particularly—demonstrates the role she has moulded for her son in life, that of Romantic hero.[10] It is a model of heroism which takes little account of conventional morality (as witnessed by the hero-worship Milton's Satan elicited in several of the Romantics).

---

[8] See also Johnson, *Charles Dickens: His Tragedy and his Triumph*, ii. 696, Harvey, 'Charles Dickens and the Byronic Hero', 309, Arnold Kettle, 'Thoughts on *David Copperfield*', *Review of English Literature*, 2 (1961), 64–74 (p. 73), Angus Wilson, 'The Heroes and Heroines of Dickens', in John Gross and Gabriel Pearson (eds.), *Dickens and the Twentieth Century* (London: Routledge & Kegan Paul, 1962), pp. 3–11 (p. 9).

[9] *The Hero in Eclipse in Victorian Fiction*, trans. Angus Davidson (London: Oxford University Press, 1956), 127.

[10] Mrs Steerforth's Romantic description of her son is echoed by other characters elsewhere. See, for example, David's description of the effect of Steerforth's manner on Ham and Mr Peggotty when they visit Salem House, which David still believes 'to have borne a kind of enchantment with it' (chapter 7, pp. 89–90).

Perhaps the most perturbing implications of Mrs Steerforth's 'casting' of her son are manifested in her melodramatic description of the sacking of Mr Mell: 'He [Steerforth] would have risen against all constraint; but he found himself the monarch of the place, and he haughtily determined to be worthy of his station. It was like himself' (chapter 20, p. 253). Her words objectify Steerforth: 'it' (his behaviour) was like 'himself' (the heroic, Romantic, and ideal Steerforth that Mrs Steerforth has created as the chosen role for her son). Mrs Steerforth fictionalizes her son, demonstrating Lionel Trilling's point that 'The hero is one who looks like a hero; the hero is an actor—he acts out his own high sense of himself.'[11] The poignant part of Steerforth's story is that he is an actor even in childhood; he experiences himself from the outside, so to speak. Steerforth's sense of himself as an actor means that he is unable to become 'genuinely' emotionally involved with other human beings, or to feel connections with them. He sees the world as a stage, and, as Heilman maintains, 'the enlarged sense of oneself as a good actor, like an enlarged sense of oneself as an evildoer, may become a disabling illness'.[12]

Indeed, despite the impression of intense subjectivity often associated with the Byronic pose, Steerforth's moments of experienced, rather than performed, Byronism—as far as we can distinguish between the two—paradoxically reflect the angst he feels at his inability to experience the world subjectively. That Steerforth's problematic relationship with his own subjectivity is rendered through David's first person narrative is easy to forget. David's characteristic inconspicuousness is a product of his external, melodramatic focus (and vice versa), and an impersonality reflexively related to Steerforth's own. Steerforth experiences his own selfhood as dislocated—or even fictional—and consequently finds it difficult to believe in the self-projections of others. His view of the world as a stage is verbalized most explicitly when he describes Doctor's Commons as staffed by 'actors' engaged in 'a very pleasant, profitable little affair of private theatricals, presented to an uncommonly select audience' (chapter 23, p. 293).

Steerforth's sophisticated performativity is largely responsible for his power over David. The friendship between the two boys, in fact,

---

[11] *Sincerity and Authenticity*, 85; Trilling's idea is based on that put forward by Robert Warshow's essay on Western films, 'The Westerner', in *The Immediate Experience* (Garden City, NY: Doubleday, 1962), 153.

[12] *Tragedy and Melodrama*, 111.

can be seen as dramatizing the hierarchical relationship which exists in our culture between the Romantic and the melodramatic mode. The young David (or 'Daisy') needs to believe in fictions in order to make life bearable: we think of him as a boy 'reading as if for life' (chapter 4, p. 48). Steerforth, by contrast, associates performativity with power and personal gain, demonstrating a cynical, adult view of the world even in childhood. It is thus not surprising that David's attitude to Steerforth is throughout the infatuation that one has for an actor or screen idol. David has an emotional need for heroes and villains. Indeed, throughout the novel, he casts characters in melodramatic roles, the insufficiency and dangerousness of which is implied by the retrospective narrative voice. He is only too happy to assume a melodramatic synonymity between appearance and reality—hence his misreading of Dora, Agnes, the Strongs, and Steerforth. In Steerforth's case, he grasps at the projected fantasy of heroism on the basis of the appearance of his name, carved in an old door in the playground: 'There was one boy—a certain J. Steerforth—who cut his name very deep and very often, who, I conceived, would read it in a rather strong voice, and afterwards pull my hair' (chapter 5, p. 68). David perfectly embodies Carey's claim that 'In the Dickens world it is only the child who does not put on a mask', as well as suggesting Bentley's insight that 'it is as children and as dreamers [. . .] that we enjoy melodrama'.[13]

The relationship between David's naivety and Steerforth's cynicism is most directly dramatized when the two meet at the theatre after the performance of *Julius Caesar* and the pantomime. Steerforth is incapable of the childlike enthusiasm for, and belief in, nineteenth-century theatricals; his contempt for the productions is that of a theatrical insider. Ignoring the overt 'content' of the production (as he earlier ignored Steerforth's immoral behaviour), David enthuses that the show enabled him to experience 'a romantic life' different from the 'miserable world' in which he feels like 'a stranger upon earth' (chapter 19, pp. 244–5). Steerforth, by contrast, claims of the performance: 'there never was a more miserable business' (chapter 19, p. 246). The inverted linguistic echoes between the friends' responses, and David's 'Romantic' description of himself in Byronic terms—as 'a stranger upon earth'—suggest the idea of a dialectical relationship between the Romantic and the melodramatic vision which, in *David Copperfield* at least, Dickens eventually subverts.

[13] 'Dickens and the Mask', 4; see also p. 51 above.

While the immature David frequently makes the reader aware of the proximity of the Romantic and the melodramatic modes, Steerforth emphasizes the gulf between the two. Envious of David's melodramatic transparency, he is yet unable, like Richard Wardour, to throw off Romantic angst and immerse himself in the simple 'acts' and ethics of melodrama.

This inability is partly related to one key respect in which he differs from Byron's heroes: he wants to be popular and admired. In chapter 21, for example, David observes that 'the consciousness of success in his determination to please, inspired him with a new delicacy of perception, and made it, subtle as it was, more easy to him' (p. 265). His need for popularity has fascinating self-reflexive implications for Dickens's own populism. Though Steerforth's desire to please brings immediate happiness to his audience, it also foregrounds the possible corrupting effects that can accompany the compulsion to be popular. David passionately exclaims that he never would have believed that 'all this was a brilliant game [. . .] played for the excitement of the moment, for the employment of high spirits, in the thoughtless love of superiority, in a mere wasteful careless course of winning what was worthless to him, and next minute thrown away' (chapter 21, p. 265). His description of Steerforth is strikingly similar to Goffman's analysis of the cynic:

It should be understood that the cynic, with all his professional disinvolvement, may obtain unprofessional pleasures from his masquerade, experiencing a kind of gleeful spiritual aggression from the fact that he can toy at will with something his audience must take seriously.[14]

The desire to please can engender a dislocation of personality which renders one's self-image completely subordinate to how one is perceived by others. The consequence of this is that performances of self are disconnected from what Wagner calls 'antecedent causes', and the performer's inability to experience him- or herself subjectively renders him or her unable to conceive of the subjective life of others either. Any sense of social or moral responsibility is thus secondary to the immediate pleasure of popularity, or 'the thoughtless love of superiority'.

But Steerforth's populism is also grounded in the desire to make emotional connections with others—and perhaps with himself. Indeed, the desire to experience life emotionally—and indeed

[14] *The Presentation of Self in Everyday Life*, 28–9.

morally—is what distinguishes Steerforth from Dickens's cannibalistic individuals. Dickens's presentation of Steerforth is complicated
by the fact that the novel is riddled with reminders of Steerforth's
own desire to achieve a state of transparent or 'melodramatic'
sincerity in which he has some belief. Steerforth ironically seems to
believe in the melodramatic law that transparency is 'good' and performativity 'bad', even while he flouts it. Perhaps his most important
statement in this respect comes again in chapter 21: 'Daisy, I believe
you are in earnest, and are good. I wish we all were!' (p. 271).
Steerforth, in other words, appreciates the value of David's childlike,
melodramatic view of the world and laments its loss in himself. His
patronage of David is thus also nostalgic, belittling and valuing a
'wholeness' of vision he has never possessed. He is arguably as
emotionally dependent on David as David is on him. David's innocence and transparency is an antidote to Steerforth's Byronism, just
as this Byronism seems to David to provide the romance his childhood has lacked. David acts as a symbol to Steerforth of his lost childhood and vice versa. A 'dark kind of earnestness' (chapter 22, p. 275)
is significantly only possible for Steerforth when he is alone. His
memorable parting comment to David—'Think of me at my best, if
circumstances should ever part us!' (chapter 29, p. 373)—suggests
Schiller's theory that 'Every individual human being [. . .] carries
with him, potentially and prescriptively, an ideal man, the archetype
of a human being, and it is his life's task to be [. . .] in harmony with
the unchanging unity of this ideal.'[15] Steerforth's problem, however,
is that he does not always believe in the heroic or ideal self he
presents to the outside world, though David of course does. In some
respects, David is more than Steerforth's ideal audience: he is more
Steerforth's ideal self than the Byronic pose he projects, while the
Byronic Steerforth is David's 'ideal man'.

　　Steerforth is in some senses the victim of a state of mind referred to
by the Romantics as 'Weltschmerz', a label which literally means
'world-weariness', but is defined in more detail by Thorslev as a

Romantic disease [. . .] an almost irreconcilable conflict between two
opposing forces [. . .]. The one force or drive is to lose oneself in some vision
of the Absolute; a longing for some intellectual and moral certainty [. . .].
The twin and opposing force [. . .] is toward a positive and passionate asser-

　　[15] F. Schiller, *On the Aesthetic Education of Man*, ed. and trans. E. M. Wilkinson and L. A.
Willoughby (Oxford: Clarendon Press, 1967), 17; quoted by Trilling, *Sincerity and Authenticity*,
5.

tion of oneself as an individual, a self-assertion which makes impossible any wholehearted commitment to dogmas or absolutes outside oneself.[16]

Interestingly, 'Weltschmerz' is the quality which attracted the Romantics to Hamlet. Steerforth, like Hamlet, is unable to commit himself to anything or anyone in his society, yet this society planted and encouraged his chameleonic individualism. Relief from 'Weltschmerz' was frequently seen, in Keats's poetry in particular, to lie in death, the only attainable absolute. It is thus in keeping with the characterization of Steerforth elsewhere in the novel that he, like Shelley, meets an early, watery death. But significantly the reader's response does not echo Ham's melodramatic judgement of Steerforth as a 'damned villain' (chapter 31, p. 387). Ham's unwitting quotation from *Hamlet*—'Oh villain, villain, smiling damned villain | [. . .] That one may smile, and smile, and be a villain' (i. v. 106–8)— reinforces the potential complexity of making moral judgements.

The reader's response to Steerforth, like David's, is ultimately bifocal. It combines the moralism of melodrama with an awareness of the incompleteness of a 'moral-conduct' view of either art or identity.[17] The final, ambivalent, verdict on Steerforth's character is pronounced by David, who has not rejected the melodramatic vision but decided to employ it self-consciously:

In the keen distress of the discovery of his unworthiness, I [. . .] did more justice to the qualities that might have made him a man of a noble nature [. . .], than ever I had done in the height of my devotion to him. [. . .] What his remembrances of me were, I have never known—they were light enough, perhaps, and easily dismissed—but mine of him were as the remembrances of a cherished friend, who was dead. (chapter 32, p. 388)

The double time scheme of the novel, of course, facilitates this double perspective, David the child viewing the world melodramatically and David the adult lamenting the unreality of this vision. Perhaps even more intriguing is the fact, reported by Forster, that Dickens told a girl that he himself cried when he read about Steerforth.[18] Both

---

[16] Peter L. Thorslev, Jr., *The Byronic Hero: Types and Prototypes* (Minneapolis: University of Minnesota Press, 1962; repr. 1965), 88–9.

[17] S. L. Goldberg distinguishes between the 'moral-conduct' and 'moral-life' view of character; the former uses action, and the latter motivation, as the basis of moral judgement. Goldberg's Romantic opposition valorizes the 'moral-life' approach, which is 'deeper' and deals with 'states of soul'—'Literary Judgement: Making Moral Sense of Poems', *Critical Review*, 28 (1986), 18–46 (p. 27).

[18] See van Amerongen, *The Actor in Dickens*, 43, Carey, *The Violent Effigy*, 172. Carey cites Dickens as saying, 'Yes, I cry when I read about Steerforth.'

David and Dickens combine moral judgement of Steerforth's conduct with a wilful nostalgia about Steerforth's performed persona. As adults, they choose melodrama with a wistful awareness of its fictionality. The sheer lack of 'impassioned purposefulness' in the condemnation of Steerforth invokes the bifocal nostalgia of Dickens's journalistic writings on melodrama. It also suggests Dickens's understanding of the complex moral, social, and emotional problems posed by Byronism.

Dickens (like Steerforth) understood the dangers of a shallow vision of humanity, of seeing human beings simply as actors or as types. At the same time, David's hero-worship of Steerforth suggests the dangers of a valorization of assumed depths—and of the 'moral-life' view of character so prominent in post-Romantic character criticism.[19] While David the novelist attaches depths to the public personae of others, Steerforth usually assumes that surfaces are just that—surfaces. Steerforth is a character who confuses the relationship between surfaces and depths. He is a complex rebuff to critics who, like Henry James, see Dickens as 'the greatest of superficial novelists'. For Steerforth, though intellectually and emotionally complex and aware of his complexity, is nevertheless, like Dickens's version of Hamlet, a literary representation of a deeply shallow person.[20] Dickens's portrayal of Steerforth is not itself superficial, but a complex exploration of the causes and effects of superficiality.

What is also at stake in the characterization of Steerforth and Dickens's other Byronic individuals is an analysis of the relationship between fictional and social models of identity. Despite the many critical attempts to categorize Steerforth as either 'villain' or 'hero', a 'theatrical' reading of Steerforth's character illustrates the fabricated nature of absolute moral categories (such as those which underpin melodrama).[21] The novel does not ultimately endorse Byronism, however. 'Sympathy' with the actor of the Byronic role, or an understanding of the social conditions which fostered it, does not make that role socially desirable. The Byronic individual in *David Copperfield* highlights the unreality yet indispensability of melodramatic fictions in a post-Romantic age.

---

[19] See n. 17 above.

[20] Compare my introductory discussion of Dickens's comments on Hamlet.

[21] See Carey, *The Violent Effigy*, 171, Harvey, 'Charles Dickens and the Byronic Hero', p. 308, Wilson, 'The Heroes and Heroines of Dickens', 8.

BYRONIC HOCUS-POCUS: HENRY GOWAN AND JAMES HARTHOUSE

Henry Gowan and James Harthouse have been compared with the sadist, the dandy, and Satan, as well as the Byronic hero.[22] On first appearance, both Harthouse and Gowan seem closer copies of the heroes of Byron's poetry than Steerforth, in so far as they openly flaunt their scepticism and disillusionment. They do not have a compulsive desire to be generally popular and admired, and unashamedly demonstrate their contempt for those who believe in concepts like sincerity and morality—usually their listeners. Paradoxically, both could be seen as *honest or sincere cynics*. Both adopt what they present as an unsentimental, rational view of the world, claiming to disbelieve that the material world has any meaning beyond itself. Harthouse demonstrates, for example, a 'genteel listlessness for the general society' (*HT*, book 2, chapter 7, p. 166) of Coketown, and a lack of belief in himself. He tells Sissy: 'I cannot say, [. . .] that I have any sanguine expectation of ever becoming a moral sort of fellow, or that I have any belief in any moral sort of fellow whatever' (book 3, chapter 2, pp. 232–3). Gowan's scepticism, likewise, results in an amoral perspective on the world at best. The narrator imitates Gowan's process of making moral judgements thus:

'I claim to be always book-keeping, with a peculiar nicety, in every man's case, and posting up a careful little account of Good and Evil with him. I do this so conscientiously, that [. . .] I find [. . .] that there is much less difference than you are inclined to suppose between an honest man and a scoundrel.' (book 1, chapter 17, p. 200)

Gowan's claims to objectivity and reason are actually emotional, motivated by malice and selfishness. Moreover, his performances of indifference about his society are in reality driven by class envy and insecurity. His 'Byronic' inability to commit himself to the work ethic results not from a rational or political objection to it but from personal resentment that he is not accepted as a member of the aristocracy:

So now Mr. Gowan, like that worn-out old coffin which never was Mahomet's nor anybody else's, hung midway between two points: jaundiced and jealous as to the one he had left: jaundiced and jealous as to the other he couldn't reach. (book 1, chapter 17, p. 202)

---

[22] Harvey, 'Charles Dickens and the Byronic Hero', 309–10; Cedric Hentschel, *The Byronic Teuton: Aspects of German Pessimism, 1800–1933* (London: Methuen, 1940), 7.

'TO be in the halting state of Mr. Henry Gowan', the narrator later points out, 'to be loitering moodily about on neutral ground, cursing both; is to be in a situation unwholesome for the mind, which time is not likely to improve' (book 2, chapter 6, p. 472). Thus Gowan constantly pities himself, wallowing in the role of 'a disappointed man' (book 1, chapter 34, p. 391). But his Byronism is only skin-deep, stemming from an over-valuing of a class system of a society that does not value him. He thus *plays the role* of the gloomy egoist, using the Byronic pose as a sign of the social and cultural capital he feels he lacks. Steerforth is also of course a poser whose Byronism is conditioned, but his Byronism becomes self-fulfilling; it is experienced as well as performed.

The superficial pettiness of Gowan's 'passions', and the fact that he constantly plays a role, mean that he is unable to identify with the emotional depths of others, and has no desire to do so. Little Dorrit speculates, for example,

that Mr. Gowan treated his wife [. . .] too much like a beautiful child. He seemed so unsuspicious of the depths of feeling which she knew must lie below that surface, that she doubted if there could be any such depths in himself. She wondered whether his want of earnestness might be the natural result of his want of such qualities, and whether it was with people as with ships, that, in too shallow and rocky waters, their anchors had no hold, and they drifted anywhere. (book 2, chapter 6, p. 480)

In *Hard Times*, Harthouse's view of Louisa is explained in almost exactly the same terms: 'To be sure, the better and profounder part of her character was not within his scope of perception; for in natures, as in seas, depth answers unto depth; but he soon began to read the rest with a student's eye' (book 2, chapter 7, p. 167). In Dickens's novels, as Chapter 4 explained, the sense of 'depths' is invariably given by Dickens's dramatization of dynamic emotional connections between people and things. Connected feeling or a feeling of connection thus constitutes the 'antecedent cause' which gives surfaces the impression of depths. Invisible emotional depths are never empirically knowable. Belief in the dimensionality of identity must be emotional rather than rational, the result of a willingness to ascribe emotion to surfaces, to construct emotional fictions—to view things 'sympathetically'. Harthouse and Gowan possess the intellectual mechanism of a sympathetic imagination without the emotional content that the word sympathy implies. They are thus incapable of

the passional acts of perception which ascribe meaning where meaning is impossible to prove empirically.

It is because of Gowan's inability to perform such passional acts of
perception that Dickens is so scathing about his artistic profession.
Indeed Gowan himself is characteristically scathing about the
means by which he earns his living. He claims that the meaning of
life is 'to keep up the pretence as to labour, and study, and patience,
and being devoted' to an art he believes is 'hocus-pocus' (book 1,
chapter 34, pp. 392–3). His diminution of art as a profession echoes
that of Thackeray, and stems in fact from the same cause—social
snobbery and a pseudo-aristocratic resentment at having to adopt
a profession at all.[23] Gowan is correct, however, in his judgement
that his art is 'hocus-pocus' and 'imposition' (book 1, chapter 34,
p. 392). He makes no emotional connection with his art, nor does he
care about the pleasure it may elicit in its viewer. His conception of
art is entirely material or commercial; his relationship with his
work enacts Marx's idea of alienated labour. To return to the
Wagnerian terms adopted in Chapter 4, Gowan's art—as opposed to
Doyce's invention—represents 'effect'. Gowan embodies and pre-
dicts Adorno's fears about the culture industry: he treats art as a
commodity and its consumers as philistines. The assumption of intellectual superiority in Gowan's attitude to those who purchase his art
suggests a fragmented model of the cultural market place wherein
taste functions as an instrument of social segregation. It is for these
reasons, therefore, that Gowan the artist is so detested, not, as
George Bernard Shaw argues, because Dickens is a philistine
who does not understand art.[24] The idea of the artist as an empty
impostor, an intellectually astute parasite who respects neither his art
nor its audience, is one which clearly disturbed Dickens, as it was
later to disturb Tolstoy in his compelling work *What Is Art?* To
Tolstoy, the 'activity of art' is 'to evoke in oneself a feeling one has
once experienced, and having evoked it in oneself, then, by means of
movements, lines, colours, sounds, or forms expressed in words, so
to transmit that feeling that others may experience the same feel-

---

[23] See George H. Ford, *Dickens and his Readers: Aspects of Novel-Criticism since 1836*
(Princeton: Princeton University Press, 1955), 24, for Dickens's attitude to Thackeray's
'pretence of undervaluing his art'.

[24] See Humphry House, 'George Bernard Shaw on *Great Expectations*', in *All in Due Time*,
201–20 (p. 202); House discusses the Introduction to *GE* written by Shaw in 1937 for the
edition of Limited Editions Club of New York.

ing'.[25] Gowan practises what Tolstoy (ironically referring to Wagner) calls 'counterfeit art'.[26]

It is fitting, therefore, that Gowan chooses the murderer Rigaud Blandois as his shadowy companion for a time. As we saw in Chapters 1 and 3, Rigaud is flagrantly inauthentic, a cannibalistic performer who personifies the horror of a hollow universe. Rigaud, however, characteristically persists in flaunting his own 'genuineness'. He tells Mrs Clennam, for example, 'I have a partiality for everything genuine. Such as I am, I am genuine myself' (book 1, chapter 30, p. 349). Though, as this book has made clear, there is some paradoxical truth in his assertions, Rigaud is patently mocking the idea of genuineness he appears to uphold. His histrionic sarcasm about genuineness has a specific target, moreover. Rigaud parodies both Romantic models of heroism and the Romantic model of the artist with which these heroic models are so closely associated. Mocking Byron's famous description, in 'The Corsair; A Tale' (1814), of Conrad's 'one virtue' amidst 'a thousand crimes'[27]—his chivalry and fidelity towards the opposite sex—Rigaud tells Jeremiah concerning Mrs Clennam: 'chivalry towards the sex is a part of my character!' (book 1, chapter 30, p. 346). Again the Romantic character is satirized, when Rigaud Blandois declares that he is not only pious, but 'sensitive, ardent, conscientious, and imaginative' (book 1, chapter 30, p. 351). In the same interview with Mrs Clennam, Rigaud claims, 'I love and study the picturesque, in all its varieties. I have been called picturesque myself' (book 1, chapter 30, p. 352). The deliberate parody employed by Dickens through Rigaud is rendered explicit in the narratorial aside: '(it was characteristic of this man, as it is of all men similarly marked, that whatever he did, he overdid, though it were sometimes by only a hair's-breadth)' (book 1, chapter 30, pp. 351–2).

Rigaud's parodic potential is seized upon by Henry Gowan who uses him to mock the manners and values of the middle classes:

He [Gowan] found a pleasure in setting up Blandois as the type of elegance, and making him a satire upon others who piqued themselves on personal graces. [. . .] That exaggeration in the manner of the man [. . .] was acceptable to Gowan as a caricature, which he found it a humorous resource to

---

[25] p. 50.
[26] Ibid. 139.
[27] *The Complete Poetical Works*, ed. Jerome J. McGann, 6 vols. (Oxford: Clarendon Press, 1981), iii (1981), 148–214 (III. xxiv. 696).

have at hand for the ridiculing of numbers of people who necessarily did more or less of what Blandois over-did. (book 2, chapter 6, p. 473)

In Gowan's view, Rigaud's 'true yet vital hollowness' simply exaggerates that of the aspirational classes. Rigaud's Romantic posturing, to Gowan, reflects the sentimental and Romantic view the middle classes have of themselves as if in a distorting mirror. At the same time, their need to believe in the myth of the Romantic artist and his productions suggests their felt anxieties about their own value and authenticity. It is as if the Romantic artist becomes a symbol of transcendence and integrity in a material world driven by a social class unsure of its own status—hanging 'midway between two points', in a 'halting state [. . .] unwholesome for the mind'.

Viewed in this way, the Byronic pose is the objective correlative of middle-class insecurity in *Little Dorrit*. Byronism functions as both a sign of social and cultural capital and a symbol of its felt lack. The performativity of the middle classes is both an instrument of power and a manifestation of felt powerlessness, in Dickens's novels. The Byronic individual thus lays claim to an autonomy or 'sincerity' which sets him apart from the class insecurities of the middle ground, whilst unwittingly symbolizing the insecurity and theatricality he is reacting against. So if Gowan's Byronism is largely a pose, it is crucial to the exploration of Byronism conducted in *Little Dorrit* as a whole. Gowan intensifies, in nucleus, all the human, artistic, and social neuroses which pervade the mood of the novel. Trilling argues that *Little Dorrit* is 'Dickens's great portrayal of what he regards as the total inauthenticity of England';[28] his words are particularly appropriate to middle England.

Gowan's relationship with Clennam is a key factor in this respect. If we recall Little Dorrit's earlier impression of Gowan discussed above (book 2, chapter 6, p. 480) we can see certain undeniable similarities between Gowan's existence and Clennam's own. It is not often observed, for example, that, for much of the novel, Clennam is 'unsuspicious of the depths of feeling' that lie beneath Little Dorrit's childish but not quite beautiful exterior. More important, however, is the fact that Clennam, like Gowan, finds it difficult to see a purpose in life both personally and professionally. He lacks belief in himself and is not 'stedfast and firm in purpose' (book 2, chapter 4, p. 455); interestingly, a footnote in the Clarendon edition of *Little Dorrit*

---

[28] *Sincerity and Authenticity*, 132.

indicates that Dickens used the word 'sincere' instead of 'firm' in MS A. In emphasizing that Clennam's 'inconsistencies, anxieties, and contradictions' (book 1, chapter 34, p. 393) make him a 'nobody', Dickens inverts the Romantic tendency to make these qualities the precondition for being a 'somebody'. The fact that Clennam sees his own malaise exaggerated in the character of Gowan intensifies and complicates his understandable hatred of the man; the 'unwholesome', 'halting' (book 2, chapter 6, p. 472) spirit of Byronism in part characterizes the two men. More disturbing for Dickens, perhaps, is the fact that Clennam's is the presiding consciousness of the novel, his mood, language, and perspective often mingling with that of the narrator. If this was a biographical book, of course, all sorts of familiar surmises could be proffered about Dickens's own state of mind in his maturity. But *Little Dorrit* radically subverts the idea that Byronism is the disease of the unique, artistic individual. The inability to believe that the world offers 'lasting realities' (book 2, chapter 3, p. 454) is instead a middle-class malaise.

UNMASKING MELODRAMA: SYDNEY CARTON AND EUGENE WRAYBURN

Dickens is undoubtedly more openly sympathetic to Sydney Carton and Eugene Wrayburn than he is to any of his other Byronic types, though this sympathy does not extend to an endorsement of Byronism. In Carton's case, sympathy is directed towards what Beth F. Herst calls 'the sense of a better nature, a *true* nature, concealed beneath the careless mask' he assumes.[29] In *Our Mutual Friend*, Dickens's sympathy with Byronism is motivated by his more aggressive questioning of the capitalist social backdrop which makes repressive, performative individualism to some extent inevitable. Eugene Wrayburn, for instance, is in many ways similar to Steerforth, Harthouse, and Harold Skimpole; Sydney Carton resembles both those just mentioned and the ill-fated Richard Carstone in *Bleak House*. But Dickens is able to show more active understanding of the 'Weltschmerz' of Carton and Wrayburn because of his obvious disillusionment, in his last works, with the materialism and fragmentation of Victorian society. This disillusionment inevitably leads,

---

[29] *The Dickens Hero: Selfhood and Alienation in the Dickens World* (London: Weidenfeld & Nicolson, 1990), 143.

furthermore, to heightened anxieties about melodrama's continued viability as a popular cultural mode.

It would, however, be wrong to assume that Carton and Wrayburn act the same role under a different name. Carton is closer to the Byronic villains of Gothic melodrama than any of Dickens's other Byronic individuals, as his passions are excessive and antisocial. They govern Carton and he makes little effort to hide his inner turmoil beneath a social mask. Indeed, Carton's lack of control over his self-projection is a symptom of his own powerlessness and lack of concern with power dynamics. He is the only non-comic Byronic character in the Dickens canon for whom the Byronic role does not function as a sign of social capital. Carton is a victim of angst, melancholy and his own sense of his wasted potential. This is not to say that his emotional life is rendered from the inside, however; Carton's Byronism is rendered melodramatically. Dickens uses the whole range of melodramatic techniques to reinforce the idea that Carton is 'genuinely' Byronic. Indeed, interestingly, Carton is the only Byronic character in Dickens whose emotional malaise is (in melodramatic terms) 'genuine'; paradoxically, that is, his angst expresses itself transparently. His language, looks, manner, and demeanour all function, therefore, as a direct index of his 'inner' nature. Dickens's visual descriptions of Carton's appearance, for example, perfectly anatomize his complex spiritual state. Near the end of the novel, Carton is 'pictured' in the very Byronic description:

Carton's face [. . .] was turned to the fire. [. . .] He wore the white riding-coat and top-boots, then in vogue, and the light of the fire [. . .] made him look very pale, with his long brown hair, all untrimmed, hanging loose about him. (book 3, chapter 9, p. 294)

The antisocial excess which characterizes Carton also manifests itself in animalistic imagery; he is evocatively compared with 'a dissipated cat' and 'an amazingly good jackal' (book 2, chapter 5, p. 81). The emphasis on Carton's physicality is in keeping with melodrama's bodily semiotics, its marginalization of the mind; even his self-abuse manifests itself physically, for example, in the alcoholism so prominent in contemporary admonitory domestic melodramas. Carton's potential as well as his demise is passionally and physically rendered. Indeed, Carton differs from relatives like the similarly named Richard Carstone in so far as his degeneration, like that of the villains of Gothic melodrama, seems to have no specific cause. Dickens's use of physiognomy and bodily semiotics is most telling in the overt physical comparison drawn between Darnay and Carton, the former's 'Double of coarse deportment' (book 2, chapter 4, p. 78).

While Carton's Byronism is characterized by emotional excess, Wrayburn's is distinguished by his relative lack of passion. Even towards the end of the novel, when Wrayburn begins to appreciate the full extent of his love for Lizzie, his resulting anguish is only thinly sketched. Wrayburn, more than Carton, masks his inner unhappiness beneath a tightly controlled persona. Like Steerforth, he appreciates that control—over one's role and one's inner life—gives power over others. Wrayburn's emotional life is, unlike Carton's, intermittently at odds with his performances of self, and indeed the dialogue between his 'private' self and his social persona is largely constitutive of his Byronism. Wrayburn's acute consciousness of the operations of power engenders a dislocation of self; he is, more-over, a more aggressive character than either Steerforth or Carton. Although Wrayburn's goading of Headstone, at a deeper level, betrays self-destructive tendencies, it is significant that he must prompt someone else to attempt to take his life. Wrayburn, unlike Carton, experiences himself primarily as a social being; his disdain for a society of which he feels a product does not prevent him from projecting his destructive tendencies the only way he knows how, externally or socially. He is thus always more potentially dangerous to others than Carton. Carton contains seeds of the tragic hero with-in his personality; Wrayburn never entirely erases traits of the stereo-typical aristocratic villain or seducer. Wrayburn is a sadist, Carton a masochist.

That Wrayburn's sadism is not damned out of hand is testimony to significant ideological shifts in Dickens's late works. These shifts are most apparent if one considers the relationship between Wrayburn and Headstone as a variation on the opposition, prevalent in melo-drama and Dickens's previous novels, between the repressed performer of self and the transparent, passionate, 'melodramatic' personality. While Edmund Wilson relates Headstone to the Gothic villain of melodrama, he is also a relative of the emotional, 'good' melodramatic character; Wrayburn is clearly a relative of the passionless villain of domestic melodrama, as well as the Byronic villain. The merging of 'opposite' types suggested by the relationship between Wrayburn and Headstone is consummated in the (melo-dramatically Byronic) John Jasper in *Edwin Drood*. While biographical critics of the school of Wilson and House interpret such contrasts as a reflection of Dickens's personal emotional make-up, this repeated 'structure of feeling' and Dickens's innovations to it are as interesting in terms of Dickens's social and cultural politics. In terms of overt class politics, then, Dickens's refinement of the conflict between the passionless aristocrat and the passionate worker shows a movement away from the unambiguously anti-aristocratic impulse of domestic melodrama. While the class enmity between Wrayburn and Headstone has roots in domestic melodrama, Wrayburn is undoubtedly more passionate—and more sympathetic—than most Byronic types in the earlier novels, just as Headstone is more repressed and immoral than earlier relatives as faithful to the work ethic. The dialectical relationship between the Romantic and the melodramatic character provisionally suggested in *David Copperfield* has become, in *Our Mutual Friend*, more accepted and explicit.

Consonant with these shifts is a reassessment of the melodramatic mode as a vehicle of cultural inclusiveness. For *Our Mutual Friend* contains a sophisticated, self-reflexive interrogation of the consequences of a misappropriation of the melodramatic mode. The implications of this are a new pessimism about the power of 'popular' culture as an instrument of social cohesion. Crucial in this respect is the use of melodramatic stereotype. In *Our Mutual Friend*, characters employ melodramatic stereotypes self-consciously and divisively as tools of power. Though Headstone is no more the clumsy, primitive man of feeling than Wrayburn is the familiar evil aristocrat, a major reason for the intense hatred between the two men is the fact that each perceives the other as a stereotype and uses that stereotype as an instrument of torture. Tellingly, Wrayburn understands how to use cultural stereotypes better than Headstone, and his socially superior status means that he speaks from a position of power. Significantly, he tells his rival that he is 'rather too passionate for a good school-master' (book 2, chapter 6, p. 292), an insult rendering explicit the (high) cultural hierarchy Dickens's novels attempt to subvert, whereby passion is associated with the uncivilized (and vice versa). Eugene labels Headstone, as if scientifically labelling a new species, 'a curious monomaniac' (p. 294). Ironically, the more Wrayburn goads the schoolmaster, the more he conforms to type by playing the role of what Carey calls the 'violent villain'.[30] Though Headstone is self-

[30] *The Violent Effigy*, 27.

conscious and self-controlled, 'watching and repressing himself daily' (book 2, chapter 6, p. 291), there is a strong sense of what Donohue calls (in melodrama) the 'climactic display of the immanent' in Headstone's dressing in Riderhood's clothes.[31]

While Headstone's murderousness could undoubtedly be read as a sign of Dickens's reactionary discomfort with working-class social mobility, it is more accurately interpreted as a symptom of pessimism about the possibility of lower-class agency. Wrayburn, for example, wields power both discursively and performatively. He appropriates stereotype and the melodramatic vision to disempower those who are already disempowered. Where David Copperfield's melodramatic vision attributes depths to surfaces, Wrayburn inverts the original function of melodrama by seeing people as surfaces only. Wrayburn uses melodrama, in other words, unsympathetically. His treatment of Headstone is not exceptional, as his insulting remarks to Riah the Jew demonstrate. Again, Wrayburn taunts another human being by stereotyping and indeed caricaturing him according to social or racial type. He calls Riah 'Mr. Aaron' (book 2, chapter 15, pp. 405–7) and later describes him as 'quite a Shylock, and quite a Patriarch' (p. 535). He explains that the name Mr Aaron 'appears to me [him] Hebraic, expressive, appropriate, and complimentary' (book 3, chapter 10, pp. 535–6). Wrayburn uses melodramatic aesthetics to increase social divisions. That his stereotyping is a self-conscious game to relieve his Byronic boredom does not lessen its effect.

Though Wrayburn uses repression to suggest autonomous individuality, his autonomy is in fact illusory. His self-image also depends on an aggressive 'Othering' of males whose social status does not rival his own—Headstone, Mr Dolls, and Riah, in particular. He clearly takes a sadistic pleasure in denying his male social inferiors their individuality; and further, his sense of his own individuality seems to demand these gratuitous demonstrations of power. In other words, Wrayburn is far from autonomous; his self-image is highly dependent on a need to confirm his social status—hence the dilemma with which Lizzie presents him. Lizzie, of course, is partly attractive to him because of the opportunity she presents of thwarting Headstone. Wrayburn actively uses the cultural capital at his disposal to attract Lizzie whilst belittling Headstone. His offer of education as an instrument of social improvement clearly entails the possibility of

---

[31] *Theatre in the Age of Kean*, 111.

sexual and social subordination (of both Lizzie and Headstone). In this respect, the offer acts as a metaphor of containment, suggesting the impossibility of working-class agency. But Wrayburn's agency is also limited; to seduce Lizzie would be to become a class stereotype, and Eugene fears (and desires) this more than anything.

Headstone offers Wrayburn a much more individual way of relieving feelings of class enmity that are closely tied up with anxieties about his masculinity. Indeed, his hatred of Headstone is clearly the one passion to which he abandons himself absolutely and 'sincerely' in the course of the novel. The relationship between Wrayburn and Headstone bears out René Girard's theory of desire as the product of rivalry and offers support to Eve Sedgwick's groundbreaking 'homosocial' reading of *Our Mutual Friend* as a novel about 'erotic rivalry' and 'anality'.[32] Wrayburn's obsession with Headstone is much in evidence when he explains his nocturnal 'cat and mouse' routine to Mortimer—'I goad the schoolmaster to madness. The amiable occupation has been the solace of my life' (book 3, chapter 10, p. 542)—and when Mortimer observes the passionate intensity of Wrayburn's sadism: Wrayburn has 'no other object on earth than to disappoint and punish him', Lightwood noted, 'with a feeling of astonishment that so careless a man could be so wary, and that so idle a man could take so much trouble' (book 3, chapter 10, p. 544).

The competitiveness between Wrayburn and Headstone is, to an extent, the dramatic expression of the logic of capitalism which clearly informs the society of *Our Mutual Friend*. This capitalist environment is formative in the reassessment of melodrama, affecting in particular Dickens's attitude to the work ethic which is so central to melodramatic ideology (and Victorian culture). The Byronic character is an inevitable focus for this reassessment and an intertextual consideration of the treatment of the work ethic makes the shifts in Dickens's thinking apparent. Perhaps the most significant variation on a theme is Wrayburn's discussion of the function of the bees, in which he virtually reproduces the opinions voiced by Skimpole in *Bleak House* (chapter 8, p. 93).[33] Wrayburn rejects Boffin's view that 'there's nothing like work. Look at the bees', arguing:

Ye-es, [. . .] they work; but don't you think they overdo it? They work so much more than they need [. . .] Regarded in the light of my conventional

---

[32] See Girard's *Deceit, Desire, and the Novel*, Eve Kosofsky Sedgwick, *Between Men: English Literature and Male Homosocial Desire*, Gender and Culture (New York: Columbia University Press, 1985), 162, 164.   [33] See Chapter 6 above.

schoolmaster and moralist, I protest against the tyrannical humbug of your friend the bee. (book 1, chapter 8, pp. 93–4)

In previous novels, Dickens had always detested this type of disparagement of the work ethic; he had no sympathy for a man 'so soon bored, so constantly, so fatally' (*OMF*, book 1, chapter 12, p. 147). Wrayburn's comment that 'they work so much more than they need', however, points to the greed and excess which permeates the work ethic in a capitalist society. Moreover, proving one's masculinity in this environment seems to entail not supporting one's family or earning a decent living, but outstripping one's perceived competitors. Thus in *A Tale of Two Cities*, Carton's opposite 'Stryver' is represented as a superficial man, whose 'striving' is motivated by the desire for social status and material gain. When we turn to *Our Mutual Friend*, Bradley Headstone, the passionate, 'earnest' schoolmaster, clearly views education as a tool of self-advancement rather than an instrument of moral and social improvement. Again, all his energy and hard work is directed towards attaining a respectability parodied by the Veneerings, who appear to do little work. But in *Our Mutual Friend*, the most pointed criticism of, or perhaps scepticism towards, the work ethic is relayed through the character of Rogue Riderhood. It is no accident that the 'catch-phrase' of Rogue Riderhood, the most transparent villain in the novel, is, 'I am a man as gets my living, and as seeks to get my living, by the sweat of my brow' (book 1, chapter 12, p. 148).[34] Once more, Dickens is not using a stereotype naively; on the contrary, Riderhood functions within a typically Dickensian, 'refractive', character cluster to satirize what Wrayburn calls, in his analysis of the bees, the 'tyrannical humbug' of the 'conventional schoolmaster and moralist' (book 1, chapter 8, pp. 93–4).

The work ethic, like education, has thus metamorphosed, in *Our Mututal Friend*, from an instrument of social cohesion to a vehicle of capitalism and materialism. Eugene Wrayburn's pronouncements against the work ethic are consequently not seen simply as a sign of his corruption, but as an indictment of society itself. It is a society in which economic and class structures militate against willed lower-class agency and the instruments of this agency. Against this social backdrop, the idea of popular culture as an instrument of cultural cohesion seems both naively fantastical and uneconomic.

On the face of it, however, the endings of *Our Mutual Friend* and

---

[34] Note that the title of this chapter is 'The Sweat of an Honest Man's Brow' (p. 144).

A Tale of Two Cities appear to reinforce melodramatic ideologies: the ideals of selflessness, communality, and the triumph of the 'good' individual over oppressive social structures are all dramatized. Both Wrayburn and Carton appear to embody the transformation of the Byronic deviant into the melodramatic hero, and the triumph of the agency that is consonant with selflessness in an ideal, ethical world. In insisting on the 'redemption' in one form or another of both Eugene Wrayburn and Sydney Carton, however, several critics have simplified the deeply ambiguous endings of the two novels in which those characters appear.[35] Far from negating his own Byronism, or nobly thwarting the conventions of society, for example, Eugene's decision to marry Lizzie is clouded by his uncertainty and dubious though well-meaning motives. Before Headstone attacks his rival, the text specifically states that Eugene feels trapped between two impossible options: 'Out of the question to marry her, [. . .] and out of the question to leave her. The crisis!' (book 4, chapter 6, p. 698). More importantly, Wrayburn is sure that he is going to die when he communicates to Jenny Wren that he wants to marry Lizzie (book 4, chapter 10, p. 742). His widely admired wish to make 'reparation' (book 4, chapter 10, p. 741), likewise, seems to me far more troubling than critics usually concede, not least because it is Lightwood rather than Eugene who uses the term and suggests the idea. Moreover, the phrase to make 'reparation' usually suggests a process of punishment or atonement, an idea of marriage which is hardly complimentary to Lizzie. A further problem with the idea of Eugene as a man 'redeemed' or even 'self-fulfilled' is the fact that, even after the marriage, Eugene seems to be in what Dickens labels in the case of Gowan a 'halting' state of doubt and uncertainty. Indeed, Lizzie has to persuade him that he wants to live (book 4, chapter 11, p. 754). Even Eugene's more positive 'protestations'—for example, 'We are shepherds both. In turning to at last, we turn to in earnest' and 'I will fight it out to the last gasp, with her and for her, here in the open field' (book 4, chapter 16, pp. 812–13)—are undermined by his avowed disbelief in 'protestations' (book 4, chapter 16, p. 811). Again, it is no accident that, in between the latter so-called 'heroic' protestations, Wrayburn compares himself to Hamlet: 'I can say to you of the healthful music of my pulse what Hamlet said of his. My blood is up,

---

[35] The term 'redemption' is used in Angus Wilson's 'The Heroes and Heroines of Dickens', 8. See also Harvey, 'Charles Dickens and the Byronic Hero', 310, 312–14, Herst, *The Dickens Hero*, 139–60, 161–84, Moers, *The Dandy*, p. 246.

but wholesomely up, when I think of it!' (book 4, chapter 16, pp. 812–13).[36] Dickens's contemptuous remark on Hamlet 'the poser' in his original version of *A Christmas Carol*,[37] as well, of course, as the play itself, suggest that this is not an altogether innocent reference. Furthermore, there is something which, far from 'heroic', is not even tasteful, about a marriage enabled (like that between Jane Eyre and Rochester) by the physical mutilation of the socially superior male. Just as Wrayburn seemed to use his class status to confirm his sense of his own masculinity, his physical mutilation seems to necessitate a relinquishment of both his class status and his related sense of his own masculinity.

Twemlow's concluding remark that 'The *feelings* of a gentleman' (italics mine) are 'sacred' (book 4, chapter the last, p. 820) is important not for its confirmation of Wrayburn's sincerity, but for its obvious idealism in the context of the 'post-sacred' society explored in the novel. Crucially, Dickens demonstrates in the late novels that feelings cannot exist in isolation; they are subject to change and can be submerged beneath a role influenced by the larger theatre of society. An exploration of the performative personality can thus entail a properly indirect exploration of the passional life and not the discovery of its absence. The later novels reveal an increased emphasis on the role of economic and class structures in determining both emotional development and the means by which individuals express personal feeling. This is nicely captured in Eugene's explanation of his father's unemotional demeanour:

M.R.F. [. . .] was so affable as to remark [. . .] that Lizzie ought to have her portrait painted. Which, coming from M.R.F., may be considered equivalent to a melodramatic blessing.

[. . .] When M.R.F. said that, and followed it up by rolling the claret [. . .] in his mouth, and saying, 'My dear son, why do you drink this trash?' it was tantamount—in him—to a paternal benediction on our union, accompanied with a gush of tears. The coolness of M.R.F. is not to be measured by ordinary standards. (book 4, chapter 16, pp. 811–12)

This passage expresses a new foregrounding of the fact that self-consciousness can constitute sincerity, and that the melodramatic rendering of emotion may be no more 'authentic' and socially constructive than repressive suggestions of the same. Dickens's early (melodramatic) distrust of 'coolness' and trust in openness have eventually been reviewed and modified. The balance between the

---

[36] Cf. *Hamlet*, III. iv. 140–1.   [37] See Introduction above.

'ambiguous' ending and the 'happy' ending exemplifies the double perspective through which Dickens renders melodrama self-conscious and self-consciousness melodramatic.

In *A Tale of Two Cities*, Carton's death is, on one level, unambiguously melodramatic. His heroic potential is realized because, like Wardour in *The Frozen Deep*, he eventually externalizes his passions for the larger social good. Carton is more consciously determined to commit himself to an absolute ideal outside himself than Wrayburn; he neither wavers nor doubts his own sincerity in sacrificing his own life to the happiness of Lucie Manette. William R. Harvey argues in familiar terms that 'Carton's death is a purposeful one', and 'results from his *selfless* dedication to Lucie. Thus Dickens diminishes much of the Byronism that surrounds Carton, one of the hallmarks of the Byronic character being his totally egocentric behaviour.'[38] There are problems, however, with the conventional reading of the ending of *A Tale of Two Cities* which sees Carton as a hero, and also with the text's sense of him as a Christlike figure. Carton's climactic, hypothetical 'heroic' remarks (book 3, chapter 15, pp. 357–8), for example, betray as much an obsession with self as 'selfless dedication to Lucie'. Carton hopes that after his death others will rewrite his life story in heroic terms. Even if one is convinced by his love for Lucie, which is only sketchily drawn in the novel, it is difficult to believe that this is a purely selfless love. The dead Carton would undoubtedly cast a shadow over the marriage of Lucie and Charles; Carton's comment, 'I know that each was not more honoured and held sacred in the other's soul than I was in the souls of both', literally places him between the couple. As interestingly, moreover, Carton wants his name to be venerated through the acts of Lucie's son; though he has been unable to believe in his society and its institutions, he wants his namesake to be the 'foremost of just judges and honoured men'.

This is not to say that Dickens is exposing Carton as a hypocrite. What Carton's hypothetical words demonstrate is the difficulty of both being true to oneself and representing oneself faithfully in a social situation. The ending of Carton's story shows the impossibility of achieving absolute selflessness, absolute sincerity, or of committing an act of heroism which lays claim to both qualities. In the words of André Gide, 'One cannot both be sincere and seem so.'[39] Carton is ultimately not immune to the applause of the theatre of society he

---

[38] 'Charles Dickens and the Byronic Hero', 311.
[39] Quoted by Trilling, *Sincerity and Authenticity*, 70.

has always appeared to disdain. He is thus most self-conscious and socially strategic when he is most melodramatic. His heroism is also recognizably Byronic in so far as it is only attainable through death. Stylistically, the emotional and pictorial directness of the speech is pure melodrama; however, the fact that 'Carton's' remarks are actually the narrator's fantastical projection draws attention to both their idealism and the silencing of this idealism in a world riddled by class enmity. Carton's death contributes to the novel's scepticism about the morally absolute stereotypes and the transparent models of identity familiar in nineteenth-century melodrama. But at the same time, the immediate euphoria it creates in the reader is dependent on his or her desire to believe in utopian possibilities.

In the late novels, Dickens foregrounds the self-consciousness of his own melodramatic art. It is important to register, however, that melodramatic strains persist and indeed coexist with Dickens's self-reflexivity. Dickens's self-consciousness constitutes one element of a double perspective via which the melodramatic and the self-conscious vision problematize each other. He never acquiesces in the subject-centred valorization of interiority of his Romantic individuals and literary forefathers, continuing to explore interiority from the outside. He recognizes that 'the turn inwards' is pervasive, but refuses to compound an involution of focus—or a mystification of this involution—which remains to him a socially divisive malaise. He interrogates innerness, that is, on his own melodramatic terms. Melodramatic aesthetics are not jettisoned but flagrantly and self-consciously relativized.

Ellen Moers argues that, though obsessed with Byronic individuals like Carton, Dickens had nothing in common with these characters 'save unspoken thoughts'.[40] The fact that these thoughts remain unspoken is testimony to Dickens's refusal to accept the suitability of Byronism as a constructive social or artistic response to an increasingly fragmented world. The fact that Byronic individuals are always presented melodramatically clearly highlights the moral and ideological problems they pose. At the same time, the ongoing dialogue between the Byronic and the melodramatic mode foregrounds the ideological and moral fantasy which constitutes melodrama's foundation. Dickens continues to employ this fantasy, but the self-consciousness with which he does so suggests its inextricability from the 'post-sacred world' it affects to counter.

[40] *The Dandy*, 250.

Sincerely Deviant Women

In *Dickens and Women*, Michael Slater provides an impressive list of stock stage types of female deviance which appear in Dickens's early novels: the nagging, tyrannical wife, 'nightmare mothers', buxom women who turn to religion, socially competitive women, cultured women, schoolmistresses, spinsters, 'grotesque men-women', solipsists, matchmaking mothers, and unattractive young women.[1] All these types are indeed evident in Dickens's fiction, and the comic cotton wool which can soften their perceived abnormalities should obviously not fool the reader into ignoring their relevance to the idealized 'norm' of femininity which Dickens presents in his novels. Dickens's supposed ideal of femininity is by now so well known and well criticized that it is scarcely worth repeating. It is perhaps in his portrayal of women that Dickens is generally thought most to deserve Trollope's nickname for him, 'Mr Popular Sentiment'; his heroines were shaped by, and in turn reinforced, the dominant ideology concerning the 'true'—angelic, domestic—nature of woman, an ideology spelt out most clearly perhaps in Coventry Patmore's *The Angel in the House* (1854–6) and Ruskin's 'Of Queens' Gardens' (1865) .

The dominant ideological myth that woman was sent from heaven to work wonders in the home was also, of course, emphasized in nineteenth-century melodrama of all varieties. Without wishing to make excuses for any immaturity or confusion in the presentation of women in Dickens's novels, this chapter will demonstrate that the nineteenth-century theatre can serve as an illuminating context for a sophisticated understanding of Dickens's novelistic women—a context at least as helpful as the familiar biographical story of Dickens's involvement with Mary Hogarth and his personal enthusiasm for young, virginal, and virtuous girls. Until recent feminist work on

[1] pp. 226–34.

Dickens's attitudes to women by Patricia Ingham and Claire Tomalin,[2] among others, the complexity of the relationship between models of femininity Dickens encountered in life and the ideals and anxieties about women found in Dickens's novels had scarcely been broached, let alone understood. My contention is that Dickens could divorce neither his conscious understanding nor his sub-conscious, creative imagination from the models of womanhood he encountered in the nineteenth-century theatre.

What makes the relationship between Dickens's female male-factors and the theatre even more complex, in some respects, than that between his male villains and stage prototypes is the specific problem of Victorian attitudes to the professional actress. While there had always been distrust of the professional actor as one who made his money pretending to be something he was not, this suspicion was intensified in the case of nineteenth-century responses to actresses. The reasons for this, generally speaking, were first, that in elevating the principles of sincerity and authenticity, the Victorians were inclined to enshrine them especially in the female sex; second, that professional actresses, by definition, denied and subverted both these principles and the consequent assumptions about women; and finally, that, simply by having a profession, the Victorian actress thwarted the doctrine that a woman's place was in the home. In contemporary responses to the Victorian theatre, we can thus see a particular degree of confusion about the relationship between the parts played by women in the theatre and the women employed to play those parts.

This confusion is encapsulated in its purest form in an unidentified article in Dickens's journal *All the Year Round* entitled 'Harlequin Fairy Morgana' (20 August 1864).[3] Young Peebles the narrator, like the young David Copperfield, is ecstatic to be at the theatre, a place of 'soft realms of celestial light, happiness, and joy!' (p. 43). When the

---

[2] Patricia Ingham, *Dickens, Women & Language* (Hemel Hempstead: Harvester Wheat-sheaf, 1992), Tomalin, *The Invisible Woman*. Ingham's *Dickens, Women & Language* includes a perceptive, long-overdue critique of simplistic biographical readings of Dickens's novelistic women, demonstrating convincingly that women in Dickens's autobiographical writings are no less fictional constructs than their novelistic sisters (see 'Postscript: Rewriting Experience', 133–44). Tomalin's *The Invisible Woman*, though a biography of Ternan, also employs a refreshingly sophisticated sense of the fluidity of the relationship between life and fiction in Dickens's worlds. Her excellent analysis of 19th-century attitudes to actresses has been more useful to this book than her biographical detective work, fasci-nating though this is.

[3] *AYR* 12 (20 Aug. 1864), 40–48.

fairy queen of the pantomime appears, the young-old narrator reflects: 'I felt a feeling—I can only liken to a sort of wrench—at my heart; and oh! from that moment I was an undone m—, boy I mean. A divinity, surely, hired secretly from somewhere up in the regions we heard of on Sundays (was this sinful?)' (p. 44). The comic tone ultimately intensifies the poignancy of the young man's disappointment when, after a great deal of fruitless pining, he finds that the real fairy queen is one of the 'sickly unwholesome creatures, dressed rather like decayed housemaids', 'in an old striped shawl, with a basket on her arm, and leading a very cold child [. . .]. She was as yellow as a guinea, and looked as if she had lately been ill.' The mature narrator laments in retrospect, 'O Harlequin Fairy Morgana, I have found a greater change than you, many and many a time since that day!' (p. 48). The real fairy queen disappoints the narrator because, though appearing to represent the ideal Victorian woman or 'divinity', in actuality, she is old rather than young and has a child, a fact which denies her sexual innocence. Her child, moreover, like herself, is neglected and unhealthy.

But the young narrator is most disillusioned by the artifice of the actress, or by her ability to manipulate his fantasies. The tone of the mature narrator's last lament suggests that this deception was not the last or the greatest played on him by women. It is interesting that this lament—'O Harlequin Fairy Morgana, I have found a greater change than you, many and many a time since that day!'—appears to be a general comment on the narrator's disappointment with life, not just with the stage. This comment is typical of the slippage or overlapping between life and the stage which characterizes Victorian attitudes to women particularly; it is interesting and ironic that Victorian audiences so often looked to stage (and fictional) representations for ideal embodiments of 'the angel in the house', and so often looked to real life, to the overworked, put-upon actress, for a symbol of female wickedness.

It is perhaps fair to say, then, that the professional actress, or the idea of the professional actress, was a more potent type of female immorality in the early and mid-nineteenth century than the female villain of melodrama. In fact, there are very few critics who pay any detailed attention to the figure of the female villain in nineteenth-century melodrama.[4] Booth points out that the villainess

[4] Daniel Duffy's 'Heroic Mothers and Militant Lovers: Representations of Lower-Class Women in Melodramas of the 1830s and 1840s', *Nineteenth Century Theatre*, 27 (1999), 41–65

never really came into her own as a melodramatic character until the second half of the nineteenth century; in early melodrama, the embryonic villainess 'is usually a dissatisfied female associate of the villain who sympathizes with the plight of the hero and heroine and actively assists them', or 'if she actually commits acts of evil her guilt is mitigated by circumstances'. 'For out-and-out female villainy', Booth argues, 'one must really begin with *Lady Audley's Secret* [1862]'.[5] Lynda Hart seems to agree, arguing that 'the Victorian woman-who-killed more often than not didn't really do it, or she did it only as an accomplice, or did it but she didn't really know what she was doing';[6] Hart's article assumes, however, that the Victorian 'villainess' is a murderess or at least a criminal. Gabrielle Hyslop's more detailed survey of the earlier plays of 'the father of melodrama', Pixérécourt, notes that, although only four evil females are repre-sented in the fifty melodramas he wrote between 1798 and 1835, 'heroines who subvert the norm' (including transvestite heroines) feature 'in a number of his most popular melodramas'.[7] Although it is undeniable that the villainess was more prominent in the second half of the century, I would argue that an 'out-and-out' female villain like Lady Audley is the offspring of earlier prototypes.

The main thread that links melodramatic wayward women throughout the nineteenth century is that, significantly (and perhaps not surprisingly, given the essentialist tendencies of melodrama), many of them are perceived as actresses.[8] For example, the arche-typal Millwood, the 'out-and-out' villainess of Lillo's *The London Merchant; or, The History of George Barnwell* (1731), had exclaimed to rapt audiences for over a century before Lady Audley was conceived: 'If to seem what one is not in order to be the better liked for what one really is, if to speak one thing and mean the contrary, be art in a woman, I know nothing of nature' (I. iv. 10–13). In Lady Clara

distinguishes interestingly between the 'antiheroine' of romantic melodrama and the villainess: 'Unlike the villainess (who does not seem to have appeared as a plebeian character in melodrama, perhaps because of this), the antiheroine neither chooses [. . .] nor revels in her agency' (p. 44).

⁵ *English Melodrama*, 156–7.

⁶ 'The Victorian Villainess and the Patriarchal Unconscious', *Literature and Psychology*, 40 (1994), 1–25 (p. 2).

⁷ 'Deviant and Dangerous Behaviour: Women in Melodrama', 69–70; Hyslop observes interestingly that 'Among the heroines who do not conform to the usual submissive model, more than half wear men's clothes at some time during the play' (p. 72).

⁸ There are, of course, many straightforwardly hotheaded female villains of the same breed as Dickens's Hortense in *BH* in Victorian melodrama, but they do not seem to me to demand the same amount of attention as their more theatrically aware sisters.

Cavendish's *The Woman of the World* (13 November 1858, Queen's), Lisa Selby, the unrepentant villainess and accomplice to the hypnotist-villain Monti, puzzles over the popularity of the virtuous heroine Joanna: 'all that she *really* is, have I not *seemed*?'[9] Lisa uses her ability to assume different roles to achieve the upward social mobility which she thinks will make her happy. J. Palgrave Simpson's *Broken Ties* (8 June 1872, Olym.), though written after Dickens's death, is interesting in this context because it crystallizes the supposed links between female immorality and the stage. The central female character—presented more as a fallen woman than a villainess—is an opera singer called La Silvia, who has left her husband and son to pursue her passion for the stage. In later life, she comes face to face with them, and, helped by an old operatic friend who now dreams only 'of cradles, little frocks, and baby eyes',[10] and by the shame of the fact that her profession will thwart her son's plans for a respectable marriage, she realizes the error of her ways. She tells her son, 'By *self*-sacrifice, I may prove a mother still', offering to 'retire from the world' and 'be dead to all' (pp. 39–40; II. ii). She is rewarded, and, indeed, taken up on these generous offers, when her son and husband take her back into the bosom of the family. In case the audience is in any doubt about the moral message of the play, her last words (ironically spoken by a professional actress) are:

> Life's fatal error is atoned at last,
> My future bless'd by pardon for the past.
> 'Tis mine again, the true treasure flung aside,
> Domestic love, true woman's dearest pride. (p. 41; II. ii)

Unsurprisingly, more subversive of the dominant ideology concerning femininity is George Soane's *Lilian, the Show Girl* (10 October 1836, Surrey). The heroine Lilian is a show girl but virtuous, and in addition, she is intelligent, strong-willed, and a vocal proto-feminist. She tells her would-be genteel seducer Everard that she will give in to him if pressed, but reminds him of his responsibility for the consequences: 'Will you corrupt the life stream of its source? will you make me that I dare not name?'[11] This so confuses Everard's neat system for stereotyping women that he, like most of the audience perhaps, does not know what to make of it all:

---

[9] *Lacy*, 38 (London: Lacy, [1859]), 9 (I. ii).
[10] *Lacy*, 96 (London: French, [1850 etc.]), 25 (II. i).
[11] *Duncombe*, 24 (London: Duncombe, [1825 etc.]), 9 (I. ii).

Is this real? can it be real? For coquetry it is the sex's instinct; [. . .] to have a girl fling herself into one's arms and say 'touch me if you dare' with a look so pure withal—so innocent! I should as soon have kissed the marble image of a saint, as have breathed upon her lips! Incredible! (p. 10; I. ii)[12]

Though the play does much to redress the popular image of the actress as whore, the potentially radical and original idea of making the heroine a professional performer is partially undermined by the revelation that Lilian is actually, unbeknown to herself, of genteel stock.[13]

Lady Audley herself contrasts fundamentally with Lilian the show girl. A social rather than professional role-player, she—like Lady Clara Cavendish's Lisa Selby—uses her theatrical talents to deceive others and gain upward social mobility. Braddon's original novel makes it quite clear that Lady Audley is an actress by nature. Robert Audley mutters to himself, 'what an actress this woman is. What an arch trickster—what an all-accomplished deceiver.'[14] In C. H. Hazle-wood's adaptation of the novel, Lady Audley, on seeing Robert, makes an obvious reference to herself as an actress, telling herself, 'here comes Robert Audley, he must not see me with a cloud upon my brow! Let me again resume the mask, which not only imposes on him, but on all the world';[15] Hazlewood also omits the secret of the insanity of Lady Audley's mother,[16] an omission which perhaps positions the daughter closer still to the actress in terms of the actress/madwoman opposition which appears to structure the tale. But the fact that Lady Audley—in the original novel and the extant stage adaptations—does, in fact, experience inner turmoil which she

[12] Note, however, Everard's assertion that 'coquetry'—a form of acting which involves manipulating one's sexual attractiveness—is 'the sex's instinct'. Everard thus assumes that all women are sexually provocative actresses at heart, at the same time that he doubts the assumption.

[13] T. W. Robertson's *Caste*—(6 Apr. 1867, Prince of Wales), *French*, 1960 (London: French, 1867)—also implies a fairly positive (though unglamorous) view of the hard-working, professional actress, though again the actress is 'rewarded' for her virtue and 'exceptional merit' (III; p. 144) by marrying her social superior, a marriage which takes her away from the stage. Interestingly, a century later, the life story of Grace Kelly/Princess Grace of Monaco is a variation on the same theme.

[14] Mary Elizabeth Braddon, *Lady Audley's Secret*, ed. David Skilton (Oxford: Oxford University Press, 1987; repr. 1991), 256 (book 2, chapter 10).

[15] *Lady Audley's Secret* (25 May 1863, Vic.), *Lacy*, Suppl. 2 (London: Lacy, [1850 etc.]), 17 (II. i).

[16] See Hart, 'The Victorian Villainess and the Patriarchal Unconscious', 11; Hart's article, though illuminating on matters of gender and psychology, does not concern itself with the class issues which are important in the novel and its adaptations.

takes great pains to hide is just one of the ways in which she is more than an 'out-and-out' villainess. Lady Audley is a victim as well as a villain, and her misdeeds result largely from her desire to escape from the miserable position allotted to her. Left indefinitely with a pathetic, drunken father by a thoughtless husband who goes off to seek 'their' fortune, robbed by society of an opportunity to use her intelligence to raise herself through honourable work, she turns her life into a lie. She mimics an idealized femininity that does not exist, becoming 'a *real impostor*'; she 'does not pretend to be someone that she is not; she is that "not-someone"'.[17] So confusing was Lady Audley to contemporary gender ideology that reviewers found her and her kind not just 'revolting' but '*impossible*'.[18] Though Lady Audley eventually presents herself as mad, Braddon handles the issue of female insanity with delicate ambiguity, enabling readers to see clearly how a diagnosis of madness could be used as a convenient fiction to oppress and marginalize women who threatened the dominant ideology and status quo.

Lady Audley does so in various ways, not least of which is the fact that she has the childish appearance of the typical heroine of stage melodrama, or, as the jealous Alicia puts it in William E. Suter's adaptation of the novel, of 'a frivolous, heartless, giggling wax doll!'[19] Booth maintains that the archetypal villainess, like Ravina in *The Miller and his Men*, has dark hair and looks.[20] Thus Lady Audley's doll-like appearance is radically subversive of the conventional assumptions about physiognomy common in novelistic and stage melodrama. Her entire character is likewise at odds with the general tendency of melodrama to externalize and simplify the inner life. Lady Audley, like most wicked women in Victorian melodrama, complicates its moral, emotional, ideological, and dramaturgic patterning to an extent unrivalled by most of the male malefactors.

This chapter will concentrate on the bad women of melodrama—and those women in Dickens's novels that derive from them—rather than the comic types of traditional farce mentioned by Michael Slater, or the fantastical types of pantomime. The principal reason for this is that the raw materials of melodrama—passion, theatri-

---

[17] Hart, 'The Victorian Villainess and the Patriarchal Unconscious', 9.

[18] Ibid. 13 and n.

[19] *Lady Audley's Secret* (21 Feb. 1863, Queen's), *Lacy*, 57 (London: Lacy [1863]), 20 (i. iv).

[20] *English Melodrama*, 20. Booth maintains that the 'raven-haired villainess, or adventuress' is often the accomplice of the villain. Duffy labels Ravina an 'antiheroine' rather than a villainess ('Heroic Mothers and Militant Lovers', 44). See n. 4 above.

cality, and moral polarity/certainty—must be fascinatingly distorted to accommodate the deviant woman. Crucially for this study, the synonymity between theatrical talent and heartless vacuity which could often be assumed in the male villain of domestic melodrama did not hold true in the female villain; passional interiority is often the hallmark of the female villain. Significantly, this interiority is neither condoned nor condemned out of hand. The social and cultural ramifications of the deviant, passionate woman of melodrama—whose ability to fashion the self was matched only by the power to destroy it—were enormous. Some of the most memorable, complex, and, to contemporaries, disturbing representations of women in the Victorian period are informed by the melodramatic model: the actress Vashti in Charlotte Brontë's *Villette* (1853),[21] Lady Isabel Vane in Mrs Henry Wood's *East Lynne* (1861), Gwendolen Harleth in Eliot's *Daniel Deronda* (1876), and Henry James's Miriam Rooth in *The Tragic Muse* (1889–90).

Although Lady Audley—in the original novel and stage adaptations—is perceived by herself and others as passionless, it is clear to novel readers and stage audiences that she is not. In Braddon's novel, the self-analysis of the story's 'good woman', Clara Talboys, would ironically sound perfectly fitting coming from the mouth of Lady Audley: 'I have grown up in an atmosphere of suppression,' she said, quietly; 'I have stifled and dwarfed the natural feelings of my heart, until they have become unnatural in their intensity' (book 2, chapter 5, p. 200). Having said this, as Lady Audley explains in the novel (book 3, chapter 3, p. 347) and in Suter's adaptation, though she does feel intense passion, it is all of self and she is incapable of feeling for others. In Suter's adaptation, when Sir Michael discovers her secrets, she tells him:

I should be sorry for you if I could, for you have been very good to me, but I can't, I can't. I can feel nothing but my own misery. I have ever been selfish, now more selfish than ever in my misery. Happy, prosperous people may feel for others—I laugh at other people's sufferings, they seem so small compared to my own. (p. 37; II. v)

These two excerpts capture several of the distinguishing characteristics of most female malefactors in Victorian melodrama: repression of passion which intensifies that passion, utter selfishness, an

---

[21] Vashti was, of course, based on the actress Rachel who was (in)famous for her passionate acting style in Dickens's day.

inability to empathize with others, and an inability to escape from biting personal misery and suffering.

Though in Wilkie Collins's first stage adaptation of his own novel *Armadale* (1864–6), the fascinating Lydia Gwilt eventually sacrifices her own life for that of the man she loves, the adaptation adopts as a major theme the continuous flux of her emotional life, and the misery which circumstances and her own nature have made an unavoidable fact of her life.[22] In addition, of course, Collins explores the tensions created by her ability to disguise her inner life and manipulate her social persona. She explains to her villainous accomplice Dr Downward, 'You know the horrors I have gone through, the miseries I have suffered, the wickedness [...] that I have committed' (pp. 11–12; 1). Dr Downward offers her no escape from her miserable isolation, however, and in fact the play explores his sadistic attempts to make her drop her actress's mask and reveal her intensely passionate nature. Lydia Gwilt in fact underestimates her own capacity for humane and generous feeling, finally making the ultimate self-sacrifice by laying down her own life.

Her suicide is not simply prompted by love, however; it is also the result of intense misery and self-loathing. Lisa Selby, the defiant villainess of *The Woman of the World*, must also die before the play is out, but her death, unusually, is caused by a burst blood-vessel rather than suicide. It is as if the playwright, Lady Clara Cavendish, cannot believe that such intense misery and hatred as Lisa feels can remain repressed without causing physical damage. Though Ravina of *The Miller and his Men* is one of the near-villainesses in melodrama who is not a role-player, she too knows the unhappiness that comes from leading a double life and disguising immorality—she tells Grindoff/Wolf, 'Content! such guilt as thine can never feel content.[23] Never will thy corroded heart have rest' (p. 63; II. ii). Her own conviction about the misery which must inevitably accompany a dishonest life is so strong that she betrays the forces of evil with 'one glorious act of repentance' (p. 65; II. iii).

It was, of course, the main aim of melodrama, as a highly moralistic genre, to portray virtue triumphant, and to promote the message that the wages of sin are misery, suffering, and very possibly death. It thus seems in keeping with the simplifying tendencies of melodrama for creators of female villains to portray their creatures as

---

[22] *Armadale* (London: Smith, Elder, 1866).   [23] See n. 20 above.

naturally or innately masochistic. If we look at the minutiae of these Victorian melodramas, however, there are very few examples of wicked women who are shown to be evil and suffering without good reason. From Ravina to Lydia Gwilt and Lady Audley, wayward women are presented, to a considerable degree, as having been forced into certain patterns of behaviour. Lady Audley is badly treated by the men in her life, Lydia Gwilt by her social superiors. Because of the common Victorian ethos that woman's place was not in the public arena, it was virtually impossible for a talented, intelligent, and poor woman to raise herself from drudgery if she did not take the path either of marriage or deceit—or indeed a deceitful marriage. In addition, whereas Victorian melodrama presents male actor-villains as, for the most part, motivelessly malignant gentlemen who repress their inner emotions in order to appear fashionable or respectable, or to heighten their sense of selfhood, female villains are presented, to differing extents, as having been obliged to act roles. Melodrama's deviant women are denied the libidinous, auto-erotic pleasures Kucich associates with repressive individualism because such pleasures derive largely from the *act* of *choice*. When repression is a necessity and not an act of choice, then pleasure is denied.[24]

Yet the oppressive structures that melodrama frequently shows bearing down on the deviant woman may not ultimately represent the proto-feminist rays of hope we may wish them to be. By removing some blame from the wicked woman, melodrama also takes away the *capacity* for self-willed deviance, reinforcing an essentialist view of women as naturally passive and good. Moreover, the partial acceptance of passional interiority suggested by the female malefactor is as consistent with the traditional association of women with emotion and privacy as it is with a radical debunking of Victorian conceptions of sincerity.

Deviant women—superficially at least—served to undermine or subvert melodrama's moral and dramaturgic scheme and its overt propaganda that women should remain angelic in feeling and demeanour, whatever their grievances.[25] But if the Victorians could push to one side the paradoxes presented by the fictional figure of the

---

[24] See *Repression in Victorian Fiction.*

[25] E. Ann Kaplan's 'Theories of Melodrama: A Feminist Perspective' also sees the dual potential of melodrama to be either subversive or oppressive; her conclusion is downbeat, however, maintaining that 'melodrama is oppressive in that it ultimately ends up teaching women to accept their subordinate position'.

villainess-actress, they could not ignore the affront to their values represented by the all-too-real, flesh-and-blood professional actress— who was not so easily sidelined in her own social drama. The actress appeared in important ways more monstrous and threatening to the establishment than the female villain—though paradoxically, the affinities of the stage villainess with the actress gave the fictional figure the subversive potential which meant she had to be marginalized. Looked at from the outside, the actress appeared to possess all the bad points, with none of the redeeming features, of the stage type she sometimes had to play: rather than suffering for assuming various masks, she was financially rewarded; she could assume a second self for an evening's performance, yet walk away afterwards without the burden of having to maintain her façade; she was courted rather than victimized by men, and, in the case of successful actresses, fame and fortune could buy her the freedom to live by her own moral and sexual rules. And of course, not the least of her sins was her wish to work outside the heaven of the home. As Kathy Fletcher puts it, 'In general, the public nature of the actress's profession set her clearly in opposition to the "domestic angel".'[26]

It goes without saying that this is a highly glamorized picture of the life of a professional actress, as the valuable recent work of feminist theatre historians has shown. Women who worked in the theatre were never free from a chorus of critical abuse; and documentary evidence suggests that they were a far greater cause of concern to those who upheld conventional Victorian values than the melodramatic or fictional villainess ever was. This was of course because the disruptive potential of the fictional 'type' could be controlled by—predominantly male—playwrights and directors in a way that the actress's subversive potential could not. The threat posed by the professional actress was thus explicit, whilst the threat of her fictional sister remained implicit. An *Encyclopaedia Britannica* article of 1797 set the theme for commentaries on professional actresses of the next century, though its tone and understanding of the moral and ideological issues involved is more subtle than those to come:

There are some very agreeable and beautiful talents, of which the possession commands a certain sort of admiration; but of which the exercise for the sake of gain is considered, whether from reason or prejudice, as a sort of public prostitution. [. . .] The exorbitant rewards of players [. . .] are

---

[26] 'Planché, Vestris, and the Transvestite Role: Sexuality and Gender in Victorian Popular Theatre', *Nineteenth Century Theatre*, 15 (1987), 9–33 (p. 15).

founded upon these two principles: the rarity and beauty of the talents, and the discredit of employing them in this manner.[27]

Tracy C. Davis's article 'Actresses and Prostitutes in Victorian London' argues convincingly that the common assumption that actresses were prostitutes was, in general, incorrect, though there are many good practical reasons why the two professions were confused: actresses were often seen with gentlemen, received gifts from them, and sometimes became their mistresses, theatres in London were often in the same areas as brothels, prostitutes frequented theatres, actresses sometimes had to wear skimpy costumes which showed off their bodies and suggested sexual pleasure, etc.[28] Another more general reason for the false synonymity perceived between actresses and prostitutes was, of course, the fact that both groups consisted of working women whose living and independence depended on physical appearance.

But independence was an illusory dream for many struggling actresses in the provinces, who became prey to exploitative managers rather than domineering husbands and were scarcely paid for their work. Despite the reality of life for many actresses—hard work and social isolation—they received little praise for either industry or talent.[29] John Styles's 1806 tract *An Essay on the Character, Immoral and Anti-Christian Tendency of the Stage*, which went to a third edition, describes the moral degradation which acting supposedly breeds:

Transform her character: let modesty, the guardian of every female virtue, retire; let the averted eye which turns disgusted from the remotest approach of evil grow confident; let that delicacy of sentiment which feels a 'stain like a wound' give place to fashionable apathy; let the love of home and taste for the sweetly interesting employments of the domestic scene be exchanged for the pursuit of theatrical entertainment, and the vagrant disposition of a fashionable belle, and the picture is reversed; the female is degraded, and society has lost its most powerful, captivating charm.[30]

In 1809, the actress Ann Holbrook herself advised women against seeking a living on the stage; interestingly, she warned them against melodrama particularly:

---

[27] Quoted by Claire Tomalin in *The Invisible Woman*, 17–18.

[28] 'Actresses and Prostitutes in Victorian London', *Theatre Research International*, 13 (1988), 221–34.

[29] Jan McDonald, 'Lesser Ladies of the Victorian Stage', *Theatre Research International*, 13 (1988), 234–49.

[30] (Newport, Isle of Wight: Medina Press, 1806), 34; quoted by Tracy C. Davis in 'Actresses and Prostitutes in Victorian London', 229.

A woman also ought to be deterred from the Stage by the fact that people in general regard Actresses, at best, but as doubtful characters. If we consider their frequent appearance in male habits, their carrying thinness of clothing to excess, and the postures in which the *new-fangled Melo-Drama* places females thus clad, we cannot wonder that the strictly prudent should avoid any intimacy with women, be their inward virtue what it may, whose outward seeming borders on licentiousness.[31] (italics mine)

The middle-class author of *The Diary of an Actress* recorded the social taint and ostracism that her choice of a career on the stage entailed; though one sister paid her a brief visit months after her mid-century debut, the other was immovable: 'She does not wish to be brought down to my level, or to hold any communication except by letter. She has even told me that men might not like to marry her girls when they grow up, if they thought they had an aunt who was an actress.'[32] The diarist Arthur J. Munby perceptively highlighted unease about the contradictions the actress appeared to present in an entry recording a meeting with a ladylike woman at a dinner party in the 1860s, whom he afterwards discovered to be the daughter of an extravaganza performer:

I took down to supper her mother, a pleasant elderly lady, of quiet gentle manners, ladylike, selfpossesst: might have been a Bishop's wife. And who was this nice old lady? Why, she was Mrs German Reed—Miss P. Horton; whose legs, as Ormsby said afterwards, used to be familiar objects at the Haymarket, years ago! nay, she is 'entertaining' still. Does this prove the versatility of women? or not rather their wellkept purity in many cases where fools allow it not? And her daughters, so dignified & free from what is theatrical & meretricious—they prove something, too, I should think![33]

Towards the end of the century, though more and more women were embarking on a stage career, their sisters were still advising them against it.[34] For example, 'A Lady', in 1885, wrote *An Appeal to the Women of England to Discourage the Stage*:

[31] Ann Catherine Holbrook, *The Dramatist; or, Memoirs of the Stage* (Birmingham: Martin & Hunter, 1809), 60; quoted by McDonald in 'Lesser Ladies of the Victorian Stage', 236.

[32] [Alma Ellerslie?], *The Diary of an Actress; or, Realities of Stage Life*, ed. H. C. Shuttleworth (London: Griffith, Farran, Okeden, & Welsh, 1885), 53; quoted by Tracy C. Davis, *Actresses as Working Women: Their Social Identity in Victorian Culture, Gender and Performance* (London: Routledge, 1991), 73.

[33] 6 July (1865–7); quoted by Fletcher, 'Planché, Vestris, and the Transvestite Role', 15, from Derek Hudson, *Munby: Man of Two Worlds* (Boston: Gambit, 1972).

[34] Jan McDonald maintains in 'Lesser Ladies of the Victorian Stage' (p. 247) that 3,696 women entered the theatrical profession in 1891 compared with 384 in 1841.

Ask yourself whether it is possible for a woman to become an actress without suffering any moral deterioration. What is a woman's greatest charm? Does it not consist in a modest, retiring disposition, and, if so, is the stage likely to foster and cherish it?[35]

As far as this book is concerned, the most important reason for Victorian animosity towards actresses is the radical denial they presented of the essentialist, patriarchal (and indeed melodramatic) idea that women embodied by their very nature a 'transparent' ideal of sincerity and authenticity. Tracy C. Davis argues that actresses, like prostitutes, 'were women whose identity, sincerity, and appearance were illusory'.[36] Claire Tomalin states that 'to pretend to be what you were not and to make a good job of it made you morally suspect', pointing to Fanny Burney's *The Wanderer* (1814), Jane Austen's *Mansfield Park* (1814), Thackeray's Becky Sharp in *Vanity Fair*, and his Emily Fotheringay, the professional actress in *The History of Pendennis* (1850), as fictional explorations of the issue.[37] But the complexity of the question of the actress's threat to the principle of sincerity is perhaps most succinctly analysed in Nina Auerbach's article 'Alluring Vacancies in the Victorian Character':

In nineteenth-century novels and in Victorian life as well, women were supposed to embody an integrity of being that offered ballast to the excruciating complexities of men and the painful falsifications of the society they made. Female identities, in art and in life, were squeezed into one-dimensional stock roles [. . .]. Actresses, those sacred monsters, [. . .] like fictional heroines, [. . .] pleased audiences by perfecting the sincere self-fabrication demanded of ordinary women as well. Woman's sincerity assured observers that a knowable self existed: her devious dimensionality inspired awe at the self's hidden boundlessness.[38]

Auerbach shrewdly perceives that the actress's 'sincere self-fabrication' and 'devious dimensionality', though gratifying to theatre audiences, ultimately threatened the very foundations of Victorian society. The actress's ability to impersonate the sincere, angelic, domestic heroine of melodrama, for example, suggested that moral and spiritual purity could (and often had to) be feigned—by professional and, perhaps more importantly, by non-professional acting women. Or, as Erving

---

[35] (London: Masters, 1855), 9; quoted by McDonald in 'Lesser Ladies of the Victorian Stage', 235.
[36] 'Actresses and Prostitutes in Victorian London', 227.
[37] *The Invisible Woman*, 16.
[38] *Kenyon Review*, 8 (1986), 36–48 (p. 36).

Goffman explains in a different context, realistic performances can be threatening because 'a competent performance by someone who proves to be an impostor may weaken in our minds the moral connection between legitimate authorization to play a part and the capacity to play it'.[39] Thus, to adopt appropriately melodramatic terms, the actress ultimately awakened the anxiety that the angel in the house could be the devil in disguise.

DICKENS'S PASSIONATE PERFORMERS

Sincerely Fiery Females

Most of the female deviants I shall be discussing have not committed what could be called 'masculine' crimes; that is, most have not, like Hortense or Madame Defarge, for example, broken the *written*, codified laws of the patriarchal society they inhabit. Many are in fact 'gender offenders'; that is, they have actively violated the *unwritten* Victorian code or ideal of femininity. They have married for money, like Edith Dombey, or had an illegitimate child, like Lady Dedlock. Then again, some are neither criminals in the eyes of the law, nor have they actually committed a 'sexual offence'; they are, like Rosa Dartle or Miss Havisham, 'gender offenders' by nature rather than by action, women who are guilty of the worst sin of all, that of *being* 'unfeminine'. Gender offenders of all kinds are more interesting, in many respects, than convicted criminals, because they are obliged to be more devious. They must act roles, wear masks, negotiate a strategy for the presentation of self in a society which does not want to acknowledge the complexity of female selfhood; to such women in such a society, selfhood is synonymous with interiority. As Lady Dedlock tells Esther, 'If you hear of Lady Dedlock, brilliant, prosperous, and flattered; think of your wretched mother, conscience-stricken, underneath that mask!' (*BH*, chapter 36, p. 512). Except when the crime is that unique sexual crime of prostitution, criminality for most women in Dickens seems perversely to offer a carnivalesque freedom from the restrictions of the patriarchal order.[40]

---

[39] *The Presentation of Self in Everyday Life*, 67.
[40] Of course, Foucault and feminists from Gilbert and Gubar onwards have argued that this freedom is illusory; criminality is always defined by the dominant social order and vice versa. The same is true of madness. See Michel Foucault, *Discipline and Punish* and *Madness and Civilization: A History of Insanity in the Age of Reason*, trans. Richard Howard, Studies in

But just what are these restrictions? The dilemma for women who do not happen to be born in the mould of the angel in the house is neatly summed up by Mrs Skewton in *Dombey and Son*: 'With all those yearnings, and gushings, and impulsive throbbings that we have implanted in our souls, and which are so very charming, why are we not more natural?' (chapter 21, p. 288). Though Victorian society enshrined the principles of sincerity and honesty in its ideal of the female sex, as we have seen, it did not expect, or allow for, extreme passion in its women—whether this passion was sexual or otherwise. Slater points out that deviant women in Dickens's fiction are often excessively passionate, channelling their passion against the structure of patriarchal society, rather than providing an anchor for it.[41] What Slater does not emphasize, however, is that Dickens's passionate women may not acceptably *unleash* their pent-up passion. In Dickens's novels (as in Victorian society), even female speech has to meet stringent, though significantly unspoken, criteria for women to gain novelistic (and social) acceptance and approval. Notably, it is the role of women to 'bring out' others in conversation, and to allow the conversational skills of men to shine. 'Theatrical' or excessive speech is, as Ingham argues, 'multiply inappropriate; it is insubordinate in its claims for the self, indelicate in its clamour for public attention and, [. . .] it is the outcome of false emotionalism. For such a complex of characteristics the *actress* was a suitable sign.'[42] Perhaps unsurprisingly, therefore, what interests Dickens as much as openly fiery women is women who repress their passion and don a social mask, women who are forced to become role-players. Such unfortunates offend against the gender code in two ways: they are violently passionate and also duplicitous, thus violating the ideals of both submissiveness and sincerity associated with femininity proper.

Yet the dilemma for these women (and also for Dickens) is that they can be seen, from one perspective, as innocent victims. Ironically, the ghastly Mrs Skewton's enquiry locates a crucial and persistent ambiguity in Dickens's portrayal of deviant women: when she talks of the 'impulsive throbbings that we have implanted in our souls', does she mean that the passions of passionate women in

Existentialism and Phenomenology (London: Tavistock, 1967), Sandra M. Gilbert and Susan Gubar, *The Madwoman in the Attic: The Woman Writer and the Nineteenth-Century Literary Imagination* (New Haven: Yale University Press, 1979).

[41] *Dickens and Women*, 354–6.

[42] *Dickens, Women & Language*, 77. In this respect (and of course many others), Little Dorrit seems to me to be a striking example of the female ideal fulfilled.

Dickens are innate or socially conditioned? In the familiar terminology of modern feminist debate, was Dickens an essentialist in his
view of women or a materialist? With refreshing precision, Ingham
sophisticates the received idea that Dickens's understanding of
gender was straightforwardly essentialist; even Dickens's 'concept of
"womanliness"', she argues, 'is based not just on a belief in inherent
female qualities but also in the belief that they need to be curbed in
order to reach it'.[43]

This chapter aims to muddy further the essentialist view of
Dickens's women by analysing those deviant women who are
passionate and, like the actress, rigorously controlled in the image of
self they project. Though they are encouraged or forced to repress
themselves in this way, the performative nature of their social,
gendered identities grants a degree of agency or control within their
marginalization. I am particularly concerned in this section with the
way in which the widely criticized 'melodramatic' or 'theatrical'
aspects of Dickens's presentation of Edith in fact enrich or complicate Dickens's investigation of her deviant femininity.[44] There are
some obvious instances of melodramatic rhetoric, from the narrator
and from Edith, which are clearly open to criticism.[45] But these
instances should not blind us to the positive side of the question: that
is, in *Dombey and Son*, Dickens employs melodrama and 'theatricality'
in an ambitious and sophisticated way, not to obscure but to explore
and reveal the character of Edith Dombey, and to analyse the performative nature of (gendered) identities generally. Edith's 'theatricality'
is in fact a highly gendered way of managing intense emotions.

Edith Dombey is passionate, cynical, and a social role-player.
While the male characters in *Dombey and Son* cast her in the stock roles
of wife and mistress alternately, literary critics have traditionally seen
her as a stock figure, a 'bought bride' and/or a near relation of the
deviant women of nineteenth-century melodrama.[46] The fact that

---

[43] *Dickens, Women & Language*, 68.

[44] F. R. Leavis, for example, argues that the theme of the 'Bought Bride [. . .] takes
Dickens into a realm where he *knows* nothing. What he takes for knowledge is wholly
external and conventional; determined, therefore, unresistingly by all the theatrical clichés
and sentimental banalities of the high-life novelette and the equivalent drama'—Leavis
and Leavis, *Dickens the Novelist*, 48. Ian Milner, 'The Dickens Drama: Mr. Dombey',
Nineteenth-Century Fiction, 24 (1970), 477–87 (p. 484), states that 'Edith is of course "melodramatic"; she makes her way in the novel accompanied by a mounting array of rhetorical
cliché.'

[45] See pp. 219–20 below for examples of both.

[46] See n. 44 above.

she 'centers the main arguments about the role of women in the strongly patriarchal world of commercial capitalism' has been commented upon.[47] Likewise, it is easy to see the general importance of her repression of emotion in a novel investigating the death or repression of feeling. Again, Edith, like Florence Dombey and Alice Marwood, is thematically significant in terms of the parent–child relationship analysed in the novel as a whole. Edith and Alice are obviously particularly relevant in this respect because both are presented as, most immediately, victims of matriarchal exploitation—though their respective family microcosms cannot be divorced, of course, from the patriarchal macrocosm of commercial capitalism depicted in *Dombey and Son*.

Dickens uses the fundamental melodramatic tension between emotional excess and restraint, in *Dombey and Son*, not simply for dramatic effect, but to investigate a crucial and real dilemma for the passionate woman in Victorian society: how far can she ever '*be* herself' in a social situation? Through the character of Edith, Dickens investigates the causes and effects of a particularly female brand of emotional repression. Edith stifles her passion for much of the time through a curious mixture of personal pride—she does not want to lose self-control—and self-loathing—she has resigned herself to the fact that she will not command such market value if she lets passion ruin her ornamental potential. Nevertheless, her sadness at the loss of her potentially 'natural heart'[48] becomes a refrain throughout the novel. When the narrator observes near the end of the novel, 'She was moved and weeping. Had she been oftener thus in older days, she had been happier now' (chapter 61, p. 825), he is not sharing any insight with the reader that Edith herself does not perceive.

However, the fact that emotional outpourings are not always so acceptable—to either the narrator or Victorian society—is reinforced through the presentation of Edith's novelistic shadow, Alice Marwood. Alice is an interesting double for two reasons in particular: first, because of the synonymity often perceived between actresses and prostitutes in Victorian Britain (in this case, Edith is a social performer who has prostituted herself on the marriage market). Second, Alice is particularly significant in the light of Dickens's

---

[47] Mary Montaut, 'The Second Mrs. Dombey', *Dickens Quarterly*, 4 (1987), 141–53 (p. 142).
[48] She upbraids her mother: 'Oh Mother, Mother, if you had but left me to my natural heart when I too was a girl [. . .] how different I might have been!' (chapter 30, p. 418).

investigation of female passion, its causes and effects. While Florence's presence in the Dombey home itself ensures that Edith's 'tempest of passion [is] hushed' (chapter 30, p. 409), Alice's wild nature is a volcano of hatred and resentment symbolizing her own ultimate, imminent eruption.[49]

Alice is less successful than Edith at stifling her own passions, though the energy she puts into the attempt is as frightening to the narrator as the passion itself. When Good Mrs Brown tells Alice that Carker is 'thriving', the narrative description which ensues could serve as a paradigmatic illustration of Dickens's ambiguous attitudes to female passion:

the face and form before her [Mrs Brown] were unshaped by rage. It seemed as if the bosom would burst with the emotions that strove within it. The effort that constrained and held it pent up, was no less formidable than the rage itself: no less bespeaking the violent and dangerous character of the woman who made it. (chapter 34, p. 471)

The word 'unshaped' accurately suggests the main and significant difference, for Dickens's narrator, between Edith and Alice. Whereas Edith is constantly compared to a statue or a frozen object, imprisoned by the form of her own beauty like a figure on Keats's Grecian urn, Alice is 'unshaped' by passion. Despite the fact that Edith is presented as suffering intensely within the urn of her social persona, the narrator finds it difficult to forgive Alice for marring her good looks with passion. The ambiguity contained within the last sentence of the above quotation echoes that of Mrs Skewton, discussed earlier; when the narrator refers to 'the woman that made it', 'it' could refer either to 'the effort' Alice makes to constrain her temper or to 'the rage' itself. If we accept the latter possibility then there is once more a suggestion that women are agents responsible for their own passions.

Despite all the attention that is paid to Alice's background, the narrative itself is consistently ambivalent about whether there can be any excuse for the extremity of Alice's negative, subversive passions— or, more to the point, whether there can be any excuse for revealing or venting such passions. For the slight but significant difference between Edith and Alice is that Alice is not an accomplished role-player like Edith, and her transparency is problematized rather than valorized. This difference can partly be explained in social and

---

[49] Ingham sees Alice's role as crucial, rather than peripheral, to the novel: she is 'pivotal to the plot' and 'though invisibly, its agent'—*Dickens, Women & Language*, 56.

legal terms: Edith is a woman of rank who has something to lose by relaxing her social image; Alice is a prostitute and convict who has nothing further to lose and no real hope of gain if she were to don a mask of calm. Critics like Nancy Armstrong and Camille Colatosti have rightly drawn attention to the way in which Dickens's feminine ideal is a bourgeois one, but the important point here, however, is this:[50] if there is one surprising characteristic that Edith and Alice have in common it is a specifically female brand of 'sincerity' which includes, and indeed necessitates, a split between the public persona and the private 'self'. At first glance, Alice appears to fit Erving Goffman's 'transparent' definition of sincerity.[51] Alice's inner being, that is to say, is at one with the social persona she projects; she is 'honest' about her thoughts and feelings and she believes in the truth of her social performances. Edith, by contrast, appears to be anything but sincere. Her social mask hides her passionate self. Like Goffman's cynic, in fact, she has no belief in her own performances and cares little about the feelings of the audience upon whom she imposes.[52]

But Edith's social hypocrisy is paradoxically superficial. Throughout the novel, Edith has an acute sense of a 'true' self which she believes herself to have betrayed; moreover, in her continuous attempts to be true to what is left of her better self, she ironically reveals a kind of sincerity more remarkable by far than the 'sincerity' of long-suffering, unquestioning Dickens heroines like Kate Nickleby or Lizzie Hexam. What is impressive about Edith is that she understands the complicating—or fabricating—factors involved in attaining a state of sincerity which is socially acknowledged; moreover, as Edith appreciates, for a woman to appear sincere in an exploitative patriarchal society is especially problematic. Such 'sincerity' can in fact be more damaging and duplicitous than Edith's thoughtful and principled refusal to play the angel in the house. In the words of Judith Butler, 'as a strategy of survival within compulsory systems, gender is a performance with clearly punitive consequences'.[53]

To understand fully Edith's particular brand of sincerity, it is

[50] Armstrong argues (mistakenly) that 'all the monstrous women [in novels written between the 1830s and 1860s . . .] have other than middle-class origins'—*Desire and Domestic Fiction*, 183; Colatosti's position on Dickens's women is more measured and persuasive—see 'Male versus Female Self-Denial: The Subversive Potential of the Feminine Ideal in the Fiction of Charles Dickens', *Dickens Studies Annual*, 19 (1990), 1–24.

[51] *The Presentation of Self in Everyday Life*, 28–9; see p. 173 above.

[52] *The Presentation of Self in Everyday Life*, 28–9; see p. 179 above.

[53] *Gender Trouble: Feminism and the Subversion of Identity* (London: Routledge, 1990), 139.

essential to appreciate that Edith's 'theatricality' is only rarely thoughtlessly histrionic; for most of the time, Edith is a calculating, self-conscious, social role-player. Edith's strategy for negotiating her precarious moral and social position is twofold: first, in social situations, she is as undemonstrative as possible, to minimize the responsibility she feels for the hawking and vending[54] in which she is centrally implicated. Dombey and Carker both misread her character, because both—in different ways—reinvent her as a two-dimensional, conventional stock type; Dombey expects her to adopt the role of wife, Carker that of mistress. But Edith erects a kind of taciturn denial of the readings that both men impose upon her. While she has often maintained silence in society rather than obliging her husband with conversational prompts, when she does question Dombey, her tone is as aggressive as it should be polite: 'Did I ever tempt you to seek my hand? Did I ever use any art to win you? Was I ever more conciliating to you when you pursued me, than I have been since our marriage? Was I ever other to you, than I am?' (chapter 40, p. 543). Dombey's construction of Edith as wife is in fact a reconstruction. Edith, like Alice for most of the novel—Alice asks Harriet Carker, 'Why should *I* be penitent, and all the world go free?' (chapter 33, p. 464)—has the courage to posit her own sense of truth against that of the world she lives in, to assert that there can and should be more than one reading of female behaviour.

Edith's second means of coping with her predicament is related to the first: she perceives herself not as a unified being but as two selves, the public and the private, or the apparent and the 'real'. She refuses to become her social persona; her mental stability and self-respect in fact depend on her conception of herself as an actress playing a role. This conception underpins her behaviour even in those passages most difficult to rescue from the accusation that they are 'melodramatic'. For example, when Edith is described

with her dark hair shaken down, her dark eyes flashing with a raging light, her broad white bosom red with the cruel grasp of the relentless hand with which she spurned it from her, pacing up and down with an averted head, as if she would avoid the sight of her own fair person, and divorce herself from its companionship. Thus, in the dead time of the night before her bridal, Edith Granger wrestled with her unquiet spirit, tearless, friendless, silent, proud, and uncomplaining. (chapter 30, p. 420)

---

[54] In chapter 27, she asks her mother, 'Have I been hawked and vended here and there, until the last grain of self-respect is dead within me, and I loath myself?' (p. 382).

her violent gestures signify more than the melodramatic masochism of a stock villainess; Dickens's narrator distinguishes, for example, between 'her own fair person' and 'herself'. Edith is tormented, as she is for much of the novel, because she wants to divorce her appearance from the self that it betrays; she wishes to destroy the beautiful shell which has imprisoned her. Frank McCombie, arguing that the novel is about specifically sexual repression, points out that in this passage the object of Edith's violence is her bosom, a symbol of her sexuality.[55]

Edith is more similar to Alice Marwood than my earlier provisional distinction between the two implied. Though Alice appears to be sincere in Goffman's terms, erasing any division between self and persona, and believing in the role she plays, she is not quite as straightforward as this description would imply. Though 'honest' about her thoughts and feelings, this does not necessarily mean, in her case, that she projects her inner self truly. For the capacity to do so, as I discussed in Chapter 7, is bound up with questions of self-knowledge and self-expression. Both Alice and Edith in fact vacillate in their attitudes to their 'essential' selves, though both intermittently suggest a belief in the essential self that is thoroughly un-postmodern. Thus, whereas the above analysis of Edith emphasizes her belief in her better self, there are also many moments in the novel when she perceives herself as wicked to the core; in the case of Alice, whilst much of the time she vents her self-loathing, her torment stems from her instinct that she has, or once had, a better self—hence her refusal to accept money from Harriet Carker. Her public persona of prostitute does not, therefore, reflect her recurring sense of her 'true' worth and her resentment of her lot is intensified.

These parallel or corollary vacillations in the images of self held by Edith and Alice go some way towards explaining the exaggerated influence of their unpleasant mothers over their lives. Alice is more straightforward than Edith in this respect. She was bred into a career of prostitution before she knew any better, but, on her return from captivity, lets her mother know that she no longer respects her maternal authority. Edith, on the other hand, is fully aware of Mrs Skewton's role as pimp in the marital prostitution that her marriage to Dombey represents, but still goes along with it. It might be argued that Edith's marriage to Dombey represents her submission to the will of the hideous yet pathetic Mrs Skewton, a submission tending to

[55] 'Sexual Repression in *Dombey and Son*', *Dickensian*, 88 (1992), 25–38.

invalidate any claim that could be made for Edith as a strong, sincere woman. Edith's marriage to Dombey suggests nothing of the sort: it represents Edith's submission to her own worst sense of self and her submission to a vision of the world which she feels offers no real freedom or happiness to the beautiful, passionate woman. No doubt Mrs Skewton played a major part in forming Edith's jaded vision of the world, but once Edith becomes conscious of the forces that have moulded her, she has the chance to reject them. Edith marries Dombey not because she is weakly submissive to Mrs Skewton but because she regards herself as a cynic. In marriage, however, her idealistic self paradoxically torments her as she longs to attain a state of transparent sincerity.

Edith and Alice are ultimately sincere in the only way possible for an intelligent, passionate, Victorian female. They are true to a hidden self, a self driven underground by the social restrictions on the behaviour of women. Of course, as I suggested in my last chapter, a sincerity which is socially acknowledged is extremely difficult—if not impossible—for men too; but Victorian males at least had greater freedom to project themselves in a way which they *believed* to be honest. For the Victorian female in particular, a sense of one's own personal sincerity often had to coexist with a consciousness of one's social hypocrisy. Edith and Alice both have as much thoughtful integrity as any of the other characters in the novel. Mrs Skewton declares in terms reminiscent of John Chester in *Barnaby Rudge*: 'The world is coming to such an artificial and ungrateful state, that I begin to think there's no Heart—or anything of that sort—left in it, positively' (chapter 37, p. 509). Both Edith and Alice, whatever wrongs they may have committed in the eyes of their society, affirm positively that there is such a thing as the human heart. Edith's ulti-mate defiance of Dombey and Carker is what Donohue identifies in melodrama as 'the climactic display of the immanent'. Though she must pay the price of becoming a social outcast, she is ultimately true to her better self; that is, female integrity necessitates social rejection/alienation. The conclusion of Alice Marwood's story, by contrast, is artistically and psychologically inappropriate. Her repentance to Harriet Carker (chapter 53, p. 718) shows Dickens try-ing to make her conform to society's *idea* of a sincere woman, rather than to the alternative model of sincerity the novel has constructed through her own character and that of Edith.

The fact that Edith can be true to herself only by becoming a social outcast is itself a radical subversion of Victorian values. Likewise, the emphasis placed on Edith's conditioning wins sympathy for her character and predicament. Edith is herself conscious of her society's tendency to squeeze women into one-dimensional roles, and she evades and manipulates its habit of stereotyping human beings. This means that she is anything but a stock type, or a fallen woman immersed in her 'role'; she privileges the private self as the most important site of identity. Finally, her defiance of Dombey and Carker, which is in effect a rejection of the Victorian world, can be interpreted as the heroic, rebellious stand of an individual against a corrupt society.

Admittedly, a more hostile feminist interpretation could maintain, with equal validity, that what Dickens is doing with the character of Edith is endowing an apparently wayward woman with the characteristics of the conventional stage heroine—or turning a genuine 'gender offender' into a cliché and disarming her by these means. For example, Dickens uses Edith's relationship with Florence to show the reader that Edith is a good woman 'deep down'.[56] Edith's love for Florence demonstrates that she possesses one of the qualities Dickens most admired in virtuous women, their feeling of sisterhood. Edith's virtual adoption of Florence as a daughter shows the maternal spirit which Dickens believed to be natural in women. In addition, her constant harping on her 'better self' suggests to the reader that she, like Nancy in *Oliver Twist*, is innately virtuous. In the same vein, the ending of Edith's story can be interpreted as a last-minute failure on Dickens's part, rather than a reflection of his social and moral radicalism.

What I want to show is the inadequacy of regarding Dickens's deviant women simply as stock types. For instance, to regard Edith as no more than the passive reflection or creature of Dickens's supposed social attitudes is itself to regard her as a stock type, though of criticism as much as of fiction. Edith Dombey herself, as we have seen, understands the inadequacy and destructiveness of perceiving women as 'flat', finite types. Tellingly, Dickens himself reveals a similar understanding, in *Little Dorrit*, when the actress Fanny superficially labels Amy a 'flat' sister (book 2, chapter 14, p. 571). The text makes clear, of course, what Nina Auerbach would call the 'devious dimensionality' behind Little Dorrit's veneer, a dimensionality

---

[56] Ingham's category 'True Mothers' is interesting in this respect (*Dickens, Women & Language*, chapter 6, pp. 111–32).

appreciated by few in the novel and which Clennam is particularly slow to perceive. There is no denying that Dickens draws on stock types of wayward womanhood, but his texts simultaneously reveal that the mythologizng or fictionalizing of femininity such clichés involve can be emotionally and morally crippling for the women (deviant or domestic) expected to conform to them.[57]

Moreoever, in an important reversal of the typical Dickensian aversion to the valorization of the inner life, the texts Dickens's deviant women inhabit seem partially to condone the privileging of interiority these women adopt by explaining it in terms of necessity rather than choice. Despite this, the greater understanding accorded to women who live life on the inside could be seen as reinforcing traditional associations between femininity and privacy. Again, the very association of interiority with female *deviance* shrouds Dickens's apparent reversal of attitudes in convenient ambiguity. However, this ambiguity offers readers an interpretative choice regarding Dickens's wayward women, rather than trapping them in the prison of essentialism.

Deviant Women as Art Objects

In *The Second Sex* (1949), Simone de Beauvoir argues that even the least sophisticated woman, when she is dressed,

> does not present *herself* to observation; she is, like the picture or the statue, or the actor on the stage, an agent through whom is suggested someone not there—that is, the character she represents, but is not. It is this identification with something unreal, fixed, perfect as the hero of a novel, as a portrait or a bust, that gratifies her; she strives to identify herself with this figure and thus to seem to herself to be stabilized, justified in her splendor.[58]

In Dickens's novels, several deviant females are presented as art objects as well as actresses. In *Dombey and Son*, for example, Edith is likened to 'a handsome statue; as cold, as silent, and as still' (chapter 30, p. 413). Elsewhere Carker notes 'a most extraordinary accidental likeness' between Edith and a woman in a picture, 'Perhaps it is a

---

[57] Critics (like Ingham and Colatosti) are finally beginning to realize that not even Dickens's heroines are as straightforward as they appear. Esther Summerson is perhaps the most obvious example of a heroine–actress, and there has been a refreshing revival of critical interest in her.

[58] Trans. H. M. Parshley, Everyman's Library, CIIIVII (London: Cape, 1953; repr. London: Campbell, 1993), 560.

Juno; perhaps a Potiphar's Wife; perhaps some scornful Nymph' (chapter 33, p. 455); this is, of course, a telling example of the tendency of Carker—and Dombey—to reinvent Edith as a type. The statuesque appearance of Edith, however, is emphasized throughout the novel; in conversation with Florence about Dombey's paternal shortcomings, Edith's face 'strove for composure until its proud beauty was as fixed as death' and her manner is 'stately and quiet, as a marble image' (chapter 35, p. 486); 'The tears that were visible in her eyes as she kept them fixed on Florence, showed that the composed face was but as a handsome mask' (chapter 35, p. 487).[59] In *Bleak House*, Guppy initially suspects a link between Lady Dedlock and Esther when he sees a portrait of the former (chapter 29, p. 406), whilst Tulkinghorn, along with fashionable society in general, regards her as 'a study' (chapter 48, p. 660). The portrait of Lady Dedlock at Chesney Wold, of course, is repeatedly and fatalistically associated with Lady Dedlock herself. Moreover, it is not only young, beautiful women in Dickens's novels who are compared with art objects; both Mrs Steerforth and Mrs Clennam are transformed into statues by their emotional breakdowns and Miss Havisham is unforgettably compared with 'some ghastly wax-work at the Fair' (*GE*, volume i, chapter 8, p. 59).[60]

Interestingly, however, given de Beauvoir's comments and subsequent feminist interest in both the representation of women as objects of the male gaze and the commodification of the female, Dickens's wayward women are not shown to be gratified by their identification with art objects. On the contrary, to confine my discussion initially to Edith Dombey and Lady Dedlock, both are presented as prisoners of their beauty. To repeat my earlier Keatsian analogy, the two women are figured as suffering selves, trapped inside the aesthetically beautiful object perceived by the outside world. At her reconciliation with Esther, for example, Lady Dedlock exclaims (as I quoted earlier), 'If you hear of Lady Dedlock, brilliant,

[59] The significance of the use of art objects in *D&S* has been commented on perceptively by Susan Nygaard, in 'Redecorating Dombey: The Power of "a Woman's Anger" versus Upholstery in *Dombey and Son*', *Critical Matrix*, 8 (1994), 40–80. She, like Frank McCombie, notes the significance of the illustrations within Phiz's illustrations—see 'Sexual Repression in *Dombey and Son*', 29–31.
[60] See also *DC*, chapter 56, p. 687—'she lay like a statue, except for the low sound now and then'—and *LD*, book 2, chapter 31, p. 772: 'There, Mrs. Clennam dropped upon the stones; and she never from that hour moved so much as a finger again, or had the power to speak one word. [. . .] Except that she could move her eyes and faintly express a negative and affirmative with her head, she lived and died a statue.'

prosperous, and flattered; think of your wretched mother, conscience-stricken, underneath that mask!' (chapter 36, p. 512). She distinguishes here between society's image of herself and her own suffering self. Lady Dedlock urges Esther to remember in future that whatever appearance she (Lady Dedlock) presents, 'the reality is in her suffering' (chapter 36, p. 512). She talks about herself in the third person here, not because she regards herself as an object, but because she is adopting the perspective on her own behaviour which she knows will be Esther's vantage point. Her bifocal view of herself has become habitual, and this device only increases the reader's sense of the poignant gap between the undoubted reality of her suffering and the appearance of passionlessness suggested by her aesthetically beautiful exterior.

The striking feature, then, of Dickens's dramatization of the objectification and commodification of women in Victorian society, in *Dombey and Son* and *Bleak House*, is that the wayward women in question are presented as subjects as well as objects—a fact which complicates any superficial reading of the texts which sees Dickens's gaze as simply turning women into objects. Indeed, the inner life of Dickens's female deviants is interestingly more introspective and self-orientated than the outwardly focused, emotionally charged storytelling which so often constitutes Dickensian 'subjectivity'.[61] In *Dombey and Son*, for example, though Dombey sees Edith as an object, Dickens emphasizes throughout the text her sense of herself as subject, her sense of a better, private self which even Carker does not fully perceive or understand. Moreover, in terms of the critique of capitalism which the novel offers, Edith's social commodification is undermined by her resentment of her status as object; here too, though Edith and the reader perceive that she is regarded socially as an object, Edith's indignation is an expression of her sense of herself as subject. As we have seen, Lady Dedlock is also presented—and indeed, like Edith, sees herself—as both object and subject throughout the novel's narratives which, it is worth remembering, are themselves apparently 'objective' and 'subjective' by turns. Again, the suffering woman's sense of herself as subject subverts society's treatment of her as object.

Having said this, Dickens's novels do not uphold a simplistic

---

[61] See Introduction and Chapter 4 for a fuller discussion of Dickens's rendering of subjectivity and interiority. I would argue that all Dickens's first person narrators express their 'subjectivity' through outwardly focused storytelling.

dichotomy between society's objectification of women, on the one hand, and female resistance to that objectification on the other. Both Edith and Lady Dedlock, as my earlier analysis maintained, are to some extent complicit in turning themselves into art objects. Indeed, Ingham argues fascinatingly of Edith, Lady Dedlock, and Louisa Gradgrind/Bounderby that 'each woman reclaims a specific identity for herself through her evident choice of a single object as the expression of a concealed self'; in Edith's case, this is a looking glass and in Lady Dedlock's a portrait.[62] In my view, however, Edith and Lady Dedlock differ crucially from Louisa in that both consciously imitate objects and adopt roles whereas Louisa is relatively transparent. They do so through a curious mixture of pride (they do not want to lose self-control) and self-loathing (both have compromised themselves by playing society's games and adhered to rules they resent). Of course, they are complicit in the process of social commodification because both appreciate that a statuesque exterior can act as a protective mask as well as a prison, an impenetrable veil which hides the secret, better self of the subject; in *Bleak House*, for example, we read about Lady Dedlock drawing 'her habitual air of proud indifference about her like a veil' (chapter 36, p. 510).

Cynthia Northcutt Malone's article ' "Flight" and "Pursuit": Fugitive Identity in *Bleak House*' uses post-structuralist theory to argue that 'the novel represents a substitutive chain of veiled ladies' to signify the illusory nature of identity.[63] Though the idea of the fiction of the self fascinated Dickens, it is important to emphasize that Edith and Lady Dedlock believe in the idea of a better, private self in a way that Dickens's dandies, for example, do not. By perceiving themselves not as unified personalities but as two selves, the public and the private, or the subject and the object, both feel able to preserve a sense that their integrity resides 'inside' the public, social veneer of the object. Thus, though neither Edith nor Lady Dedlock is shown to be gratified by their identification with objects, both perceive themselves in a way consistent with de Beauvoir's analysis of female self-objectification. Neither believes her inner self to be on display; each is, in de Beauvoir's words, 'like the picture or the statue, or the actor on the stage, an agent through whom is suggested someone not there—that is, the character she represents, but is not'.[64] This

---

[62] *Dickens, Women & Language*, 97–8. In Louisa's case, the 'object' is fire.

[63] *Dickens Studies Annual*, 19 (1990), 107–24 (p. 107).

[64] Ingham argues similarly of the 'passionate women', Edith, Lady Dedlock, and

is a particularly female brand of social hypocrisy, however, which situates selfhood privately. To Dickens's male hypocrites, appearance is all; to Dickens's deviant women, the inner sanctum of the self is of paramount importance.

Edith Dombey and Lady Dedlock are not then, like de Beauvoir's female, motivated by conditioned vanity. Their self-objectification is pragmatic, allowing them a secret, private self within the inevitable, unavoidable prison of the object. Thus, if the woman's representation of herself as an object can be seen as a compromise or even surrender to the male gaze, from another perspective it can be seen as a pragmatic seizure of limited potential power; by manipulating her own appearance, the female subject can at least make her prison private and protective—as well as oppressive. Moreover, whereas I have emphasized the protective possibilities of self-objectification, Nygaard rightly stresses the aggressive force of such a practice: 'Edith turns Dombey's upholstery against him by playing her role to extremes; since he has acquired her to add to his decor, she violently and obviously objectifies herself.'[65]

Such subtleties in Dickens's treatment of the idea of the woman as object have, until recently, been overlooked by some influential critics, who have perceived a familiar theme and assumed a familiar handling of it. To give just one example, when John Carey observes in the characterization of Edith 'a tendency to freeze her into a work of art',[66] he does not consider the question of who exactly is doing the freezing, and the importance of that question. Though Carker, Dombey, and Edith herself are all complicit, for their different reasons, in the commodification of the female, the text's simultaneous emphasis on the suffering female as subject precludes any simplistic reading of the novel which assumes that the author himself perceives deviant women as art objects.

I emphasize the word 'deviant' because it is significant that Dickens's wayward women are likened to works of art, whereas typically his 'good' women are not.[67] This is, of course, something to

Louisa—*Dickens, Women & Language*, 100. In my view, Louisa is far more transparent and less defiant than the others, and has more in common with Dickens's fallen women than with his fully adult, deviant actresses.

[65] 'Redecorating Dombey', 59.

[66] *The Violent Effigy*, 87.

[67] The association of the statuesque with both deviance and actresses is explored by Gail Marshall in *Actresses on the Victorian Stage: Feminine Performance and the Galatea Myth*, Cambridge Studies in Nineteenth-Century Literature and Culture, XVI (Cambridge: Cambridge

do with a primitive dichotomy between the natural and the artificial, the angel and the whore. But Dickens's manipulation of the idea of the woman as art object is also connected with his investigation of female repression of passion, the social enforcement of female interiority, fashionable society's admiration of the statuesque, and commercial society's valuing of the female as a commodity. Whereas Dickens's male characters are presented and present themselves as (art) objects to suggest the fictionality of the inner emotional self, when Dickens's female characters are connected with art objects, the primacy of the private, feeling self is paradoxically suggested.

The primacy of the secret emotional self is suggested even in the case of some of Dickens's older, less beautiful, female artefacts (Mrs Skewton and Mrs Merdle are obvious exceptions). Mrs Steerforth and Mrs Clennam end their days as statues not because they are inhuman or passionlessness, but because the intensity of conflicting passions which they have repressed for years finally erupts and breaks them.[68] It is in fact as statues that they paradoxically become most sympathetic as human beings, because it is then that their status as monstrous victims is crystallized. Likewise, Miss Havisham's presentation of herself as 'ghastly wax-work' is an attempt to parade, freeze, and immortalize the pain she has experienced; she turns herself into a monument of female suffering at the hands of men and ultimately becomes a monument of female masochism.

WOMEN AS SEX OBJECTS

Angus Wilson argues that there is no character in Dickens's novels who 'gives woman the true dignity of a whole body and a whole

University Press, 1998): 'on the Victorian stage [. . .], it was precisely the "statuesque" actress who was a highly charged icon of sexual desirability, whose own "erotic energy" was variously camouflaged, denied, even facilitated by her access to the theatrical rhetoric of statuary' (p. 4).

[68] I disagree here with Carol Hanbery MacKay's view that 'Miss Havisham's powerlessness—her isolation and position as a social outcast—denies her sexual possibilities'—'Controlling Death and Sex: Magnification v. the Rhetoric of Rules in Dickens and Thackeray', in Regina Barrreca (ed.), *Sex and Death in Victorian Literature* (Houndmills: Macmillan, 1990), 120–39 (p. 122). To me, it is Miss Havisham's very 'sexual possibilities' that result in her isolation in the first place. MacKay's remarks here also seem inconsistent with her subsequent observation that Miss Havisham 'exercises power by [. . .] transferring the contained erotic component so effectively that Estella becomes the cold-hearted temptress, who in turn manipulates social rules and boundaries to self-destructive ends' (p. 122).

mind'.[69] John Carey comments in a related vein on the 'erotic paternalism'[70] Dickens feels towards his mindless, bodiless women, while Maria Nicholls maintains that 'Dickens is either incapable or unwilling to portray any erotic urge on the part of a woman'.[71] These critics are all expressing the received idea concerning Dickens's attitude to sexuality in (novelistic and extra-novelistic) women; Dickens, the story goes, deeply traumatized by the death of his wife's 17-year-old sister Mary Hogarth, with whom he was obsessed, could never regard women who did not look like children as sexually attractive partly because he found sexual desire in women repugnant. The revelations about his later relationship with the young actress Ellen Ternan only added weight to this theory (though in many ways, given that Ternan was an actress, this later relationship should have complicated analyses of Dickens's taste in women, as Claire Tomalin makes clear).

In no area of Dickens studies have naive biographical approaches warped criticism of Dickens's texts more glaringly or more damagingly, in my view.[72] The main problem haunting traditional, author-based interpretations of Dickens's attitude to female sexuality, as that attitude is expressed in the novels themselves, is that of logically linking the two halves of the recurring critical argument. The argument maintains, on the one hand, that Dickens's angelic child-women are 'about as tempting as wax fruit', and on the other, that Dickens himself is upholding these sterilized creatures as the sole objects of sexual desire in his novels. This train of thought begs the question: if Dickens's child-women are no more sexually appealing than plastic dolls, how can critics then deduce that Dickens intends them to be regarded otherwise?

There is, of course, no doubt that those child-women Kate Millett labelled 'insipid goodies'[73] are regarded by other characters within the texts themselves as sexually attractive.[74] The image of Quilp leering at Little Nell, for instance, is difficult to forget, and there are countless other examples: Kate Nickleby is ogled by Sir Mulberry

---

[69] *The World of Charles Dickens* (London: Secker & Warburg, 1970), 103.

[70] *The Violent Effigy*, 158.

[71] 'Lady Dedlock's Sin', *Dickensian*, 89 (1993), 39–94.

[72] See n. 2 above.

[73] *Sexual Politics* (Garden City, NY: Doubleday, 1970), 90.

[74] Ingham's chapter (2) on 'nubile girls' is highly perceptive on the contradictions inherent in the figuration of Dickens's heroines/nubile girls; at the same time as they are desired by others, they must be innocently unaware of their desirability—*Dickens, Women & Language*, 17–37.

Hawk, Dolly Varden is rough-handled by the savage Hugh, Pet Meagles is desired by both Gowan and Clennam, and Bella Wilfer's flirtation with her father rather nauseatingly suggests her awareness of her own sexuality.

But if it is true that the virtuous heroine, however childlike and however insipid, is often regarded as the focus of male sexual desire in the texts themselves, it is also true that Dickens's deviant women are presented as objects of sexual attraction. The critical common-place that Dickens was unable to associate maturity with sex has often blinded commentators to the fact that it is not only suffering heroines in Dickens's novels who are regarded as objects of sexual desire. Dickens's deviant women are adults, aware of their own sexuality and sexual attractiveness. They are also agents and Dickens 'makes a degree of agency the concomitant to identity as a sexual being'.[75] To give several examples: Edith Dombey is conscious of the sexual aspect of both Carker's voyeurism and his sadism; Lady Dedlock's relationship with Tulkinghorn contains similar elements, though Tulkinghorn has none of Carker's sensuality; the serpentine Rosa Dartle attracts both Steerforth and the young David, who felt himself 'falling a little in love with her' (*DC*, chapter 24, p. 304); Miss Wade is the ex-lover of Gowan and her relationship with Tattycoram is strongly sexually charged; Estella is a flirtatious *femme fatale* who, even as a young girl, possesses an adult's awareness of how to manipulate her sexuality, with ruinous effects on Pip's happiness.

In the words of *The Violent Effigy*, sex in Dickens's novels 'is not banished but driven underground, to emerge in perverted and inhibited forms'.[76] As Dickens's wayward women are frequently enmeshed in perverted male–female power relations, it is not surprising that they often act as a textual locus for an implicit investigation of adult sexual relationships in Victorian society. Perhaps the most intense sexual energy, in Dickens's novels, is expressed through the fraught struggles for power between adult men and adult women; and these power struggles frequently take a sado-masochistic form. Of course, Dickens's 'good' heroines too, like the heroines of stage melodrama, are the ultimate masochists and suffer interminably at the hands of sadistic men. As Laura Peters observes, the 'pattern of power relations involving a self-tormenting female evidently fasci-

---

[75] *Dickens, Women & Language*, 61.   [76] Carey, *The Violent Effigy*, 171.

nated Dickens'.[77] What distinguishes the power relations involving Dickens's deviant women, however, is that these women refuse to surrender power completely; indeed, they crave power for themselves. The resulting friction is the most intense and disturbing glimpse of adult sex that the novels have to offer.

Perhaps the most striking example of the emergence of sex in a perverted and inhibited form is presented as a rare and brief journey into the realm of sexual fantasy:

> Did the phantom of such a woman flit about him on his ride; true to the reality, and obvious to him?
>
> Yes. He saw her in his mind, exactly as she was. She bore him company, with her pride, resentment, hatred, all as plain to him as her beauty; with nothing plainer to him than her hatred of him. He saw her sometimes haughty and repellent at his side, and sometimes down among his horse's feet, fallen and in the dust. But he always saw her as she was, without disguise, and watched her on the dangerous way that she was going. (*D&S*, chapter 46, p. 618)

This is Carker fantasizing about Edith. But the striking feature of his sado-masochistic daydream is that it could be that of several male characters in Dickens's novels who are both attracted by, and desire to punish, the active, deviant woman—indeed, to force her into her properly passive role. The memorable, throbbing scar on Rosa Dartle's lip is indelible evidence of the blow Steerforth inflicted on her—and more complexly, it symbolizes Steerforth's assertion of power over a woman he possibly loved, a woman whose tool of power is her sharp tongue, her control over language. Indeed, Rosa's ironic interrogations of David and Steerforth seem to me among the most remarkable examples of female speech in the Dickens canon, as threatening as her passionate sexuality (also symbolized by the vaginal association of her 'lips').[78] Carker's 'secret sense of power in her [Florence's] shrinking from him' (chapter 37, p. 502) is one he clearly enjoys over Edith herself.[79] It is also that experienced by

---

[77] 'The Histories of Two Self-Tormentors: Orphans and Power in *Little Dorrit*', *Dickensian*, 91 (1995), 187–97.

[78] It is surprising that Ingham, like most critics, omits discussion of Rosa's irony in *Dickens, Women & Language*, commenting only on Rosa's scar as 'the physical index of her passionate nature' (p. 60). Barbara Black's 'A Sisterhood of Rage and Beauty: Dickens's Rosa Dartle, Miss Wade, and Madame Defarge', *Dickens Studies Annual*, 26 (1998), 91–106, is an exception to the general critical neglect of Rosa, discussing both her scar and her use of irony perceptively.

[79] See *D&S*, p. 502: 'Proudly as she opposed herself to him, [. . .] the triumph and superiority were his, and [. . .] he knew it full well.'

Tulkinghorn in the presence of Lady Dedlock. Miss Wade is conquered by Gowan, as she records in her 'History of a Self-Tormentor' (*LD*, book 2, chapter 21, pp. 644–51). But these women often experience a parallel and corollary desire to dominate. Edith's final triumph over Carker and his death under a train would in fact have appealed to the craving for power displayed by nearly all Dickens's deviant women. These women desire, use, and abuse power; they are sadists when given the opportunity. Edith Dombey obviously derives some relish from her thwarting of the expectations of both Dombey and Carker; Rosa Dartle's wish to have Little Emily whipped until she is dead (*DC*, chapter 50, p. 616) is, on one level, an expression of the intensity of her sexual desire for Steerforth; Miss Wade's victimization of Tattycoram positions her firmly in the centre of an abuse cycle; Madame Defarge's sadistic violence is a reaction against the rape of her sister, the murder of her family, against aristo-cratic and male power. Finally, *Great Expectations* as a whole is a superbly subtle investigation of the crippling effects of sado-masochistic relations between men and women; a perfect integration of plot and theme is achieved by making nearly all the characters either agents or victims (or both) in a plot the very stuff of which is abuse.

In 'The Subjection of Women' (1869), John Stuart Mill, that most merciless of contemporary critics of Dickens's attitudes to women, argues that lack of liberty for women can only result in distorted cravings for power.[80] Mill's arguments are ironically borne out in Dickens's texts, where women who desire liberty in an oppressive society can only console themselves through perverted power games. Dickens's wayward women consistently focus his investigation of adult sexual relationships and the perverted and inhibited forms they take in the patriarchal world of Victorian England.

In *Sexual Politics*, Kate Millett argued that, though Dickens achieves 'a nearly perfect indictment of both patriarchy and capitalism in *Dombey and Son*', he does so 'without ever relinquishing the sentimental version of women which is the whole spirit of Ruskin's "Of Queens' Gardens"'. 'It is one of the most disheartening flaws in the master's work', she goes on, 'that nearly all the "serious" women in Dickens' fiction, with the exception of Nancy [. . .] and a handful of her criminal sisters, are insipid goodies carved from the same soap as

---

[80] *On Liberty and Other Essays*, 471–582 (p. 578).

Ruskin's Queens.'[81] For Millett, Dickens's sentimentalized portrayal of women is ultimately far more important than his indictment of patriarchy; and his 'insipid goodies' are more noteworthy than that 'handful of criminal sisters' who do not conform to the Victorian ideal of femininity. She despises Dickens's admiration of 'insipid goodies' whereas the more traditional critic may not; but the striking thing is that both are reading Dickens in the same way. This approach is perhaps understandable in one of the pioneers of feminist criticism, but it has been an ironically persistent feature of criticism of Dickens's women that, until recently, it has adopted essentially the same perspective on Dickens's texts as he would have done himself.[82] One of my principal aims in this chapter is in keeping with more recent work on Dickens's women: I have aimed to prove that mere repetition of the received idea concerning Dickens's representation of women—in whatever kind of intonation—is ultimately a disservice to his novels and the variety they encompass.

Though I agree with the general interpretation of the significance of Dickens's 'good' heroines as angels in their patriarchal houses, I have taken this reading for granted in order to concentrate on a more neglected area of Dickens's texts. There is no reason why, because Dickens attempts to marginalize some of his deviant women, feminist critics should do likewise. Surely the contrary should be true. And indeed, characters like Edith Dombey, Lady Dedlock, Miss Havisham, and so forth could never be said to be at the margins of their respective texts. As Kate Flint suggests: 'within and outside Dickens' texts, we do discover the presence of those whose deviance is so pronounced that they have the effect of denying this supposed or desired norm [of femininity].'[83]

It may finally be impossible to give any definitive response to the question of whether or not Dickens's deviant women are powerful enough presences within their respective texts, or within his work as a whole, to subvert the supposed ideal or 'norm' of femininity embodied in the 'good' heroines. What is more appropriate is to avoid rigidity of interpretation or perspective and emphasize the

---

[81] pp. 89–90.

[82] David Holbrook's *Charles Dickens and the Image of Woman* (New York: New York University Press, 1993), with its frequent references to the reader as 'he', is perhaps the most shocking example of the stagnation which has pervaded criticism of Dickens's women; it is completely untouched by the most rudimentary developments in feminist (and Dickens) criticism.

[83] *Dickens* (Brighton: Harvester Press, 1986), 113.

protean and fluctuating nature of the texts themselves. In my de-polarization of those supposed 'opposites' sincerity and artificiality, object and subject, sexual and asexual, sadist and masochist, I have however tried to avoid the current tendency to reinvent Dickens as a (pre-)postmodernist for whom experience is a free play of meta-morphic, fictional constructs. Dickens's texts contain idealized, 'static' models of femininity who create the impression of monopathy or 'wholeness'; at the same time, the novels contain performative female characters whose dislocated sense of selfhood problematizes the transparent, one-dimensional construction of femininity which was the cornerstone of Victorian gender ideology. Once again, the ideal or utopian figure coexists in Dickens's novels with the character who throws the fictionality of the ideal into relief. It is neither neces-sary nor desirable to prioritize one of these strains in Dickens's work, however. In the case of Dickens's women in particular, it would surely be ironic if the twenty-first-century reader—especially the twenty-first-century female reader—chose to adopt one critical role or perspective when other ways of seeing and being are freely available to her.

Afterword

Edwin Drood's John Jasper appears to embody perfectly the idea behind this book: that Dickens associates interiority, particularly the psychological variety, with deviance. Jasper is a pillar of the chocolate-box community of Cloisterham, but he is also an opium addict and probably a murderer. As a man with a double life, he is a role-player par excellence. Jasper's double life makes him an especially fitting vehicle of the double perspective Dickens so often adopts towards melodrama. But the novel, unlike Dickens's first person narratives, does not generally offer us a double perspective on its initial protagonist John Jasper. Jasper represents the merging of the Romantic and the melodramatic types which function dialectically in so many of Dickens's late novels. Unusually for a central character in a Dickens novel, he has many of the traits of the Romantic individual—he is interested in altered states of consciousness, artistically sensitive, cultured, and inwardly focused. But Dickens is not adopting Romantic aesthetics: what is interesting about Jasper is that his typically 'Romantic' traits are melodramatically rendered. On the evidence of the first drug-induced scene it is tempting to argue that Dickens has adapted conventional melodramatic aesthetics to render what Brooks calls 'melodrama of consciousness'.[1] Even this scene, however, is inside the deviant mind only as it paradoxically attempts to escape from itself. The rest of the novel returns to business as usual. As a mystery story and a detective tale, it tends to rely on melodramatic aesthetics—plot, action, visual description, and dramatic confrontation—to imply insights into the character's 'psychology'. Indeed, from one perpective, it is possible to see Jasper as a purely melodramatic creation—a Gothic villain of the type disparaged by Wilson, but a reconstructed Gothic villain whose implied interiority gives him, to post-Romantic readers, 'reality'.

What distinguishes *Edwin Drood* from Dickens's previous novels is the prominence given to a deviant character whose mind we seem to be asked to read. This is not the same as saying that Dickens foregrounds interiority—he does not—but that he asks us to prioritize

[1] *The Melodramatic Imagination*, 160.

the problem of the self-consumed, performative personality in our responses to the novel. Rather than marginalizing the type in an attempt to diminish his or her importance, Dickens decides to foreground his exploration of the social effects of the secretive roleplayer. While this approach risks reinforcing the increasing nineteenth-century obsession with interiority, its advantage is that it makes the consequences of a life lived on the inside melodramatically obvious. While Jasper's centrality, and the incompleteness of the novel, have inevitably acted as an invitation to many critics to psychoanalyse Jasper, a more fruitful line of enquiry seems to me to lie in the novel's exploration of the social causes and effects of repressive deviance.

From this perspective, Jasper is most interesting as a symbol of the canker at the heart of British—or, more specifically, English—society. Jasper is an 'insider', trusted within his family and community. In the novel, he personifies the duality and corruption inherent in Victorian ideas of both respectability and Englishness. Dickens is commonly associated with an idea of 'Englishness' which the claustrophobically cloistered town of Cloisterham appears to uphold. But *Edwin Drood*, perhaps more than any other Dickens novel, challenges traditional notions of the English 'community'. Dickens's notion of community is not necessarily, as this book has implied, either democratic or egalitarian; likewise his notion of cultural inclusivity. But the social pessimism of the complete late novels is not reinforced, in my account, in *Edwin Drood*. Rather Dickens's unfinished novel explores alternative models of community and communality and critically interrogates the notion of cultural inclusivity so crucial to his art and politics. Who is included in English culture and society and where are they included? There is a sense in *Edwin Drood* of a community turned inside out; the centre may be rotten but the margins may stop the rot. The repressive English lack the passionate vitality of the outwardly focused, 'Landless' outsiders. The 'foreign' brother and sister pairing do not function simply as the colonial 'Other'. The English may regard them as a threat, but the novel positions them as crucial to the regeneration and survival of the community. Helena Landless is particularly important here. She inverts many of Dickens's gender and racial stereotypes: she is active, slightly masculine, and foreign, but despite all this, virtuous, heroic, and possibly a detective. Whatever Dickens's precise plans for her, there is no doubt that she features centrally in the novel's blurring of gender and racial stereotypes. She is crucial, that is, to Dickens's new, multifaceted model of English community. The fact that she is a woman and 'Landless' gives a sense of modernity to Dickens's last vision of community.

Whether Dickens's novels have indeed furthered the cause of cultural inclusivity is, of course, a matter of debate. A dominant strand of cultural theory relates the 'popularity' of popular culture to the reassurance offered by its conservative ideologies. Though Dickens's novels undoubtedly include both this reassurance and the conservative ideologies which are its precondition, Dickens's cultural politics are, this book has argued, both contradictory and central to an understanding of modern cultural formations. Inevitably, I will have raised as many questions as I have answered. But my hope is that when the definitive book on Dickens and popular culture does materialize, questions surrounding 'aesthetic' categories like character will not seem entirely extraneous to it. The melodramatic Dickens character plays a crucial part in both Dickens's politics and in the cultural politics informing his critical reception. However inconsistent or problematic the politics of Dickensian character, the sheer scale of Dickens's appeal suggests that he was far from ignorant about the pragmatics of cultural inclusivity. A love of 'dramatic entertainments', it seems, is not peculiar to the 'common people', but constitutes more inclusively what people have in common.

Bibliography

Works by Dickens

'The Amusements of the People', *HW* 1 (30 Mar. 1850), 13–15; *HW* 1 (13 Apr. 1850), 57–60.

Charles Dickens: The Public Readings, ed. Philip Collins (Oxford: Clarendon Press, 1965).

Charles Dickens as Editor: Being Letters Written by Him to William Henry Wills his Sub-editor, selected and ed. R. C. Lehmann (London: Smith & Elder, 1912).

'The Demeanour of Murderers', *HW* 13 (14 June 1856), 505–7.

'Dullborough Town', in *The Uncommercial Traveller and Reprinted Pieces* (Oxford: Oxford University Press, 1958; repr. 1987), 116–26.

(With Wilkie Collins), *No Thoroughfare* (New Royal Adel., 26 Dec. 1867), in *Complete Plays and Selected Poems of Charles Dickens* (London: Vision Press, 1970), 171–222.

'Preliminary Word', *HW* 1 (30 Mar. 1850), 1.

The Speeches of Charles Dickens: A Complete Edition, ed. K. J. Fielding (Hemel Hempstead: Harvester Wheatsheaf, 1988).

'The Spirit of Fiction', *AYR* 18 (27 July 1867), 118–20.

'Two Views of a Cheap Theatre', in *The Uncommercial Traveller and Reprinted Pieces* (Oxford: Oxford University Press, 1958; repr. 1987), 29–39.

The Village Coquettes (6 Dec. 1836, St J.), in *Complete Plays and Selected Poems of Charles Dickens* (London: Vision Press, 1970), 41–89.

Plays

À BECKETT, GILBERT ABBOTT, *Oliver Twist* (26 Mar. 1838, St J.), LC Add. MS 42945, fos. 683–707b.

[Anon.], *Oliver Twist* (1855, intended for Stand.), LC Add. MS 52, 955 H.

[Anon.], *Oliver Twist*, (21 Apr. 1868, Garrick), LC 53067 P.

BAILLIE, JOANNA, *De Monfort* (29 Apr. 1800, DL) (London: Longman, Hurst, Rees, & Orme, 1807).

BARRYMORE, WILLIAM, *The Forest of Bondy; or, The Dog of Montargis* (30 Sept. 1814, CG), Hodgson's Juvenile Drama (London: Hodgson, *c.*1825).

——— *Gilderoy; or, The Bonnie Boy* (25 June 1822, Cob.), *Richardson Minor*, 2 (London: Richardson, [1829]).

BERNARD, WILLIAM BAYLE, *The Farmer's Story* (13 June 1836, Lyc.), *Dicks*, [no.] 434 (London: Dicks, [1883?]).

Booth, Michael R. (ed.), *English Plays of the Nineteenth Century*, 5 vols. (Oxford: Clarendon Press, 1969–76).

—— *Hiss the Villain: Six English and American Melodramas* (London: Eyre & Spottiswoode, 1964).

Buckstone, J. B., *Jack Sheppard* (28 Oct. 1839, Adel.), *Acting Nat. Drama*, 7 (London: Chapman & Hall, [1840?]).

Bulwer (Lytton), Edward, *Not so Bad as We Seem; or, Many Sides to a Character* (16 May 1851, Devonshire House) (London: Chapman & Hall, 1851).

Cavendish, Lady Clara, *The Woman of the World* (13 Nov. 1858, Queen's), *Lacy*, 38 (London: Lacy, [1859]).

Collins, Wilkie, *Armadale* (London: Smith, Elder, 1866).

—— *The Frozen Deep* (6 Jan. 1857, Tavistock House), in *The Frozen Deep and Other Tales* (London: Chatto & Windus, 1905), 1–75.

Fitzball, Edward, *Jonathan Bradford; or, The Murder at the Roadside Inn* (12 June 1833, Surrey), *Dicks*, [no.] 370 (London: Dicks, [1883?]).

—— *Paul Clifford* (28 Oct. 1835, CG), *Dicks*, [no.] 367 (London: Dicks, [1883?]).

Grangé, E., and Montépin, Xavier de, *The Corsican Brothers* (10 Aug. 1850, Théâtre Historique, Paris), trans. Charles Webb, *Cumberland*, 47 (London: Music-Publishing, [1860?]).

Haines, J. T., *The Factory Boy; or, The Love Sacrifice* (8 June 1840, Surrey), *Dicks*, [no.] 641 (London: Dicks, [1885]).

Hazlewood, C. H., *Lady Audley's Secret* (25 May 1863, Vic.), *Lacy*, Suppl. 2 (London: Lacy, [1850 etc.]).

Jerrold, Douglas, *Black-Eyed Susan; or, All in the Downs* (8 June 1829, Surrey), in Michael Booth (ed.), *English Plays of the Nineteenth Century*, 5 vols. (Oxford: Clarendon Press, 1969–76), i (1969), 151–200.

—— *Fifteen Years of a Drunkard's Life!* (24 Nov. 1828, Cob.), *Dicks*, [no.] 220 (London: Dicks, [1877?]).

—— *The Rent Day* (25 Jan. 1832, DL) (London: Chapple, 1832).

Lewis, Leopold, *The Bells* (25 November 1871, Lyc.), in Michael Booth (ed.), *Hiss the Villain: Six English and American Melodramas* (London: Eyre & Spottiswoode, 1964), 343–82.

Lewis, M. G., *The Castle Spectre* (14 Dec. 1797, D. L.), 4th edn. (London: Bell, 1798).

Lillo, George, *The London Merchant; or, The History of George Barnwell* (1731), ed. William H. McBurney, Regents Restoration Drama (London: Arnold, 1965).

Maturin, R. C., *Bertram; or, The Castle of St. Aldobrand* (9 May 1816, DL) (London: Murray, 1816).

Moncrieff, W. T., *Zoroaster; or, The Spirit of the Star* (19 Apr. 1824, DL), 2nd edn. (London: Limbird, 1824).

Murrey, W. H., *Obi; or, Three-Fingered Jack* (2 July 1800, H.2), *Dicks*, [no.] 478 (London: Dicks, [1883]).

OXENFORD, JOHN, *Oliver Twist* (11 Apr. 1868, Queen's), LC 53066U.

PHILLIPS, WATTS, *Lost in London* (16 Mar. 1867, Adel.), in Michael R. Booth (ed.), *Hiss the Villain: Six English and American Melodramas* (London: Eyre & Spottiswoode, 1964), 203–69.

PITT, G. DIBDIN, *Rookwood!* (24 Feb. 1840, SW), *Dicks*, [no.] 307 (London: Dicks, [1882?]).

—— *Sweeney Todd: The Demon Barber of Fleet Street* (22 Feb. 1847, Britannia), ed. Montagu Slater (London: Howe, 1928).

POCOCK, ISAAC, *The Miller and his Men* (21 Oct. 1813, CG), in Michael R. Booth (ed.), *English Plays of the Nineteenth Century*, 5 vols. (Oxford: Clarendon Press, 1969–76), i (1969), 29–72.

ROBERTSON, T. W., *Caste* (6 Apr. 1867, Prince of Wales), *French*, 1960 (London: French, 1867).

SHEPHERD and CRESWICK, *Oliver Twist* (5 May 1868, Surrey), LC 53068 F.

SIDDONS, HENRY, *The Sicilian Romance; or, The Apparition of the Cliffs* (28 May 1794, CG) (London: Barker, 1794).

SIMPSON, J. PALGRAVE, *Broken Ties* (8 June 1872, Olym.), *Lacy*, 96 (London: French, [1850 etc.]).

SLATER, MONTAGU (ed.), *Maria Marten; or, The Murder in the Red Barn* (London: Heinemann, 1971; repr. 1973).

SOANE, GEORGE, *Lilian, the Show Girl* (10 Oct. 1836, Surrey), *Duncombe*, 24 (London: Duncombe, [1825 etc.]).

SUTER, WILLIAM E., *Lady Audley's Secret* (21 Feb. 1863, Queen's), *Lacy*, 57 (London: Lacy, [1863]).

TAYLOR, T. P., *The Bottle* (1 Oct. 1847, CL), *Lacy*, 17 (London: Lacy, [1850 etc.]).

WALKER, JOHN, *The Factory Lad* (15 Oct. 1832, Surrey), in Michael R. Booth (ed.), *English Plays of the Nineteenth Century*, 5 vols. (Oxford: Clarendon Press, 1969–76), i (1969), 201–33.

Eighteenth- and Nineteenth-Century Criticism

À BECKETT, GILBERT ABBOTT, *The Quizziology of the British Drama* (London: Punch, 1846).

[Anon.], 'Harlequin Fairy Morgana', *AYR* 12 (20 Aug. 1864), 40–8.

[Anon.], 'Lacenaire', *AYR* 5 (27 July 1861), 417–22.

[Anon.], '*Oliver Twist*', *Quarterly Review*, 64 (1839), 83–102.

ASSELINEAU, CHARLES, *Charles Baudelaire: sa vie et son œuvre* (Paris: Lemerre, 1869).

BENTHAM, JEREMY, *Bentham's Theory of Fictions*, ed. C. K. Ogden (London: Kegan Paul, 1932).

BULWER (LYTTON), EDWARD, *England and the English*, 2 vols. (London: Bentley, 1833).

BYRON, Lord GEORGE GORDON, 'English Bards, and Scotch Reviewers', in

The Works of the Right Honourable Lord Byron (Philadelphia: Thomas, 1820), 1–86.

CARLYLE, THOMAS, *Sartor Resartus* (1833–4), ed. Kerry McSweeney and Peter Sabor (Oxford: Oxford University Press, 1987; repr. 1991).

CHESTERFIELD, Lord PHILIP DORMER STANHOPE, *Lord Chesterfield's Letters* (1774), ed. David Roberts (Oxford: Oxford University Press, 1992).

[CHESTERTON, GEORGE LAVAL], 'Coolness amongst Thieves', *HW* 3 (17 May 1851), 189–90.

COLERIDGE, SAMUEL TAYLOR, *Biographia Literaria; or, Biographical Sketches of my Literary Life and Opinions* (1817), in *The Collected Works of Samuel Taylor Coleridge*, ed. James Engell and W. Jackson Bate, 16 vols., Bollingen Series, LXXV (London: Routledge & Kegan Paul, 1983), vii.

—— Lecture on *Hamlet* (2 Jan. 1812), repr. in *Samuel Taylor Coleridge*, ed. H. J. Jackson, The Oxford Authors (Oxford: Oxford University Press, 1985), 655–9.

—— *Table Talk*, 2nd edn. (1836); repr. in *The Romantics on Shakespeare*, ed. Jonathan Bate (Harmondsworth: Penguin, 1992).

DE QUINCEY, THOMAS, 'On Wordsworth's Poetry', *Taits's Magazine* (Sept. 1845), repr. in *Collected Writings*, ed. David Masson, 14 vols. (London: Black, 1896–7), xi (1897), 294–325.

DOLBY, GEORGE, *Charles Dickens as I Knew Him: The Story of the Reading Tours in Great Britain and America, 1866–70* (London: Fisher Unwin, 1885).

ELIOT, GEORGE, 'The Natural History of German Life', *Westminster Review*, 10 (1 July 1856), 51–79; repr. in *Selected Essays, Poems and Other Writings*, ed. A. S. Byatt and Nicholas Warren (Harmondsworth: Penguin, 1990), 107–39.

FORSTER, JOHN, *The Life of Charles Dickens*, ed. J. W. T. Ley (London: Palmer, 1928).

GARCÍA, GUSTAVE, *The Actor's Art: A Practical Treatise on Stage Declamation, Public Speaking and Deportment*, 2nd edn. (London: Simpkin, Marshall, 1888).

[HALLIDAY, ANDREW], 'Mr. Whelks over the Water', *AYR* 15 (30 June 1866), 589–92.

HAZLITT, WILLIAM, 'British Institution' (1814), in *Complete Works of Hazlitt*, ed. P. P. Howe, 21 vols. (London: Dent, 1930–4), xviii (1933), 10–16.

—— 'A View of the English Stage; or, A Series of Dramatic Criticisms' (1814(–17)), in *Complete Works of Hazlitt*, ed. P. P. Howe, 21 vols. (London: Dent, 1930–4), v (1930), 169–379.

HORNE, R. H. (ed.), *A New Spirit of the Age*, The World's Classics, CXXVII (London: Oxford University Press, 1907).

HUNT, LEIGH, 'Patent Theatres and Mr. Arnold' (27 Jan. 1831), in *Dramatic Criticism*, ed. Lawrence Huston Houtchens and Carolyn Washburn Houtchens (New York: Columbia University Press, 1949), 256–60.

—— 'Lounging through Kensington', *HW* 7 (6 Aug. 1853), 533–8.

JAMES, HENRY, '*Our Mutual Friend*', *Nation*, 1 (21 Dec. 1865), 786–8.

—— 'Some Notes on the Theatre', *Nation* (11 Mar. 1875), repr. in Montrose J. Moses and John Mason Brown (eds.), *The American Theatre as Seen by its Critics, 1752–1934* (New York: Norton, 1934), 122–6.

LAMB, CHARLES, 'On the Custom of Hissing at the Theatres, with Some Accounts of a Club of Damned Authors' (1811), in *The Works of Charles and Mary Lamb*, ed. E. V. Lucas, 6 vols. (London: Methuen, 1912), i. 101–7.

—— 'On the Tragedies of Shakespeare, Considered with Reference to their Fitness for Stage Representation', *Reflector* (Oct.–Dec. 1811); repr. in David Bromwich (ed.), *Romantic Critical Essays*, Cambridge English Prose Texts (Cambridge: Cambridge University Press, 1987), 56–70.

LEWES, G. H., 'Dickens in Relation to Criticism', *Fortnightly Review*, 11 (Feb. 1872), 141–54.

—— *On Actors and the Art of Acting* (1985), Evergreen, LXI (New York: Grove Press, 1957).

LISTER, T. H., 'Dickens's Tales', *Edinburgh Review*, 68 (1838), 75–97.

[LYNN, ELIZA], 'A Few Pleasant French Gentlemen', *HW* 15 (18 Apr. 1857), 366–9.

MAGINN, WILLIAM, 'Mr. Edward Lytton Bulwer's Novels; and Remarks on Novel-Writing', *Fraser's Magazine*, 1 (June 1830), 509–32.

MAYHEW, EDWARD, *Stage Effect; or, The Principles which Command Dramatic Success in the Theatre* (London: Mitchell, 1840).

MAYHEW, HENRY, *London Labour and the London Poor: A Cyclopaedia of the Condition and Earnings of Those That Will Work, Those That Cannot Work, and Those That Will Not Work*, 3 vols. (London: Morning Chronicle, 1851).

MILL, JOHN STUART, 'Of Individuality, as One of the Elements of Well-Being', in *On Liberty and Other Essays* (1859), ed. John Gray (Oxford: Oxford University Press, 1991), 62–82.

—— 'On the Subjection of Women' (1869), in *On Liberty and Other Essays*, ed. John Gray (Oxford: Oxford University Press, 1991), 471–582.

[MORLEY, HENRY], 'A Criminal Trial', *HW* 13 (21 June 1856), 529–34.

REDE, LEMAN THOMAS, *The Road to the Stage; or, The Performer's Preceptor* (London: Smith, 1827).

[SALA, GEORGE A.], 'Strollers at Dumbledowndeary', *HW* 9 (3 June 1854), 374–80.

SCOTT, Sir WALTER, 'An Essay on the Drama', in *Essays on Chivalry, Romance and the Drama*, in *The Miscellaneous Prose Works of Sir Walter Scott, Bart.*, 28 vols. (Edinburgh: Cadell, 1834–36), vi (1834), 217–395; first pub. in the Supplement to the *Encyclopaedia Britannica* (1819).

SIDDONS, HENRY, *Practical Illustrations of Rhetorical Gesture and Action*, 2nd edn. (London: Sherwood, Neely & Jones, 1822).

SMITH, ALBERT, *The Natural History of the Gent* (London: Bogue, 1847).

TAINE, HIPPOLYTE, 'Charles Dickens, son talent et ses œuvres', *Revue des deux mondes*, 1 (1 Feb. 1856), 618–47; repr. in Stephen Wall (ed.), *Charles Dickens Critical Anthology* (Harmondsworth: Penguin, 1970), 99–103.

THACKERAY, WILLIAM MAKEPEACE, 'Horae Catnachianae', *Fraser's Magazine*, 19 (Apr. 1839), 407–24.

TOLSTOY, LEO, *What is Art?*, trans. Aylmer Maude (Chicheley: Minet, 1971).

WAGNER, RICHARD, *Opera and Drama* (1851), in *Richard Wagner's Prose Works*, trans. William Ashton Ellis, 8 vols. (London: Kegan Paul, 1893), ii.

WORDSWORTH, WILLIAM, and COLERIDGE, S. T. (1802), preface to the *Lyrical Ballads*, ed. Michael Mason (London: Longman, 1992), 55–93.

Twentieth-Century Criticism

ACKROYD, PETER, *Dickens* (London: Guild Publishing, 1990).

ADAMS, JAMES ELI, *Dandies and Desert Saints: Styles of Masculinity* (Ithaca, NY: Cornell University Press, 1995).

ADORNO, THEODOR, *The Culture Industry* (1941; London: Routledge, 1991).

ARAC, JONATHAN, 'Hamlet, *Little Dorrit*, and the History of Character', in Michael Hays (ed.), *Critical Conditions: Regarding the Historical Moment* (Minneapolis: University of Minnesota Press, 1992), 82–96.

ARMSTRONG, ISOBEL, *Victorian Poetry: Poetry, Poetics and Politics* (London: Routledge, 1993).

ARMSTRONG, Nancy, *Desire and Domestic Fiction: A Political History of the Novel* (Oxford: Oxford University Press, 1987).

AUERBACH, NINA, 'Alluring Vacancies in the Victorian Character', *Kenyon Review*, 8 (1986), 36–48.

AXTON, WILLIAM, *Circle of Fire: Dickens' Vision and Style and the Popular Victorian Theatre* (Lexington: University of Kentucky Press, 1966).

BAKHTIN, MIKHAIL, *The Dialogic Imagination*, ed. Michael Holquist, trans. Caryl Emerson and Michael Holquist (Austin: University of Texas Press, 1981).

——*Rabelais and his World*, trans. Hélène Iswolsky (London: MIT Press, 1968).

BARTHES, ROLAND, *The Pleasure of the Text* (1973), trans. Richard Miller (Farrar, Strauss & Giroux, 1975; Oxford: Blackwell, 1990).

——'The Reality Effect', in Lilian R. Furst (ed.), *Realism*, Modern Literatures in Perspective (London: Longman, 1992), 135–41.

BAUDRILLARD, JEAN, 'Simulacra and Simulations' (1981), repr. in Peter Brooker (ed.), *Modernism/Postmodernism* (Harlow: Longman, 1992), 151–62.

BEAUVOIR, SIMONE DE, *The Second Sex* (1949), trans. H. M. Parshley, Everyman's Library, CIIIVII (London: Jonathan Cape, 1953; repr. London: Campbell, 1993).

BENTLEY, ERIC, *The Life of the Drama* (New York: Atheneum, 1964).

BERGSON, HENRI, 'Laughter', in Wylie Sypher (ed.), *Comedy*, trans. Fred Rothwell (Garden City, NY: Doubleday, 1956), 59–190.

BERMEL, ALBERT, 'Where Melodrama Meets Farce', in Daniel Gerould (ed.), *Melodrama, New York Literary Forum*, 7 (1980), 173–8.

BERNSTEIN, ROBERT, '*Oliver* Twisted: Narrative and Doubling in Dickens's Second Novel', *Victorian Newsletter*, 79 (1991), 27–34.

BLACK, BARBARA, 'A Sisterhood of Rage and Beauty: Dickens's Rosa Dartle, Miss Wade, and Madame Defarge', *Dickens Studies Annual*, 26 (1998), 91–106.

BOOTH, MICHAEL R., *English Melodrama* (London: Jenkins, 1965).

—— 'Melodrama and the Working-Class', in Carol Hanbery MacKay (ed.), *Dramatic Dickens* (Houndmills: Macmillan, 1989), 96–109.

BRATTON, JACKY, COOK, JIM, and GLEDHILL, CHRISTINE (eds.), *Melodrama: Stage, Picture, Screen* (London: British Film Institute, 1994).

BROOKS, PETER, *The Melodramatic Imagination: Balzac, Henry James, Melodrama and the Mode of Excess* (New Haven: Yale University Press, 1976).

BROWNE, NICK, 'Society and Subjectivity: On the Political Economy of Chinese Melodrama', in Jacky Bratton, Jim Cook, and Christine Gledhill (eds.), *Melodrama: Stage, Picture, Screen* (London: British Film Institute, 1994), 167–96.

BUTLER, JUDITH, *Gender Trouble: Feminism and the Subversion of Identity* (London: Routledge, 1990).

CAREY, JOHN, 'Dickens and the Mask', *Studies in English Literature*, 59 (1983), 3–18.

—— *The Violent Effigy: A Study of Dickens' Imagination* (London: Faber & Faber, 1973).

CHANDLER, F. W., *The Literature of Roguery*, 2 vols. (London: Constable, 1907).

CHESTERTON, G. K., *Appreciations and Criticisms of the Works of Charles Dickens* (London: Dent, 1911).

CHITTICK, KATHRYN, *The Critical Reception of Charles Dickens, 1833–1841* (New York: Garland, 1989).

—— *Dickens and the 1830s* (Cambridge: Cambridge University Press, 1990).

CLARK, ANNA, 'The Politics of Seduction in English Popular Culture, 1748–1848', in Jean Radford (ed.), *The Progress of Romance* (London: Routledge & Kegan Paul, 1986), 47–70.

CLARK, TIMOTHY, 'Dickens through Blanchot: The Nightmare Fascination of a World without Interiority', in John Schad (ed.), *Dickens Refigured: Bodies, Desires and Other Histories* (Manchester: Manchester University Press, 1996), 22–38.

COLATOSTI, CAMILLE, 'Male versus Female Self-Denial: The Subversive Potential of the Feminine Ideal in the Fiction of Charles Dickens', *Dickens Studies Annual*, 19 (1990), 1–24.

COLLINS, P. A. W., 'Dickens as Editor: Some Uncollected Fragments', *Dickensian*, 56 (1960), 85–96.

COLLINS, PHILIP, *Dickens and Crime*, 2nd edn. (London: Macmillan, 1965).

—— ' "Inky Fishing-Nets": Dickens as Editor', *Dickensian*, 61 (1965), 120–8.

CONNOR, STEVEN, Review essay on Harry Stone's *The Night Side of Dickens: Cannibalism, Passion, Necessity* (Columbus: Ohio State University Press, 1994), *Dickensian*, 91 (1995), 127–30.

—— ' "They're All in One Story": Public and Private Narratives in *Oliver Twist*', *Dickensian*, 85 (1989), 3–16.

DART, GREGORY, *Rousseau, Robespierre and English Romanticism*, Cambridge Studies in Romanticism, XXXII (Cambridge: Cambridge University Press, 1999).

DAVIES, JAMES A., *The Textual Life of Dickens's Characters* (Houndmills: Macmillan, 1989).

DAVIS, EARLE, *The Flint and the Flame: The Artistry of Charles Dickens* (London: Gollancz, 1964).

DAVIS, TRACY C., 'Actresses and Prostitutes in Victorian London', *Theatre Research International*, 13 (1988), 221–34.

—— *Actresses as Working Women: Their Social Identity in Victorian Culture*, *Gender and Performance* (London: Routledge, 1991).

DAWSON, S. W., *Drama and the Dramatic*, The Critical Idiom Series, XI (London: Methuen, 1970).

DEN HARTOG, DIRK, *Dickens and Romantic Psychology: The Self in Time in Nineteenth Century Literature* (Houndmills: Macmillan, 1987).

DEXTER, WALTER, *Some Rogues and Vagabonds of Dickens* (London: Palmer, 1927).

DISHER, MAURICE WILLSON, *Blood and Thunder: Mid-Victorian Melodrama and its Origins* (London: Muller, 1949).

DONOHUE, JOSEPH, *Theatre in the Age of Kean* (Oxford: Blackwell, 1975).

DUFFY, DANIEL, 'Heroic Mothers and Militant Lovers: Representations of Lower-Class Women in Melodramas of the 1830s and 1840s', *Nineteenth Century Theatre*, 27 (1999), 41–65.

EASTHOPE, ANTONY, *Literary into Cultural Studies* (London: Routledge, 1991).

EDGECOMBE, RODNEY STENNING, 'Dickens, Hunt and the "Dramatic Criticism" in *Great Expectations*: A Note', *Dickensian*, 88 (1992), 82–90.

EIGNER, EDWIN M., *The Dickens Pantomime* (Berkeley and Los Angeles: University of California Press, 1989).

—— *The Metaphysical Novel in England and America: Dickens, Bulwer, Melville, and Hawthorne* (Berkeley and Los Angeles: University of California Press, 1978).

ELFENBEIN, ANDREW, *Byron and the Victorians*, Cambridge Studies in Nineteenth-Century Literature, IV (Cambridge: Cambridge University Press, 1995).

ELIOT, T. S., 'Ben Jonson', in *The Sacred Wood: Essays on Poetry and Criticism*, 7th edn. (London: Methuen, 1950; repr. 1969), 104–22.

—— 'The Metaphysical Poets' (1921), in *Selected Prose*, ed. John Hayward (London: Penguin, 1953), 111–20.

ELIOT, T. S., 'Wilkie Collins and Dickens' (1929), in *Selected Essays*, 3rd edn. (London: Faber & Faber, 1951; repr. 1965), 460–70.

ENGELL, ELLIOTT, and KING, MARGARET F. *The Victorian Novel before Victoria: British Fiction during the Reign of William IV, 1830–37* (London: Macmillan, 1984).

FIETZ, LOTHAR, 'On the Origins of English Melodrama in the Tradition of Bourgeois Tragedy and Sentimental Drama: Lillo, Schröder, Kotzebue, Sheridan, Thompson, Jerrold', in Michael Hays and Anastasia Nikolopoulou (eds.), *Melodrama: The Cultural Emergence of a Genre* (Hound-mills: Basingstoke, 1996), 83–101.

FELDMAN, JESSICA R., *Gender on the Divide: The Dandy in Modernist Literature* (Ithaca, NY: Cornell University Press, 1993).

FITZ-GERALD, S. J. ADAIR, *Dickens and the Drama* (London: Chapman & Hall, 1910).

FLINT, KATE, *Dickens* (Brighton: Harvester Press, 1986).

FLETCHER, KATHY, 'Planché, Vestris, and the Transvestite Role: Sexuality and Gender in Victorian Popular Theatre', *Nineteenth Century Theatre*, 15 (1987), 9–33.

FORD, GEORGE H, *Dickens and his Readers: Aspects of Novel-Criticism since 1836* (Princeton: Princeton University Press, 1955).

FORSTER, E. M., *Aspects of the Novel*, Pelican (Harmondsworth: Penguin, 1962).

FORTIER, MARK, *Theory / Theatre* (London: Routledge, 1997).

FOUCAULT, MICHEL, *Discipline and Punish: The Birth of the Prison* (1975), trans. Alan Sheridan (London: Penguin, 1991).

——*Madness and Civilization: A History of Insanity in the Age of Reason*, trans. Richard Howard, Studies in Existentialism and Phenomenology (London: Tavistock, 1967).

——'What is Enlightenment?', in *The Foucault Reader*, ed. Paul Rabinow (Harmondsworth: Penguin, 1984), 32–50.

FRANK, LAWRENCE, *Charles Dickens and the Romantic Self* (Lincoln: University of Nebraska Press, 1984).

GARIS, ROBERT, *The Dickens Theatre: A Reassessment of the Novels* (Oxford: Clarendon Press, 1965).

GEROULD, DANIEL, 'Melodrama and Revolution', in Jacky Bratton, Jim Cook, and Christine Gledhill (eds.), *Melodrama: Stage, Picture, Screen* (London: British Film Institute, 1994), 185–98.

GILBERT, SANDRA M., and GUBAR, SUSAN *The Madwoman in the Attic: The Woman Writer and the Nineteenth-Century Literary Imagination* (New Haven: Yale University Press, 1979).

GILMOUR, ROBIN, 'Between Two Worlds: Aristocracy and Gentility in *Nicholas Nickleby*', *Dickens Quarterly*, 5 (1988), 110–18.

——*The Idea of the Gentleman in the Victorian Novel* (London: Allen & Unwin, 1981).

GIRARD, RENÉ, *Deceit, Desire, and the Novel: Self and Other in Literary Structure*, trans. Yvonne Freccero (Éditions Bernard Grasset, 1961; Baltimore: Johns Hopkins University Press, 1961; repr. 1988).

GISSING, GEORGE, *Charles Dickens: A Critical Study* (London: Gresham, 1903).

GLAVIN, JOHN, *After Dickens: Reading, Adaptation and Performance*, Cambridge Studies in Nineteenth-Century Literature and Culture, XX (Cambridge: Cambridge University Press, 1999).

GOFFMAN, ERVING, *The Presentation of Self in Everyday Life*, Pelican (Anchor, 1959; Harmondsworth: Penguin, 1987).

GOLDBERG, S. L., 'Literary Judgement: Making Moral Sense of Poems', *Critical Review*, 28 (1986), 18–46.

GRUBB, GERALD GILES, 'Dickens's Editorial Methods', *Studies in Philology*, 40 (1943), 79–100.

—— 'The Editorial Policies of Charles Dickens', *PMLA* 58 (1943), 1110–24.

HADLEY, ELAINE, *Melodramatic Tactics: Theatricalized Dissent in the English Marketplace, 1800–1885* (Stanford, Calif.: Stanford University Press, 1995).

HALL, STUART, 'Notes on Deconstructing the Popular', in Raphael Samuel (ed.), *People's History and Socialist Theory* (London: Routledge & Kegan Paul, 1981), 227–40.

HARDY, BARBARA, 'Dickens and the Passions', *Nineteenth-Century Fiction*, 24 (1970), 449–66.

—— *Forms of Feeling in Victorian Fiction* (London: Owen, 1985).

HART, LYNDA, 'The Victorian Villainess and the Patriarchal Unconscious', *Literature and Psychology*, 40 (1994), 1–25.

HARVEY, WILLIAM R., 'Charles Dickens and the Byronic Hero', *Nineteenth-Century Fiction*, 24 (1969), 305–16.

HAYS, MICHAEL, and NIKOLOPOULOU, ANASTASIA (eds.), *Melodrama: The Cultural Emergence of a Genre* (Basingstoke: Macmillan, 1996).

HEILMAN, ROBERT, *Tragedy and Melodrama: Versions of Experience* (Seattle: University of Washington Press, 1968).

HENTSCHEL, CEDRIC, *The Byronic Teuton: Aspects of German Pessimism, 1800–1933* (London: Methuen, 1940).

HERST, BETH F., *The Dickens Hero: Selfhood and Alienation in the Dickens World* (London: Weidenfeld & Nicolson, 1990).

HOLBROOK, DAVID, *Charles Dickens and the Image of Woman* (New York: New York University Press, 1993).

HOLLINGSWORTH, KEITH, *The Newgate Novel, 1830–1847: Bulwer, Ainsworth, Dickens, and Thackeray* (Detroit: Wayne State University Press, 1963).

HOUSE, HUMPHRY, 'George Bernard Shaw on *Great Expectations*', in *All in Due Time: The Collected Essays and Broadcast Talks of Humphry House* (London: Rupert Hart-Davis, 1955), 201–20.

—— 'The Macabre Dickens', in *All in Due Time: The Collected Essays and Broadcast Talks of Humphry House* (London: Rupert Hart-Davis, 1955), 183–9.

HOWARTH, W. D., 'Word and Image in Pixérécourt's Melodramas: The Dramaturgy of the Strip-Cartoon', in David Bradby, Louis James, and Bernard Sharratt (eds.), *Performance and Politics in Popular Drama: Aspects of Popular Entertainment in Theatre, Film and Television, 1800–1976* (Cambridge: Cambridge University Press, 1980), 17–32.

HYSLOP, GABRIELLE, 'Deviant and Dangerous Behaviour: Women in Melo-drama', *Journal of Popular Culture*, 19 (1985), 65–77.

—— 'Pixérécourt and the French Melodrama Debate: Instructing Boule-vard Audiences', in James Redmond (ed.), *Melodrama*, Themes in Drama (Cambridge: Cambridge University Press, 1992), 61–85.

—— 'Researching the Acting of French Melodrama, 1800–1830', *Nineteenth Century Theatre*, 15 (1987), 85–114.

INGHAM, PATRICIA, *Dickens, Women & Language* (Hemel Hempstead: Harvester Wheatsheaf, 1992).

JACOBSON, DAN, 'What's Eating Lara? (or Lord Byron's Guiltiest Secret)', in *Adult Pleasures: Essays on Writers and Readers* (London: Deutsch, 1988), 31–9.

JAMES, LOUIS, 'Was Jerrold's *Black Ey'd Susan* More Popular than Words-worth's *Lucy*?', in David Bradby, Louis James, and Bernard Sharratt (eds.), *Performance and Politics in Popular Drama: Aspects of Popular Entertainment in Theatre, Film and Television, 1800–1976* (Cambridge: Cambridge University Press, 1980), 3–16.

JOHN, JULIET (ed.), introduction to *Cult Criminals: The Newgate Novels, 1830–1847*, 6 vols. (London: Routledge, 1998), i, pp. v–lxxi.

JOHNSON, EDGAR, *Charles Dickens: His Tragedy and his Triumph*, 2 vols. (London: Gollancz, 1953).

JOHNSON, EDGAR, and JOHNSON, ELEANOR *The Dickens Theatrical Reader* (London: Gollancz, 1964).

KAPLAN, E. ANN, 'Theories of Melodrama: A Feminist Perspective', *Women and Performance*, 1 (1983), 40–8.

KETTLE, ARNOLD, 'Thoughts on *David Copperfield*, *Review of English Literature*, 2 (1961), 64–74.

KINCAID, JAMES R., *Dickens and the Rhetoric of Laughter* (Oxford: Clarendon Press, 1971).

—— 'Performance, Roles, and the Nature of the Self in Dickens', in Carol Hanbery MacKay (ed.), *Dramatic Dickens* (Houndmills: Macmillan, 1989), 11–26.

KREUTZ, IRVING W., 'Sly of Manner, Sharp of Tooth: A Study of Dickens's Villains', *Nineteenth Century Fiction*, 22 (1968), 331–48.

KUCICH, JOHN, 'Dickens', in John Richetti (ed.), *The Columbia History of the British Novel* (New York: Columbia University Press, 1994), 381–406.

—— *Excess and Restraint in the Novels of Charles Dickens* (Athens: University of Georgia Press, 1981).

—— *Repression in Victorian Fiction: Charlotte Brontë, George Eliot, and Charles*

Dickens (Berkeley and Los Angeles: University of California Press, 1987).

LANDA, M. J., *The Jew in Drama* (London: King, 1926).

LANE, LAURIAT, Jr., 'Dickens's Archetypal Jew', *PMLA* 73 (1958), 94–100.

LANGER, SUSANNE K., *Feeling and Form: A Theory of Art Developed from 'Philosophy in a New Key'* (London: Routledge & Kegan Paul, 1953).

LANSBURY, CORAL, 'Pecksniffs and Pratfalls', in Carol Hanbery MacKay (ed.), *Dramatic Dickens* (Houndmills: Macmillan, 1989), 45–51.

LEAVIS, F. R., *The Great Tradition*, Peregrine (London: Chatto & Windus, 1948; Harmondsworth: Penguin, 1962).

LEAVIS, F. R., and LEAVIS, Q. D., *Dickens the Novelist* (London: Chatto & Windus, 1970).

LEAVIS, Q. D., *Fiction and the Reading Public* (London: Chatto & Windus, 1932).

LITVAK, JOSEPH, 'Bad Scene: *Oliver Twist* and the Pathology of Entertainment', *Dickens Studies Annual*, 26 (1998), 33–49.

LOHRLI, ANNE (comp.), *Household Words: A Weekly Journal, 1850–1859, Conducted by Charles Dickens: Table of Contents, List of Contributors and their Contributions Based on the 'Household Words' Office Book* (Toronto: University of Toronto Press, 1973).

LUCAS, JOHN, *The Melancholy Man: A Study of Dickens's Novels* (London: Methuen, 1970).

McCARTHY, PATRICK, 'Dombey and Son: Language and the Roots of Meaning', *Dickens Studies Annual*, 19 (1990), 91–106.

McCOMBIE, FRANK, 'Sexual Repression in *Dombey and Son*', *Dickensian*, 88 (1992), 25–38.

MacDONALD, DWIGHT, 'A Theory of Mass Culture', in Bernard Rosenberg and David Manning White (eds.), *Mass Culture: The Popular Arts in America* (Glencoe, Ill.: Free Press, 1957), 59–73.

McDONALD, JAN, 'Lesser Ladies of the Victorian Stage', *Theatre Research International*, 13 (1988), 234–49.

MacKAY, CAROL HANBERY, 'Controlling Death and Sex: Magnification v. the Rhetoric of Rules in Dickens and Thackeray', in Regina Barreca (ed.), *Sex and Death in Victorian Literature* (Houndmills: Macmillan, 1990), 120–39.

McKNIGHT, NATALIE, *Idiots, Madmen and Other Prisoners in Dickens* (New York: St Martin's Press, 1993).

McMASTER, ROWLAND, 'Dickens, the Dandy, and the Savage: A Victorian View of the Romantic', in Juliet and Rowland McMaster, *The Novel from Sterne to James: Essays on the Relation of Literature to Life* (London: Macmillan, 1981), 54–70.

MALONE, Cynthia Northcutt, ' "Flight" and "Pursuit": Fugitive Identity in *Bleak House*', *Dickens Studies Annual*, 19 (1990), 107–24.

MARCUS, STEVEN, *Dickens: From Pickwick to Dombey* (London: Chatto & Windus, 1965).

MARSHALL, GAIL, *Actresses on the Victorian Stage: Feminine Performance and the Galatea Myth*, Cambridge Studies in Nineteenth-Century Literature and Culture, XVI (Cambridge: Cambridge University Press, 1998).

MEIER, STEFANIE, *Animation and Mechanization in the Novels of Charles Dickens*, Swiss Studies in English, CXI (Zurich: Francke Verlag Bern, 1982).

MEISEL, MARTIN, *Realizations: Narrative, Pictorial and Theatrical Arts in Nineteenth-Century England* (Princeton: Princeton University Press, 1983).

MILLER, D. A., *The Novel and the Police* (Berkeley and Los Angeles: University of California Press, 1988).

MILLER, J. HILLIS, *Charles Dickens: The World of his Novels* (Cambridge, Mass.: Harvard University Press, 1958; repr. 1965).

——'J. Hillis Miller on the Fiction of Realism', in Lilian R. Furst (ed.), *Realism*, Modern Literatures in Perspective (London: Longman, 1992), 287–318; repr. from 'The Fiction of Realism: *Sketches by Boz, Oliver Twist,* and Cruikshank's Illustrations', in Ada Nisbet and Blake Nevius (eds.), *Dickens Centennial Essays* (Berkeley and Los Angeles: University of California Press, 1971), 85–126.

MILLETT, KATE, *Sexual Politics* (Garden City, NY: Doubleday, 1970).

MILNER, IAN, 'The Dickens Drama: Mr. Dombey', *Nineteenth-Century Fiction*, 24 (1970), 477–87.

MOERS, ELLEN, *The Dandy* (London: Secker & Warburg, 1960).

MONTAUT, MARY, 'The Second Mrs. Dombey', *Dickens Quarterly*, 4 (1987), 141–53.

MORTIMER, JOHN (ed.), *The Oxford Book of Villains* (Oxford: Oxford University Press, 1992).

NICHOLLS, MARIA, 'Lady Dedlock's Sin', *Dickensian*, 89 (1993), 39–94.

NICOLL, ALLARDYCE, *A History of Early Nineteenth-Century Drama, 1800–1850*, 2 vols. (Cambridge: Cambridge University Press, 1930).

——*A History of English Drama*, 2nd edn., 6 vols. (Cambridge: Cambridge University Press, 1952–9).

NIKOLOPOULOU, ANASTASIA, 'Historical Disruptions: The Walter Scott Melodramas', in Michael Hays and Anastasia Nikolopoulou (eds.), *Melodrama: The Cultural Emergence of a Genre* (Basingstoke: Macmillan, 1996), 121–43.

NYGAARD, SUSAN, 'Redecorating Dombey: The Power of "a Woman's Anger" versus Upholstery in *Dombey and Son*', *Critical Matrix*, 8 (1994), 40–80.

OPPENLANDER, ELLA ANN, *Dickens's 'All the Year Round': Descriptive Index and Contributor Book* (Troy, NY: Whitston, 1984).

PATTEN, ROBERT L., ' "I Thought of Mr Pickwick and Wrote the First Number": Dickens and the Evolution of Character', *Dickens Quarterly*, 3 (1986), 18–25.

PETERS, LAURA, 'The Histories of Two Self-Tormentors: Orphans and Power in *Little Dorrit*', *Dickensian*, 91 (1995), 187–97.

PRAZ, MARIO, *The Hero in Eclipse in Victorian Fiction*, trans. Angus Davidson (London: Oxford University Press, 1956).

PYKETT, LYN, 'The Real versus the Ideal: Theories of Fiction in Periodicals, 1850–1870', *Victorian Periodicals Review*, 15 (1982), 63–74.

RADFORD, JEAN (ed.), *The Progress of Romance: The Politics of Popular Fiction* (London: Routledge & Kegan Paul, 1986).

RAHILL, FRANK, *The World of Melodrama* (University Park: Pennsylvania State University Press, 1967).

REID, J. C., *Charles Dickens: 'Little Dorrit'*, Studies in English Literature, XXVIIII (London: Arnold, 1967).

REM, TORE, 'Melodrama and Parody: A Reading that *Nicholas Nickleby* Requires?', *English Studies*, 3 (1996), 240–54.

—— 'Playing around with Melodrama: The Crummles Episodes in *Nicholas Nickleby*', *Dickens Studies Annual*, 25 (1996), 267–85.

ROACH, JOSEPH R., *The Player's Passion: Studies in the Science of Acting* (Newark: University of Delaware Press, 1985).

ROSENBERG, BRIAN, *Little Dorrit's Shadows: Character and Contradiction in Dickens* (Columbia: University of Missouri Press, 1996).

ROWELL, GEORGE, *The Victorian Theatre, 1792–1914: A Survey* (London: Oxford University Press, 1956).

SCHAD, JOHN (ed.), *Dickens Refigured: Bodies, Desires and Other Histories* (Manchester: Manchester University Press, 1996).

SCHLICKE, PAUL, 'Crummles Once More', *Dickensian*, 86 (1990), 2–16.

—— *Dickens and Popular Entertainment* (London: Allen & Unwin, 1985).

SEDGWICK, EVE KOSOFSKY, *Between Men: English Literature and Male Homosocial Desire*, Gender and Culture (New York: Columbia University Press, 1985).

SHATTUC, JANE, ' "Having a Good Cry over The Color Purple": The Problem of Affect and Imperialism in Feminist Theory', in Jacky Bratton, Jim Cook, and Christine Gledhill (eds.), *Melodrama: Stage, Picture, Screen* (London: British Film Institute, 1994), 147–56.

SHEPHERD, SIMON, 'Pauses of Mutual Agitation', in Jacky Bratton, Jim Cook, and Christine Gledhill (eds.), *Melodrama: Stage, Picture, Screen* (London: British Film Institute, 1994), 25–37.

SLATER, MICHAEL, *Dickens and Women* (London: Dent, 1983).

SPIVACK, BERNARD, *Shakespeare and the Allegory of Evil: The History of Metaphor in Relation to his Major Villains* (New York: Columbia University Press, 1958).

STEPHENS, JOHN RUSSELL, *The Censorship of English Drama* (Cambridge: Cambridge University Press, 1980).

STONE, DONALD D., *The Romantic Impulse in Victorian Fiction* (Cambridge, Mass.: Harvard University Press, 1980).

SUCKSMITH, HARVEY PETER, 'The Melodramatic Villain in *Little Dorrit*', *Dickensian*, 71 (1975), 76–83.

SUTHERLAND, JOHN, *The Longman Companion to Victorian Fiction* (Harlow:

Longman, 1988).

Sypher, Wylie, 'Aesthetic of Revolution: The Marxist Melodrama', *Kenyon Review*, 10 (1948), 431–44.

Tambling, Jeremy, *Dickens, Violence and the Modern State: Dreams of the Scaffold* (Houndmills: Macmillan, 1995).

Thorslev, Peter L., *The Byronic Hero: Types and Prototypes* (Minneapolis: University of Minnesota Press, 1962; repr. 1965).

Tomalin, Claire, *The Invisible Woman: The Story of Nelly Ternan and Charles Dickens* (Harmondsworth: Penguin, 1991).

Tracy, Robert, ' "The Old Story" and Inside Stories: Modish Stories and Fictional Modes in *Oliver Twist*', *Dickens Studies Annual*, 17 (1988), 1–33.

Trilling, Lionel, *Sincerity and Authenticity: The Charles Eliot Norton Lectures, 1969–70* (Oxford: Oxford University Press, 1972; rev. edn. 1974).

van Amerongen, J. B., *The Actor in Dickens: A Study of the Histrionic and Dramatic Elements in the Novelist's Life and Works* (London: Palmer, 1926).

van Ghent, Dorothy, *The English Novel: Form and Function* (New York: Rinehart, 1953).

Vlock, Deborah, *Dickens, Novel Reading and the Victorian Popular Theatre*, Cambridge Studies in Nineteenth-Century Literature and Culture, XIX (Cambridge: Cambridge University Press, 1998).

Watt, Ian, *The Rise of the Novel: Studies in Defoe, Richardson and Fielding* (Berkeley and Los Angeles: University of California Press, 1957).

Williams, Raymond, *Culture and Society, 1780–1950* (London: Chatto & Windus, 1958).

——*Marxism and Literature* (Oxford: Oxford University Press, 1977; repr. 1986), pp. 128–35.

Wilson, Angus, 'The Heroes and Heroines of Dickens', in John Gross and Gabriel Pearson (eds.), *Dickens and the Twentieth Century* (London: Routledge and Kegan Paul, 1962), 3–11.

—— *The World of Charles Dickens* (London: Secker & Warburg, 1970).

Wilson, Edmund, 'Dickens: The Two Scrooges', in *The Wound and the Bow: Seven Studies in Literature* (Cambridge, Mass.: Riverside Press, 1929; repr. 1941), 1–104.

Worth, George, *Dickensian Melodrama: A Reading of the Novels*, University of Kansas Humanistic Studies, L (Lawrence: University of Kansas Press, 1978).

Index